"The threat of spirals of political violence between antagonistic groups has aroused growing concern in recent years. But discussions of 'cumulative extremism' in liberal democracies have so far lacked empirical and theoretical depth. Analysing a range of British case studies, this book admirably helps to fill this gap."

—*Roger Eatwell, University of Bath, UK*

"This book could hardly be more timely. Combining precise empirical case studies with deft theoretical observations, Carter's analysis comprises a major step forward in the scholarship on 'cumulative extremism' and 'reciprocal radicalisation'."

—*Joel Busher, Coventry University, UK*

"At a time of increasing political polarisation in many Western societies, this book offers a valuable, historically-contextualised and carefully-argued critical analysis of what 'cumulative extremism' is and under what conditions it can develop. This book will be helpful to both researchers and to policy-makers and practitioners aiming to prevent extremism."

—*Paul Thomas, University of Huddersfield, UK*

CUMULATIVE EXTREMISM

This book frames several historical incidents of violent movement-countermovement conflicts within the concept of 'cumulative extremism' – the mutually reinforcing dynamic of radicalisation that can develop between two or more antagonistic groups.

Drawing on several in-depth case studies, including the contests between British fascist and anti-fascist groups in the interwar period and from 1967 to 1979 and 1980 to 2000; the Troubles in Northern Ireland from the late 1960s to mid-1970s; and Islamist extremists and the far-right counter-jihad movement in Britain since 2009, this book presents the first in-depth academic analysis of the concept of 'cumulative extremism' and constructs a theoretical framework through which to assess its development.

This is a groundbreaking volume which will be of particular relevance to scholars with an interest in the extreme right, social movements, political violence and criminology. It will also be of interest to policy makers and to practitioners dealing with extremism and radicalisation, including youth workers, prevent coordinators, community support officers and police officers.

Alexander J. Carter completed his PhD at Teesside University's Centre of Fascism, Anti-Fascism and Post-Fascism Studies. He has published research on radicalisation, terrorism and extremism.

ROUTLEDGE STUDIES IN FASCISM AND THE FAR RIGHT

Series editors: **Nigel Copsey**, *Teesside University*, and **Graham Macklin**, *Center for Research on Extremism (C-REX), University of Oslo.*

This new book series focuses upon fascist, far right and right-wing politics primarily within a historical context but also drawing on insights from other disciplinary perspectives. Its scope also includes radical-right populism, cultural manifestations of the far right and points of convergence and exchange with the mainstream and traditional right.

Titles include:

The Lives and Afterlives of Enoch Powell
The Undying Political Animal
Edited by Olivier Esteves and Stéphane Porion

Latin American Dictatorships in the Era of Fascism
The Corporatist Wave
António Costa Pinto

The Far Right and the Environment
Politics, Discourse and Communication
Edited by Bernhard Forchtner

Vigilantism against Migrant and Minorities
Edited by Tore Bjørgo and Miroslav Mareš

Trumping Democracy
From Ronald Reagan to Alt-Right
Edited by Chip Berlet

A.K. Chesterton and the Evolution of Britain's Extreme Right, 1933–1973
Luke LeCras

Cumulative Extremism
A Comparative Historical Analysis
Alexander J. Carter

CasaPound Italia
Contemporary Extreme-Right Politics
Caterina Froio, Pietro Castelli Gattinara, Giorgia Bulli and Matteo Albanese

The International Alt-Right
Fascism for the 21st Century?
Patrik Hermansson, David Lawrence, Joe Mulhall and Simon Murdoch

For more information about this series, please visit: https://www.routledge.com/Routledge-Studies-in-Fascism-and-the-Far-Right/book-series/FFR

CUMULATIVE EXTREMISM

A Comparative Historical Analysis

Alexander J. Carter

Routledge
Taylor & Francis Group

LONDON AND NEW YORK

First published 2020
by Routledge
2 Park Square, Milton Park, Abingdon, Oxon OX14 4RN

and by Routledge
52 Vanderbilt Avenue, New York, NY 10017

Routledge is an imprint of the Taylor & Francis Group, an informa business

British Library Cataloguing-in-Publication Data
A catalogue record for this book is available from the British Library

Library of Congress Cataloging-in-Publication Data
A catalog record has been requested for this book

ISBN: 978-1-138-38606-8 (hbk)
ISBN: 978-1-138-38612-9 (pbk)
ISBN: 978-0-429-06012-0 (ebk)

Typeset in Bembo
by Lumina Datamatics Limited

For my wife, Isbelis Carter-Lopez

CONTENTS

LIST OF FIGURES

ACKNOWLEDGEMENTS

I would like to express my gratitude to the following people for their help, comments and suggestions: Nigel Copsey, Matthew Feldman, Craig Fowlie, Roisín Higgins, Graham Macklin, Charlie McGuire, Paul Thomas, and Lewis Young.

I also owe my thanks to the staff at the following archives and libraries: The National Archives, the British Library, the London School of Economics Library, the London Metropolitan Archives, the University of Northampton Searchlight Archive, the Linen Hall Library, and the Wiener Library.

For their support and assistance, I would also like to thank my father, Pat, and my sisters Miranda, Josie and Tess. Special thanks must also go to Liz.

LIST OF ABBREVIATIONS

AFA	Anti-Fascist Action
AM	Al-Muhajiroun
ANL	Anti-Nazi League
ARA	Anti-Racist Alliance
AYM	Asian Youth Movement
BF	Britain First
BUF	British Union of Fascists
B&H	Blood and Honour
BM	British Movement
BoD	Board of Deputies of British Jews
C18	Combat 18
CE	Cumulative Extremism
CJM	Counter-Jihad Movement
CPGB	Communist Party of Great Britain
CRM	Civil Rights Movement
CSB	Cable Street Beat
CSJ	Campaign for Social Justice
DCAC	Derry Citizens' Action Committee
DFLA	Democratic Football Lad's Alliance
FLA	Football Lad's Alliance
FLAF	Football Lads and Lasses Against Fascism
HO	Home Office
IFL	Imperial Fascist League
ILP	Independent Labour Party
IMG	International Marxist Group
INLA	Irish National Liberation Army
IRA	Irish Republican Army

IS	International Socialists (later the Socialist Workers' Party)
IWA	Indian Workers' Association
JLC	Jewish Labour Council
JPC	Jewish People's Council Against Fascism and Anti-Semitism
M/CM	Movement–Countermovement
MCB	Muslim Council of Britain
MfE	March for England
MRF	Military Reconnaissance Force
NCCL	National Council of Civil Liberties (later Liberty)
NICRA	Northern Ireland Civil Rights Association
NA	National Action
NF	National Front
NI	Northern Ireland
NP	New Party
NSDAP	Nationalsozialistische Deutsche Arbeiterpartei (National Socialist German Workers' Party, or Nazi Party)
OIRA	Official Irish Republican Army
PIRA	Provisional Irish Republican Army
POA	Public Order Act
RA	Red Action
RAC	Rock Against Communism
RAR	Rock Against Racism
RHC	Red Hand Commando
RUC	Royal Ulster Constabulary
SAS	Special Air Service
SMO	Social Movement Organisation
SPG	Special Patrol Group
SWP	Socialist Workers' Party
SYM	Southall Youth Movement
TUC	Trades Union Congress
UAF	Unite Against Fascism
UCDC	Ulster Constitution Defence Committee
UDA	Ulster Defence Association
UDR	Ulster Defence Regiment
UPV	Ulster Protestant Volunteers
UVF	Ulster Volunteer Force
YRE	Youth Against Racism in Europe

1

INTRODUCTION

The summer of 2001 bore witness to 'the most serious outbreaks of disorder in Britain since the widespread inner-city disturbances of the early 1980s.'[1] These episodes involved clashes between groups of British Pakistani, Bangladeshi and white youths. The Home Secretary David Blunkett's response included the setting up of a Community Cohesion Review Team, led by Ted Cantle, to investigate the disturbances. Their findings were subsequently published in the Home Office document *Community Cohesion: A Report of the Independent Review Team*.[2] As the name suggests, the report viewed the incidents through the lens of 'community cohesion', and argued that the main issues were the 'physical segregation' and communal 'polarisation' which result in 'communities operat[ing] on the basis of a series of parallel lives'.[3] Given these conditions, the report argued, there 'is little wonder that the ignorance about each others' communities can easily grow into fear'.[4] Many observers felt that this emphasis on 'community cohesion' came at the expense of a more nuanced analysis of the factors leading to the disturbances, and had downplayed the part that issues such as discriminatory housing policies by the local councils, poverty and unemployment, racially motivated '[h]arassment and aggression from the police' and 'fascist antagonism' played in provoking the violence that occurred.[5]

It was the incidence of the latter issue, 'fascist antagonism', and the relationship this had with the public disorder in Oldham, that the political scientist Roger Eatwell first used as an example to illustrate the concept of 'cumulative extremism' (CE), which he described as 'the way in which one form of extremism can feed off and magnify other forms'[6] As Eatwell stated:

> Bradford in 2001 serves as a good example of how the extreme right helped to provoke tensions among ethnic minorities... For some time before the troubles broke out, both the BNP and NF had been active in the area.

Although a provocative NF march was banned shortly before the riots began, NF activists still gathered with the intention of fomenting trouble.[7]

Later, Eatwell and Goodwin stated that the '2001 riots in northern towns showed the potential for a spiral of violence', and even went so far as to argue that cumulative extremism 'is more threatening to the liberal democratic order than attacks from lone wolf extreme right-wingers or even al-Qaeda-inspired spectacular bombings.'[8]

Since Eatwell coined the concept of CE in 2006, the idea (also referred to as 'cumulative radicalisation', 'tit-for-tat radicalisation', and 'reciprocal radicalisation')[9] has gained wider currency amongst both academics and policymakers, with the relationship between far-right groups and Islamic extremists in Britain taking centre stage.[10] However, despite the growing acceptance of the idea, there has been surprisingly scant empirical investigation into it. Furthermore, the extant research has produced ambiguous conclusions over the development of processes of CE, with academics urging caution in the application of the concept.[11]

There are certainly studies amongst the small body of existing work on cumulative extremism that seem to support Eatwell's theory. Since 2009, many academics have noted that the formation of the English Defence League (EDL) in response to the provocative protests held by Islamist extremists, as well their subsequent interactions with those Islamists, may provide a further example of Eatwell's dynamic of CE.[12] Further, Littler and Feldman have analysed data collected by the anti-Muslim hate monitoring organisation Tell MAMA 'from the periods immediately before and after jihadi Islamist attacks in Sydney, Paris and Copenhagen'.[13] They found that, if 'of varied magnitude, the data nevertheless registers a spike in the number of reported anti-Muslim cases in the periods immediately following each high-profile jihadi Islamist attack', which provides 'further empirical evidence in support of the 'cumulative extremism' hypothesis.'[14] In broader terms, many academics working in fields such as social psychology[15] and social movement theory[16] have noted the development of mutually radicalising relationships developing between antagonistic groups. Furthermore, the concept has been adopted by the British Government for their counter-terrorism strategy[17] and found wider currency within the mainstream national media.[18]

However, the most in-depth and focused investigations into CE have been far more critical of the concept. Macklin and Busher have explored the most violent movement-countermovement (M/CM) contests between antagonistic social movements in Britain in the post-war era and demonstrated that, contrary to what proponents of the idea of CE might expect, there have been no real spirals of violence in these cases. They concluded that further 'research is required on these patterns and processes of interactive escalation… In the meantime, policymakers, practitioners and academics alike might do well to err on the side of caution when making claims about CE and "spirals of violence".'[19] Elsewhere

Bartlett and Birdwell have examined the M/CM interactions between far-right and Islamist Groups in Britain and found that the evidence for the existence of the dynamic of CE developing to be 'varied', and warned that 'care is needed with respect to this new concept. There may even be countervailing trends. Rather than leading to greater levels of support for each group, it could be that an extremist group's actions only serve to isolate them further.'[20]

Given the dissonance between some of these experts' conclusions and how seriously CE is being taken by policy makers, other academics, and journalists, there is clearly a pressing need for a much greater understanding of the phenomenon. In the first place, if counter-terrorism strategies are being informed by a threat that 'is being exaggerated… the consequence will be unnecessary fears, unnecessary powers and the allocation of excessive resources to the counter-terrorism machine.'[21] Secondly, as Macklin and Busher warn, if the study of cumulative extremism is not conducted in a robust manner, and as such presents spirals of violence as the inevitable outcome of interactions between opposing groups, this may actually exacerbate M/CM hostilities by encouraging and legitimating the narratives propagated by extremist groups 'themselves that cohere around and depend upon apocalyptic warnings of inevitable ethnic and religious violence.'[22] Of course, it is also possible that an insufficiently nuanced understanding of the factors which influence the development of cumulative extremism could have the opposite effect and lead to a downplaying of the threat of terrorism and political violence posed by the escalation of M/CM contests. The more accurate the understanding of CE the easier it will be to design context-sensitive and effective policy measures by which to manage the interactions of opposing groups within a society.

Researching cumulative extremism

To approach this concept, there needs to be a firm idea of its parameters. Only loosely discussed in his introductory article on the subject, Eatwell nevertheless sketched the contours of how to approach the study of cumulative extremism. In the first instance, Eatwell's article described the three processes which he seemed to consider to be the core of cumulative extremism: interactive radicalisation (when the actions of one group can provoke a more extreme reaction from an opposing group); the potential mobilisation or involvement of an increasing number of people; and communal polarisation.[23]

However, despite this, there has been a great deal of ambiguity in the literature over exactly what 'cumulative extremism' refers to. The first academic reports to include the terminology tended to do so only in passing, and the analysis of the concept often only extended to the observation that the emergence of the English Defence League in response to the activities of Islamist extremists seemed to confirm Eatwell's thesis. For example, Goodwin argued that '[The EDL's] formation, therefore, is an example of … 'cumulative extremism', whereby the activities of one extremist group trigger the formation of another manifestation, and possibly thereafter a spiral of counter-mobilization or even conflict.'[24]

Similarly, Copsey observed that the 'founding of the EDL represents a type of interaction that political scientist Roger Eatwell has usefully described as 'cumulative extremism', that is to say, a process by which one type of extremism (Islamist) can spark off another type of extremism.'[25] Holbrook and Taylor also warned of 'the potential danger of reciprocal radicalization, where far-right extremist groups with anti-Islamic agendas emerge in response to Islamist-inspired violent extremism, triggering further radicalization within some Islamic communities.'[26]

Subsequent investigations have managed to drill down further into the concept, and these studies can, broadly speaking, be divided into two groups. The first group of writers have tended to focus more on the narratives, messages and stories of the groups involved. Writing within this vein of CE scholarship, Paul Jackson has defined 'tit-for-tat radicalisation' as a 'reciprocal relationship between two or more extremist groups that actively feed off each other's messages and ideologies'.[27] Cook and Blanquart warn of 'the danger of "cumulative extremism" from vehicles such as Twitter through narrative exchanges that focus on fear and retaliation as common themes for discussion.'[28] Kundnani has similarly described cumulative extremism as 'the possibility that right-wing extremism and radical Islamism reinforce each other through a dynamic in which each one's narrative encourages support in the opposing group, in a spiral of fear and mutual demonization.'[29] More recently, Julia Ebner has argued that because 'victimisation and demonisation work well together, extremists are in a mutually beneficial relationship. To tell a coherent story, the victim needs a perpetrator as much as the perpetrator needs a victim. In extremism, this leads to an effect called reciprocal radicalisation.'[30]

By contrast, the second group of researchers have focused more on the strategies, actions and behaviour of opposing groups. Of these, Matthew Feldman and Mark Littler have described CE as 'the cyclical ratcheting up of violent activity between opposing communities, with acts of violence perpetrated by a sub-group (however small) of a given community against members of another community, triggering acts of violent retribution by members of a sub-population of the second community against members of the first community.'[31] Elsewhere, Macklin and Busher have specifically argued that 'while the journey of individuals or groups up or down the narrative and action pyramids might at times be closely interrelated, they are nonetheless distinct and discernible phenomena whose correlation with one another (let alone their causal relationship) is far from straightforward'.[32] In subsequent empirical research into CE, Busher and Macklin have stated that they 'limit our focus to processes of tactical escalation. We do not explicitly examine processes of ideological radicalisation.'[33]

This book follows this second group of writers in primarily focusing on the tactical escalation of the actors involved, rather than 'ideological radicalisation' or the mutually beneficial nature of opposing extremist narratives. This is for two reasons: firstly, the main dependent variable here is political violence, not extreme views. As has been noted, while ideological and behavioural radicalisation are linked, the former is hardly a perfect predictor of the latter. They are separate phenomena. Grasping the relationship between the two is not within the purview of this book, and accordingly the bulk of efforts will be spent on assessing interactive tactical escalation. Where the narrative output for a group directly precedes a tactical escalation on the part of an opponent, and there is strong evidence for a causal link between the two, this shall be included in the analysis. But increasingly extreme narratives alone are not the focus here. Secondly, ideological radicalisation is an extremely difficult thing to assess using documentary research. While evidence for tactical radicalisation is relatively easy to come by – newspapers are often replete with reports of an organisation engaging in violent activity after a particular episode – it would require interviewing subjects to really get to the bottom of processes of ideological radicalisation, and, with one exception, this methodology was not employed in this project due to constraints on time and resources.

Even when it *is* actors' actions, rather than their attitudes, which are under the microscope, there is still some ambiguity over precisely *who* is being affected by processes of cumulative extremism. For some writers, it is the social movements who engage in increasingly radical tactics through interactions with their opponents. As Goodwin and Eatwell warn, then, 'the potential danger of cumulative extremism is highlighted by the activity of the English Defence League (EDL), an organization with links to the football 'casuals' movement and which organizes street-based demonstrations against violent Islamism….'[34] Similarly, Macklin and Busher examine 'patterns of escalation during four waves of movement–countermovement contests involving' specific antagonistic organisations such as the far-right National Front and the far-left Socialist Workers Party in the 1970s.[35] However, in their investigation into CE, Feldman and Littler examine individual acts of violence perpetrated against Muslims: '[t]aking the date and time of [an Islamist extremist] attack as a starting point, we compared the number of reports of anti-Muslim attacks in the 7 days following each attack, as against the number of reports in the preceding 7 days.'[36] This individual-level data does not necessarily suggest meso-level tactical escalations on the part of opposing organisations at all.

Here, the focus shall be on developments at the meso, or organisational, level. Eatwell himself suggested that CE largely stems from actions and decisions made at the group/organisational level – for example, it was the groups of the 'extreme right' such as the 'the British National Party' and the 'the National Front' who had been 'active … fomenting trouble', and 'extremist "anti-fascists"', such as the Socialist Workers Party, 'who not only sought to encourage Muslim resistance but also to attack extreme right activists'.[37] Although they cannot be divorced from micro- and macro-level factors, such as the actions of a solo-actor terrorist or the decision by a government to be unresponsive to a movement's demands, it is the strategic development of social movement organisations (SMOs) that drives the evolution of M/CM contests: the decision to hold provocative marches or to form a martial body; or, conversely, the commitment to nonviolent means such as holding music festivals or organising sit-ins. These same actions and decisions also may or may not attract more people to mobilise as part of the movement. Because the SMOs and political parties which constitute social movements are (generally) centralised and consciously adopt or reject different behavioural policies, then, they are the main sites of action and innovation, and thus are the primary movers in terms of the development of CE. The behaviour of broader communities, such as ethnic groups, is much more diffuse, and of course tends to be more reactive than proactive.

Approaching the subject from an entirely different angle, Liz Fekete criticises CE for focusing too much on social movements at the expense of legitimate critiques of the state's role in contentious episodes:

> [t]he diagnosis that the real threat we face today is from cumulative extremism has different consequences in different European contexts. In the UK, for example, we are told that there is a symbiotic relationship between Islamist extremism and the English Defence League, whose ideologies mirror one another and who feed off each other in a spiral of violence. In fact this viewpoint is merely a reworking of tired frameworks used before in Northern Ireland. Remember all those filmmakers, journalists and academics who sought to present the 'Troubles' in Northern Ireland as part of an everlasting cycle of Catholic and Protestant religious fanaticism, thereby denying that British troops, British policies and entrenched discrimination against Catholics were the engine of the conflict.[38]

Fekete raises a valid concern here, especially given the interest that policy makers have taken in cumulative extremism. There is a danger that CE could be employed by states to frame conflicts in a way that suits their specific agendas – casting themselves as neutral arbiters amongst feuding groups – thereby damaging the analytic power of the concept or undermining any policy solutions arrived at through use of the concept. Thus, there needs to be an acknowledgement that the state may well play a formative part in the escalation of social movements' protest repertoires – as well as being susceptible to tactical escalation itself.

The definition of CE employed by this book, accordingly, is as follows:

> the dynamic of escalation that can develop between competing social movement organisations and their (prospective) social bases as they interact with each other, the state, and third party groups. The escalation involves the adoption of increasingly radical and violent repertoires of contention as well as the mobilisation of larger numbers of activists; both of which can provoke, and in turn be fuelled by, communal polarisation.

Given these points, the research questions driving this study are: What variables can help to foster a situation whereby interactive escalation between organisations, on the one hand, and communal polarisation, on the other, reinforce each other?

What are the key factors which are likely to escalate an M/CM contest towards the use of increasingly violent and radical means, or de-escalate towards more moderate tactics? Under what conditions are opposing movements likely to draw in larger numbers of supporters and so further expand the conflict?

To answer these questions this book will conduct a 'comparative-historical analysis' of several different case studies.[39] The movement-countermovement contests between British fascist and anti-fascist groups in the inter-war period and from the 1970s to the 1990s shall be considered alongside the Troubles in Northern Ireland from its onset in the 1960s through to its peak as a lethal M/CM contest between 1972 and 1976. Finally, this book will use the exploration of these different case studies as the basis for an analysis of movement-countermovement dynamics between the Islamist extremist and the counter-jihad movements in Britain since 2009. The overarching aim of these analyses shall be to identify the factors which are central to the development of processes of CE and to then construct a theoretical framework through which to assess the likelihood of cumulative extremism emerging between two or more antagonistic groups. This framework shall then be clearly laid out in the book's conclusion.

The case study of British fascists and anti-fascists was included as it involved mass-mobilisations of opposing groups of people, as well as a degree of violent radicalisation, but never escalated to the point of SMOs adopting lethal violence as part of their protest repertoires; this will highlight the factors that inhibit M/CM contests developing processes of CE. The Troubles in Northern Ireland, however, have been included as a case study precisely because the conflict did intensify to the point of becoming a protracted lethal conflict. Further, the Troubles have been cited by academics such as Matthew Goodwin as representing the possible end result of processes CE.[40] The case of Islamists and the counter-jihad have been included for two reasons: firstly, because it has become the focus of the majority of academic work on CE since the formation of the English Defence League in 2009. Secondly, because at the time of writing this case study is still ongoing, it provides a useful opportunity to apply the framework developed through analysis of the previous case studies so as to test its utility.

An historical cross-case comparison is necessary for this investigation because, as Rueschemeyer argues, 'only by going beyond the first case does the impact of factors on the outcomes of interest come into view that does not show up in within-case analyses because these factors are – completely or largely – held constant.'[41] Further, in the literature on cumulative extremism there has not yet been any attempt to compare cases where cumulative extremism has developed with cases where it has not. Thus, this book will attempt to fill this gap in the literature.

To that end, this study will primarily adopt a qualitative analysis of documentary sources such as newspaper articles, minutes, personal correspondences, and other relevant primary and secondary sources. There is also data from an interview with one anti-fascist and former member of Anti-Fascist Action. These will be analysed closely to assess the motivations, perceptions, and emotional reactions to events of the individuals and groups involved. This should make it possible to gain a deeper understanding of the factors which may be driving or inhibiting CE.

Literature review

Extremism and radicalism

The first concept that needs to be interrogated, given its central place in the analysis developed through this book, is 'extremism', or 'radicalism' (in this book these terms shall be used interchangeably, although the term 'radicalisation' shall be used to refer to the process of becoming 'radical' or 'extreme'). The term radicalisation has only gained wide usage relatively recently, largely due to the spur in analyses of terrorism and terrorists prompted by the events of 9/11 and the subsequent attacks in London and Madrid. As Kundnani notes, in the aftermath of these developments the 'concept of 'radicalisation' emerged as a vehicle for policy-makers to explore the process by which a terrorist was made and to provide an analytical grounding for preventative strategies that went beyond the threat of violence or detention.'[42] However, Kundnani also argues that the context in which this concept was developed led to it being 'circumscribed by the demands of counter-terrorist policy-makers rather than [used in] an attempt to objectively study how terrorism comes into being.'[43] In particular, the concept was narrowly applied to Islamist extremists (and their broader communities) rather than terrorists in general.[44]

Similarly, Silva has argued 'that the circular relationship between government counter-radicalisation research and media reflects a broader preoccupation with problematising radicalisation as a predominantly religious issue, one that affects (mostly) Muslim communities'.[45] Hoskins and O'Loughlin go even further, describing the concept of radicalisation as a 'myth', and arguing that there is a 'mediatized political trend in the UK in conflating disaffection amongst certain groups with an idea of 'radicalization'.[46] There are some reasonable criticisms made by these analysts, which highlight the importance of not allowing 'normative assessment to creep into our analysis and not to develop essentializing theories of actors and their behaviour.'[47] Nevertheless, as Neumann argues, 'radicalization is not a myth, but its meaning is ambiguous, and all the major controversies and debates that have sprung from it are linked to the same inherent ambiguity. The principal conceptual fault-line is between notions of radicalization that emphasize extremist beliefs ("cognitive radicalization") and those that focus on extremist behaviour ("behavioural radicalization").'[48]

Indeed, as with the division of focus in the literature on cumulative extremism, so too is there some disagreement over whether extremism and radicalism refer to behaviour or opinions. As Bartlett, Birdwell and King explain, the 'journey into terrorism is often described as a process of "radicalisation". However, to be a radical is to reject the status quo, but not necessarily in a violent or even problematic manner. The process of radicalisation is obviously a problem when it leads to violence… [b]ut the last decade in particular has also seen a growth in many types of nonviolent radicalisation.'[49] Distinguishing between the two is important, as while there is certainly a great deal of overlap between people with radical or extreme views and those who use extreme methods to achieve their goals, the former by no means guarantees the latter. As Bartlett and Miller correctly argue, while some 'radicals conduct, support, or encourage terrorism… many others do no such thing, and actively and often effectively agitate against it.'[50]

Many academics have written about how a lack of a coherent definition of extremism – one which takes into account the difference between attitudes and behaviour – has hindered British policy makers' counter-terrorism efforts. In particular, the 'Prevent' stream of the governments' CONTEST counter-terrorism strategy, which focuses on the prevention of radicalisation, has been criticised for failing to pay sufficient attention to this distinction.[51] For example, Qurashi has criticised Prevent training courses which some people working in 'Higher Education Institutions' have been obliged to take, in which they are ostensibly given 'an understanding of the signs that would indicate a person was vulnerable to terrorism and [so might require] some kind of support and safeguarding', as they 'ignore academic literature which problematises the linear relationships and notions of a conveyor belt to terrorism, and which shows that radicalisation and extremism are not precursors for terrorism'.[52]

This is by no means mere academic hair-splitting; counter-terrorism policy based on an insufficiently nuanced understanding of radicalisation and extremism can not only be ineffective, it can actually be counterproductive. As Kundnani argues, the focus on non-violent extremism in the Prevent agenda, through reference to ill-defined notions of 'Britishness', may actually engender feelings of disaffection among British Muslims: 'Some organisations have withdrawn from the Prevent programme as this cultural aspect has become more prominent… In practice, this approach to preventing violent extremism is counter-productive as it ends up expecting Muslims in general to mobilise around notions of Britishness imposed from above, thereby alienating the very people that need to be won over.'[53]

Elsewhere, Richards has explicitly argued that the Prevent agenda 'appears to extrematize activity, whatever activity that might be, if it is carried out for an extremist cause (hence a peaceful, public and legal protest in support of extremist views itself becomes an act of extremism), at the same time as excluding the possibility of extremist activity carried out in the cause of a non-extremist doctrine… Thus, if we are to engage with the concept of extremism, and most particularly in a counterterrorism context, a clearer distinction needs to be made between extremism of (non-violent) thought and extremism of method, because it is surely violence and the threat of violence (integral to terrorism) that should be of primary concern to counterterrorism.'[54]

Building on the criticisms raised by these writers, then, this study shall be concerned first and foremost with the behaviour of the actors involved in the case studies, and should therefore avoid blurring 'the important distinction between "extremism" of thought and "extremism" of method' which many have argued has led to 'a loss of focus in UK counterterrorism efforts'.[55] Accordingly, this book borrows the definition of 'radicalisation' employed by the social movement theorists Eitan Y. Alimi, Charles Demetriou, and Lorenzo Bosi: 'We hold radicalization to be the process that leads to and includes political violence. Accordingly, we hold "radical" to be the (organizational) actor who has adopted the use of political violence.'[56] Similarly, and drawing on the recent work of Busher, Holbrook and Macklin, 'extremist groups' 'refer to those groups in which a significant proportion of members have shown a willingness to deploy or support illegal [and violent] strategies of action'.[57] Thus, an organisation may be dedicated to the advancement of a fascist state or a fundamentalist Caliphate, but if they use only legal and non-violent methods to attempt to bring about this goal then they are not an extremist group, nor have they been radicalized, *under the definition employed here.*

Movement-countermovement contests and political violence

With regard to the study of the radicalisation of social movements, Charles Tilly's and Sidney Tarrow's pioneering work on the concept of 'contentious politics' is of great use. They define 'contentious politics' as those 'interactions in which actors make claims bearing on someone else's interests, leading to coordinated efforts on behalf of shared interests or programs, in which governments are involved as targets, initiators of claims, or third parties'.[58] Tilly and Tarrow have observed that different contentious episodes often display striking similarities to other episodes which have occurred in different times and places. These regularities are explored using the conceptual tools which they have dubbed 'contentious performances' and 'contentious repertoires'.[59] 'Contentious performances' are established and relatively well known routines which one set of political actors employ to make claims upon a different group, such as delivering a petition or organising a demonstration. In examining many particular instances of collective claim making, Tilly and Tarrow argue that it is clear that 'particular instances improvise on shared scripts'.[60] Although groups do innovate, often performances are repetitions of extant claim-making forms. Further, and crucially, performances are not always peaceful – actors can innovate their contentious repertoires to involve more violent performances or indeed draw on existing instances of violent claim making.

'Contentious repertoires' are the sets of contentious performances which a particular group of political actors are aware of. While repertoires do vary across episodes of contention, generally speaking 'when people make collective claims, they innovate within limits set by the repertoire already established for their place, time and [claimant–object] pair';[61] thus, social movements operating in the West often employ very similar performances such as petitions, mass demonstrations and sit-ins or 'occupations', but would be much less likely to consider suicide bombing, assassination, or kidnapping.[62] This of course begs the question as to how and why different tactical innovations occur within relatively stable social settings from peaceful protest repertoires towards increasingly violent and maybe even lethal ones, and more specifically whether the competition between opposing social movements is likely to accelerate these tactical innovations? If this is found to be the case, why does this happen in some cases but not others? In Northern Ireland there was a cascade of tactical innovations as an entirely peaceful civil rights movement engaged with the state and loyalist counter-protestors, and within a few years this had escalated to the level of a civil war between republican and loyalist paramilitary groups. Yet fascist and anti-fascist groups in England more-or-less eschewed lethal violence for the entire twentieth century. What accounts for these differences?

Of those who have specifically examined the relationships between movements and countermovements, Zald and Useem were the first. They argued that the mobilisation of any significant social movement will likely provoke the mobilisation of a countermovement. This is because social movements, by their very nature, exist to challenge some established interests, and so provide 'organizational entrepreneurs' with the grievances and opportunities necessary to 'define countermovement goals and issues'.[63] Further, in successfully mobilising, a social movement demonstrates to the potential constituents of a countermovement that mobilising for collective action is possible.[64] Zald and Useem started to develop a robust idea of 'movement-countermovement' (M/CM) interaction by carefully comparing it to other instances of social conflict. M/CM interaction is, they argue, similar to wars in that social movement organisations (SMOs) and countermovements (CMs) each control pools of resources which they expend in various 'battlefields' or 'arenas' (e.g. courtrooms, streets, news media). Importantly for the study of CE, Zald and Useem argue that violent conflict is most likely to occur when the movement and countermovement encounter each other face-to-face 'on the streets' at demonstrations and counter-demonstrations, because in such circumstances the groups have a heightened awareness of each other, and because these public spaces are often not so tightly regulated by the authorities so as to prevent close and personal (and sometimes violent) interactions.

That an M/CM dynamic may begin to exert a mutually radicalising influence on the movements in question is something that Donatella della Porta has also observed. In her book *Social Movements, Political Violence and the State,* della Porta observes how the regular meeting of hostile opponents can lead to the development of a dynamic which strengthens in-group loyalties while simultaneously 'creating an "abstract" and "absolute" image of the other side as the "enemy".'[65] If these encounters continue with regularity there is the possibility that movements will engage in the 'gradual reciprocal adaptation to increasingly dangerous weapons' in an interactive manner – that is, one group may feel threatened enough by their opponents to bring low-key weapons to a counter-demo, thereby provoking their enemies to bring more dangerous weapons themselves to the next encounter in order to protect themselves (or for explicitly offensive purposes).[66] This can cause M/CM conflicts to escalate in a 'logic of hatred, a logic of death'.[67] Similarly, the work of the social psychologists McCauley and Moskalenko suggests that when a movement engages in 'conflict with an outgroup' it can lead to strong emotions such as 'hate' for said outgroup developing.[68] This is activated through prolonged conflict and is the deepening of hostile sentiments towards a specified outgroup which, in extreme cases, can be manifested in an attempt to dehumanise them.[69] McCauley and Moskalenko cite theorists who conceptualise it as 'an extreme form of negative identification', whereby the 'enemy' is seen to have a 'bad essence'.[70] This view suggests that there is an evocation of positive emotions when bad things happen to the outgroup, making violence much more likely.

These studies that have focused specifically on the radicalisation of opposing social movements provide a useful starting point for the study of CE, and suggest further lines of inquiry to develop the analysis. Zald's and Useem's assertion of street-based mobilisations being more conducive to violent confrontations are no doubt correct, but why do some marches and demonstrations generate violence and others not? What other 'arenas' of collective action might produce hostility? Similar questions can be asked of della Porta's, McCauley's and Moskalenko's observations. There are many examples throughout history of movements and countermovements who have not experienced the extreme emotional responses to each other as these theorists describe (for example environmentalists and climate change sceptics or the anti-nuclear movement and the pro-nuclear lobby). Clearly the presence of two or more opposing movements who mobilise regularly against each other is a necessary but not sufficient condition for the development of CE.

Broadening the analysis somewhat, but remaining focused on the interactions between social movement organisations, Eitan Y. Alimi, Lorenzo Bosi, and Charles Demetriou draw attention to how the competition between organisations within the same movement can have a radicalising effect: 'A central mechanism, then, is *competition for power* among movement actors. Challengers sometimes complement and sometimes undercut each others' strategies as they struggle over whose strategy and tactics will dominate and as they vie for the support of yet uncommitted adherents and allies… competition for power can also support violence against movement competitors'.[71] Other theorists have made similar observations. Mia Bloom describes a process called 'outbidding' whereby groups competing over the same social base may use radicalisation as a tool to win over converts.[72] Donatella della Porta describes a process she terms 'competitive escalation', which she defines as the 'causal mechanism that locates the escalation of protest repertoires within an organisational competition'.[73] This mechanism is in large part rooted in *within-movement* competition: for instance, as established social movement organisations such as trade unions monopolise moderate and established forms of collective action, other organisations feel the need to employ more radical forms of collective action in order to outflank them to gain support from their shared social base.[74] This area of within-movement dynamics is an important area to explore with regard to CE, one which Eatwell's original article did not include. The most relevant questions raised from these observations is that once radicalisation through *within-movement competition* had occurred, is violence *between* social movements more likely? Will the actors involved become socialised to use violence in general?

The relationship between the social and political structures in which movements act and how they develop is an area which has also been explored by academics. Building on the work of Zald and Useem, David S. Meyer and Suzanne Staggenborg argue that one of the key factors in understanding movement-countermovement relationships is the 'political opportunity structure' in which the groups operate. Political opportunity structures are the arrangement of various exogenous factors which influence the 'development, tactics and impact' of social movements; these consist of stable and structural elements of political opportunity, such as the openness of political institutions, and more dynamic aspects such as the shifting currents of public opinion and political discourse.[75]

Most pertinently, Meyer and Staggenborg posit that the elements of the political opportunity structure which influence a social movement's tactical decision to engage in direct action, including the use of political violence, are the efficacy of institutional means of campaigning and the point at which the movement's protest cycle is at. On the whole, if institutional channels of redress (such as lobbying politicians) are closed to movements, they will likely start to employ tactics of direct action and civil disobedience. The more closed to them these institutional channels are, the more likely adherents of social movements are to engage in political violence.[76]

Similarly, della Porta demonstrates how structural and environmental factors such as the availability of 'environmental' and 'organizational resources',[77] a movement's position in its 'protest cycle',[78] and the style in which movements are policed all to a greater or lesser extent affect the tactical decisions of social movement organisations.[79] These writers all usefully draw our attention to the role that the structure of political opportunities and other environmental factors play in shaping interactions between movements and countermovements, but more can be said on this point in relation to cumulative extremism. For instance, this study will investigate how the structure of political opportunities may differ for international and domestic movements and countermovements; i.e. how is an M/CM conflict affected when one movement has an international dimension and the opposing movement is very much rooted in domestic affairs, such as the Northern Irish Civil Rights movement and their loyalist opponents?[80]

Interestingly, McCauley and Moskalenko have posited that social movement organisations may in fact use processes of cumulative extremism in an instrumental or strategic way, to shape how a conflict develops; specifically, a strategy that they refer to as 'Jujitsu Politics'. McCauley and Moskalenko argue that smaller groups, when threatened by an outgroup, tend to increase their group cohesion, as well as their respect for ingroup leaders, their penalties for ingroup deviates, and 'idealization of ingroup norms'.[81] Larger groups tend to respond in a similar manner, with an increase in ingroup identification such as nationalism or patriotism.[82] McCauley and Moskalenko argue that this response can be strategically used to the advantage of political groups with an aggressive agenda. A terrorist organisation can be fairly sure that in attacking a population they will provoke a counterattack. In turn, this will radicalise members of their own community who were previously not as committed to their aims. McCauley and Moskalenko argue that the perpetrators of 9/11 had just such a dynamic in mind when planning their attack:

> Dr. Ayman Al Zawahiri enunciated this strategy... If the shrapnel of war reach American homes, he opined, Americans will either give up their aims in Muslim countries or will come out from behind their Muslim stooges to seek revenge. If Americans move into Muslim countries, he predicted, the result will be jihad ... the U.S. move into Iraq has indeed been associated with increasing support for radical Islam in Muslim countries.[83]

These observations suggest that a key aspect of how and why CE may develop is the relationship between an SMO and a broader community or population. McCauley and Moskalenko further enforce this point when they describe terrorist groups as occupying the apex of a pyramid of activists and supporters:

> The base of the pyramid is composed of all who sympathize with the goals the terrorists say they are fighting for. In Northern Ireland, for instance, the base of the pyramid of support for the IRA was all those who agreed "Brits out."... From base to apex, higher levels of the pyramid are associated with decreased numbers but increased radicalization of beliefs, feelings, and behaviors.[84]

Importantly, McCauley and Moskalenko are perhaps not quite presenting the full picture in their theorising of the 'pyramid of support'. While the pyramid of supporters of the IRA does of course include all those who agree 'Brits out', the pyramid also contained many people who were included by virtue of their ascriptive ethnic identities rather than their ideological commitments. That is, young Catholics who knew very little about republicanism in general or the specific ideologies of the Official or Provisional IRA in specific, joined the paramilitaries out of revenge for the murder of their kin by loyalists or British soldiers.[85] It would seem to be the case, then, that the nature of the conflict cleavage between the opposing movements is an important factor with regard to the potential development of processes of CE.

Ascriptive and non-ascriptive divisions

Central to the analysis of CE is an understanding of the nature of the division between the opposing groups involved. For the purposes of this investigation, the quality which is of most interest is whether the conflict cleavage(s) are of an ascriptive or non-ascriptive nature, as this has a baring over the likelihood of a mutually radicalising relationship developing between oppositional movements. What 'distinguishes ascriptive identity groups is that they organize around characteristics that are largely beyond people's ability to choose, such as race, gender, class, physical handicap, ethnicity, sexual orientation, age, and nationality.'[86] It should be noted that acknowledging the ascriptive nature of certain groups does not mean that one is uncritically reifying terms such as 'race' and 'ethnicity', nor does it mean accepting them as being biologically-rooted 'facts' – indeed, it is widely accepted that all such categories are to a greater or lesser extent socially constructed. Nevertheless, the involuntary nature of these identities brings with them a certain longevity and enduring power. As Gutmann argues:

> To say that racial, gender, ethnic, and national identities are social constructions … is not to say that they are any easier to change than our genetic inheritance or physiognomy. Most African Americans, women, and deaf people cannot 'pass' for white, men, or hearing individuals; they can reinterpret their ascriptive identities but it is difficult if not impossible to give them up.[87]

Non-ascriptive groups, however, are voluntarist in nature; people decide whether to become members. This is something that Anderson refers to as 'practical identification': 'Practical identification occurs when people see themselves as members of the same collective agency – as participants in a common cooperative enterprise such as a firm or interest group, in a shared practice such as a hobby, sport, or artistic endeavor, or as committed to living and hence reasoning together about what to do, as in a democracy.'[88] There have been many instances where social movements have mobilised against each other across non-ascriptive conflict cleavages, such as across political divisions as with communists and fascists or over single-issue campaigns such as the pro-choice and pro-life movements with regard to abortion laws.

The reason this distinction is important is that it can influence how a conflict is structured. Two or more social movement organisations or political parties competing over the same community (i.e. two opposing political groups competing over the electorate) may be more reluctant to engage in violent or illegal tactics to achieve their goals than organisations claiming to represent distinct and separate social groups fighting across that cleavage. Indeed, the literature on ethnic conflict has shown that when a society is deeply divided along ethnic lines, competing parties often try to exploit the situation by positioning themselves as the group most dedicated to the interests of their ethnic community and the most hard-line with respect to other ethnic communities – a process that is called 'outbidding', and which may end in violent inter-ethnic conflict.[89]

This is an issue that is influenced far more by the nature of the society in which the conflict occurs than by the nature of the organisations involved, though.

Indeed, many organisations have attempted to exacerbate tensions along ascriptive lines between different communities so as to capitalise on resultant feelings of animosity. However, if these cleavages are not particularly salient within a society, these efforts are far less likely to be successful. Many far-right groups in Western Europe have attempted to engender hostility between white and non-white communities with the aim of starting a 'race war' and gaining support as the defenders of 'white' interests. However, this is not a lens through which sufficient numbers of citizens have viewed these societies, and consequently these endeavours have fallen on stony ground. In societies which are more significantly structured around such ascriptive divisions, it may be easier for organisations or movements to present themselves as representing the 'material and symbolic interests' of broader communities (be they based on ethnic, national, or other ascriptive identities).[90] As such, they may find it easier to exploit these divisions or otherwise mobilise broader communities behind them. Indeed, a significant difference between conflicts fought along ascriptive and non-ascriptive lines is that the former may be more likely to have large extant communities to draw support from or to mobilise.

'White working class'

Throughout some of the chapters in this book the concept of the 'white working class' is used and, due to the highly contested nature of the concept, it requires some discussion here. The first and most obvious criticism which can be levelled at the concept is that it is never entirely clear exactly who is included within it. Even the 'white' part of the term, which is ostensibly clear in its denotation, is more obscure than it may at first appear. For instance, 'in the United Kingdom, the arrival of Poles and Lithuanians ... often occupying occupational and experiential positions that would align them with the 'white working class' has thrown into relief the problems with such forms of categorisation, complicating an already ambiguous terrain populated by the liminal 'whiteness' historically ascribed to Jewish, Irish and Gypsy/Traveller populations.'[91] Perhaps less surprisingly, there is also often a great deal of ambiguity over just who is considered to be 'working class'. As Thomas *et al.* warn, many observers writing about the 'white working class' focus 'only on the poorest elements receiving free school meals rather than on a broader understanding of the working class'.[92]

Aside from ambiguities over exactly where the boundaries of the 'white working class' lie, another problem with the label is that it is seldom used in a neutral fashion, but rather is often deployed in pursuit of a specific ideological or discursive goal. Rogaly and Taylor argue that elites have often employed evocations of struggling 'white working class' communities as part of cynical attempts to evoke feelings of communal competition and thus divide workers. 'Such representations of white British working-class people, in opposition both to black and minority ethnic British people and foreign nationals of all classes, are usefully divisive for owners of capital … Such divisions enable the maintenance of low pay and insecure working conditions.'[93]

Elsewhere, writing from a Critical Race Theory perspective, Gillborn describes the ways in which a system of white supremacy is in part maintained by elites through 'popular discourses that present the working class as, on one hand, innocent victims of unfair racial competition and, on the other hand, degenerate threats to social and economic order.'[94] The 'White poor', argues Gillborn, have never been unambiguously accepted as white by the group's gatekeepers, but have rather 'long existed on the boundaries of Whiteness'.[95] When it has suited middle class interests, such as when certain tax or welfare policy reforms have been sought, a distinction between the 'respectable working class' and the 'undeserving poor' or a 'feral underclass'[96] has been constructed and repeated through the media. Yet conversely, when middle class interests have been best served by shifting public attention away from economic inequality, then a discourse of a struggling 'white working class' which has been 'left behind' by multiculturalism and 'politically correct' 'race equality measures' has been employed.[97] That the 'white working class' can be portrayed so easily by the same parties as being both victims and deviants demonstrates that frequently when the concept is employed, rather than being part of a genuine attempt to understand social actors and processes, it is intentionally warped to fit a specific agenda. As Gillborn notes, for many of those who employ it, the 'flexibility of the discourse, its lack of precision, is one of its strengths'.[98]

Further, it is not just elites who employ the concept instrumentally. Lawler has averred that 'whiteness' is symbolically applied to the 'working class' so as to obscure the 'whiteness of the middle classes'.[99] Middle-class anxieties over English national identity have grown recently, argues Lawler, due to factors such as increasing demand for regional devolution. Discourses that construct working-class whiteness as an 'extreme whiteness, or hyper-whiteness, that works as a counterpoint to 'ordinary' (and middle-class) whiteness', and which is 'framed as an unreflexive, axiomatically racist whiteness', are an effective way of dealing with these middle-class anxieties.[100]

But perhaps the most significant criticism that should be levelled at the concept of the white working class is the way in which it presents a picture of a homogenous group with consistently similar attitudes and aims. As Rhodes points out, this has been demonstrated recently by the 'academic, journalistic and policy accounts of the relationship between the 'white working class' and far-right political parties such as the British National Party (BNP) and the English Defence League (EDL),' despite membership of the 'white working class' being a poor statistical predictor for involvement with such groups.[101]

Nevertheless, both the material realities and the perceptions of social class and ethnicity do affect certain social processes; and there certainly are trends which develop amongst low-income white communities. For instance, as Thomas et al. observed, there are 'clear currents of anxiety, even resentment, within low income White communities across Europe around growing ethnic diversity'.[102] The question arises, then, how to investigate the social processes in question without reifying the concept of the 'white working class'? Rhodes argues that the answer lies in Brubaker's distinction between the concepts of 'groupism' and 'groupness'. Rhodes posits that the use of the 'white working class' as a label often 'bear all the traits of what Brubaker terms "groupism"'.[103] That is, the term displays 'the tendency to take discrete, sharply differentiated, internally homogeneous and externally bounded groups as…fundamental units of social analysis'.[104] In doing this with the 'white working class', analysts risk 'missing the complexity of social relations and practices' by overlooking 'the various fragments and fault lines that serve to make it only a rough approximation of lived realities across a spectrum of differences'.[105] This analytical oversimplification *can* be avoided, however, by considering the 'white working class' to be a 'category' not 'a group'; by thinking, 'not in terms of substantial groups or entities but in terms of practical categories, cultural idioms, cognitive schemas, discursive frames, organizational routines, institutional forms, political projects and contingent events'.[106] Doing this 'means taking as a basic analytical category not the 'group' as an entity but groupness as a contextually fluctuating conceptual variable.'[107] The distinction between 'groupism' and 'groupness' enables us to separate out the ways in which 'groupness' is constructed from the actual labels themselves, to gain an understanding of the 'organising powers' of social categorisations such as the 'white working class' without presenting them as a homogenous unit or uncritically reifying or reproducing them.[108]

The preceding discussion demonstrates that there is a rich literature on social movements, political violence and radicalisation to draw upon in exploring the dynamic of cumulative extremism. Conceptual tools and the embryo of a theoretical framework through which to proceed are provided, but most importantly many questions are raised. While these studies have done a fine job in laying the groundwork, none of them have specifically put the interactive escalation of M/CM movements and the attendant effect this process can have on extant broader social groups under the microscope.

Conclusion

The concept of cumulative extremism, recently coined by Roger Eatwell, is an important one in many respects. It can shed light on how antagonism between groups with mutually exclusive goals may sharpen to the point of political violence. It asks interesting and significant questions about the nature of the relationship between social movements, social movement organisations, and the wider social groups that they claim to represent and court for support and resources. Further, and most importantly, in-depth investigation into the concept may help to suggest policy solutions that may interrupt pathways to radicalisation, perhaps ultimately saving lives.

Despite these points, and the growing use of the concept, there has been insufficient empirical investigation into it. This book will conduct a comparative investigation across several different case studies using a qualitative methodology to address this gap in the literature. In so doing it will demonstrate some of the key factors which lead to the escalation, non-escalation or de-escalation of movement–countermovement contests; what developments contribute to M/CM contests mobilising increasing numbers of people for either or both opposing movements; and how and why these contests may cause communal polarisation.

The book's first chapter shall examine the interplay between fascists and anti-fascists in the inter-war period, largely focusing on the development of, and responses to, the British Union of Fascists (BUF) from 1932 to 1939. The next two chapters shall focus on the two cycles of mobilisation that occurred between the far right and far left in Britain between 1967 and 2000. The formation and rise of the National Front from 1967 provoked a concomitant growth in anti-fascism in the form of the Anti-Nazi League and Rock Against Racism, just as the British National Party's growth from 1982 generated the formation of Anti-Fascist Action and other anti-fascist groups. For the fourth chapter, the book's focus shifts over to Ulster in the early 1960s and the interactions between the Catholic civil rights movement and the Protestant loyalist movement. Careful attention shall be paid to the factors at play in Northern Ireland between 1960 and 1976 that caused the situation to escalate from peaceful protests to lethal civil war, with paramilitary groups emerging from both communities. Chapter five shall assess the more recent case of the far-right counter-jihad movement in Britain which formed in response to the actions of British Islamist extremists. Finally, the conclusion shall present a framework for assessing the development of cumulative extremism, constructed using the observations and analyses of the preceding chapters.

Notes

1 Thomas, Paul. 'From Petrol Bombs to Performance Indicators: The 2001 Riots and the Emergence of Community Cohesion', in *Rioting in the UK and France: A Comparative Analysis*, Edited by David Waddington, Fabien Jobard and Mike King (London: Routledge, 2011), p. 82.
2 Cantle, Ted. *Community Cohesion: A Report of the Independent Review Team* (London: Her Majesty's Stationery Office, 2001).
3 Ibid., p. 9.
4 Ibid., p. 9.
5 Ramamurthy, Anandi. *Black Star: Britain's Asian Youth Movements* (London: Pluto Press, 2013), p. 194.
6 Eatwell, Roger. 'Community Cohesion and Cumulative Extremism in Contemporary Britain', *Political Quarterly*, 77, no. 2 (2006), p. 205.
7 Ibid., p. 213.
8 Eatwell, Roger and Matthew J. Goodwin. 'Conclusion', in *The New Extremism in 21st Century Britain*, Edited by Roger Eatwell and Matthew J. Goodwin (London: Routledge, 2010), p. 243.
9 Busher, Joel and Graham Macklin. 'The Missing Spirals of Violence: Four Waves of Movement–Countermovement Contest in Post-war Britain', *Behavioral Sciences of Terrorism and Political Aggression*, 7, no. 1 (2015), p. 53.

10 Goodwin, Matthew. *The Roots of Extremism: The English Defence League and the Counter-Jihad Challenge* (London: Chatham House, 2013), p. 5; Copsey, Nigel, *The English Defence League: Challenging Our Country and Our Values of Social Inclusion, Fairness and Equality* (London: Faith Matters, 2010), p. 11.

11 Bartlett, Jamie and Jonathan Birdwell. *Cumulative Radicalisation Between the Far-Right and Islamist Groups in the UK: A Review of Evidence* (London: Demos, 2013), p. 12.

12 Bartlett, Jamie and Mark Littler. *Inside the EDL: Populist Politics in a Digital Age* (London: Demos, 2011) p. 13; Feldman, Matthew. *From Radical-Right Islamophobia to Cumulative Extremism* (London: Faith Matters, 2012), p. 4; Copsey, *The English Defence League*, p. 11.

13 Feldman, Matthew and Mark Littler. *Tell MAMA Reporting 2014/2015: Annual Monitoring, Cumulative Extremism, and Policy Implications* (Middlesbrough: Centre for Fascist, Anti-Fascist and Post-Fascist Studies, 2015), p. 3.

14 Ibid., p. 3.

15 McCauley, Clark and Sophia Moskalenko. *Friction: How Radicalisation Happens to Them and Us* (Oxford: Oxford University Press, 2011), pp. 117–119.

16 Alimi, Y. Eitan, Charles Demetriou and Lorenzo Bosi. *The Dynamics of Radicalization: A Relational and Comparative Perspective* (Oxford: Oxford University Press, 2015), pp. 48–49.

17 See: HM Government. *Contest: The United Kingdom Government's Strategy for Countering Terrorism: Annual Report* (London: TSO, 2013), p. 22; and Home Affairs Select Committee. *The Roots of Violent Radicalisation* (London: TSO, 2012), pp. 20–21.

18 See: Goodwin, Matthew. 'Woolwich Attack and the far Right: Three Points to Consider When the Dust Settles', *Guardian Online* [https://www.theguardian.com/commentisfree/2013/may/23/woolwich-attack-far-right-three-points] (23 May 2013), Accessed on 5 February 2017; and Malik, Nikita. 'The Real Terrorist Risk in Europe Is "Reciprocal Radicalisation", Where far Right and Islamist Extremists Boost each other's Popularity', *The Independent* [http://www.independent.co.uk/voices/berlin-christmas-market-attack-terrorism-terrorist-refugees-far-right-neo-nazi-extremes-reciprocal-a7489946.html] (22 December 2016), Accessed on 14 February 2017.

19 Busher, Joel and Graham Macklin. 'The Missing Spirals of Violence: Four Waves of Movement–Countermovement Contest in Post-war Britain', *Behavioral Sciences of Terrorism and Political Aggression*, 7, no. 1 (2015), pp. 65–66.

20 Bartlett, Jamie and Jonathan Birdwell. *Cumulative Radicalisation Between the Far-Right and Islamist Groups in the UK: A Review of Evidence* (London: Demos, 2013), p. 7 and p. 12.

21 Anderson, David. *The Terrorism Acts in 2012: Report of the Independent Reviewer on the Operation of the Terrorism Act 2000 and Part 1 of the Terrorism Act 2006* (London: TSO, 2013), p. 42.

22 Busher, Joel and Graham Macklin. 'Interpreting "Cumulative Extremism": Six Proposals for Enhancing Conceptual Clarity', *Terrorism and Political Violence*, 27, no. 5 (2014), p. 886.

23 Eatwell, Roger. 'Community Cohesion and Cumulative Extremism in Contemporary Britain', *Political Quarterly*, 77, no. 2 (2006), pp. 213–215.

24 Goodwin, Matthew. *The Roots of Extremism: The English Defence League and the Counter-Jihad Challenge* (London: Chatham House, 2013), p. 5.

25 Copsey, Nigel. *The English Defence League: Challenging Our Country and Our Values of Social Inclusion, Fairness and Equality* (London: Faith Matters, 2010), p. 11.

26 Holbrook, Donald and Max Taylor. 'Introduction', in *Extreme Right-Wing Political Violence and Terrorism*, Edited by Max Taylor, P. M. Currie and Donald Holbrook (London: Bloomsbury, 2013), p. 7.

27 Jackson, Paul. *The EDL: Britain's 'New Far Right' Social Movement* (Northampton: RNM Publications, 2011), p. 75.

28 Blanquart, Gabrielle and David M. Cook. 'Twitter Influence and Cumulative Perceptions of Extremist Support: A Case Study of Geert Wilders', *Australian Counterterrorism Conference*, 22 (2013), p. 3.

29 Kundnani, Arun. *Blind Spot? Security Narratives and Far-Right Violence in Europe* (The Hague: International Centre for Counter-Terrorism, 2012), pp. 9–10.

30 Ebner, Julia. *The Rage: The Vicious Circle of Islamist and Far-Right Extremism* (London: I.B.Tauris, 2017), p. 10.

31 Feldman, Matthew and Mark Littler. *Tell MAMA Reporting 2014/2015: Annual Monitoring, Cumulative Extremism, and Policy Implications* (Middlesbrough: Centre for Fascist, Anti-Fascist and Post-Fascist Studies, 2015), p. 13.

32 Busher, Joel and Graham Macklin. 'Interpreting "Cumulative Extremism": Six Proposals for Enhancing Conceptual Clarity', *Terrorism and Political Violence*, 27, no. 5 (2014), p. 887.

33 Busher, Joel and Graham Macklin. 'The Missing Spirals of Violence: Four Waves of Movement–Countermovement Contest in Post-war Britain', *Behavioral Sciences of Terrorism and Political Aggression*, 7, no. 1 (2015), p. 55.

34 Eatwell, Roger and Matthew J. Goodwin. 'Conclusion', in *The New Extremism in 21st Century Britain*, Edited by Roger Eatwell and Matthew J. Goodwin (London: Routledge, 2010), p. 7.

35 Busher, Joel and Graham Macklin. 'The Missing Spirals of Violence: Four Waves of Movement–Countermovement Contest in Post-War Britain', *Behavioral Sciences of Terrorism and Political Aggression*, 7, no. 1 (2015), p. 54.

36 Feldman, Matthew and Mark Littler. *Tell MAMA Reporting 2014/2015: Annual Monitoring, Cumulative Extremism, and Policy Implications* (Middlesbrough: Centre for Fascist, Anti-Fascist and Post-Fascist Studies, 2015), p. 14.

37 Eatwell, Roger. 'Community Cohesion and Cumulative Extremism in Contemporary Britain', *Political Quarterly*, 77, no. 2 (2006), p. 213.

38 Fekete, Liz. 'Anti-Fascism or Anti-Extremism?' *Race & Class*, 55, no. 4 (2014), p. 33.

39 Mahoney, James. 'Comparative-Historical Methodology', *Annual Review of Sociology*, 30 (2004), p. 81.

40 Goodwin, Matthew. 'Woolwich Attack and the Far Right: Three Points to Consider When the Dust Settles', *Guardian Online* [https://www.theguardian.com/commentisfree/2013/may/23/woolwich-attack-far-right-three-points] (23 May 2013), Accessed on 5 February 2017.

41 Rueschemeyer, Dietrich. 'Can One or a Few Cases Yield Theoretical Gains?' in *Comparative Historical Analysis in the Social Sciences*, Edited by James Mahoney and Dietrich Rueschemeyer (Cambridge: Cambridge University Press, 2003), p. 307.

42 Kundnani, Arun. 'Radicalisation: The Journey of a Concept', *Race and Class* 54, no. 2 (2012), p. 4.

43 Ibid., p. 5.

44 Ibid., p. 5.

45 Silva, Derek M. D. '"Radicalisation: The Journey of a Concept", Revisited', *Race and Class*, 59, no. 4 (2018), p. 48.

46 Hoskins, Andrew and Ben O'Loughlin. 'Media and the Myth of Radicalization', *Media War & Conflict*, 2, no.2 (2009), pp. 107–110.

47 Alimi, Eitan Y., Charles Demetriou and Lorenzo Bosi. *The Dynamics of Radicalization: A Relational and Comparative Perspective* (Oxford: Oxford University Press, 2015), p. vii.

48 Neumann, Peter R. 'The Trouble with Radicalization', *International Affairs*, 89, no. 4 (2013), p. 873.

49 Bartlett, Jamie, Jonathan Birdwell and Michael King. *The Edge of Violence: A Radical Approach to Extremism* (London: Demos, 2010), p. 7.

50 Bartlett, Jamie and Carl Miller. 'The Edge of Violence: Towards Telling the Difference Between Violent and Non-Violent Radicalization', *Terrorism and Political Violence*, 24, no. 1 (2011), p. 2.

51 Communities and Local Government Committee. *Preventing Violent Extremism: Sixth Report of Session 2009–10* (London: TSO, 2010).
52 Qurashi, Fahid. 'Just Get On with It: Implementing the Prevent Duty in Higher Education and the Role of Academic Expertise', *Education, Citizenship and Social Justice*, 12, no. 3 (2017), p. 205.
53 Kundnani, Arun. *Spooked! How Not to Prevent Violent Extremism* (London: Institute of Race Relations, 2009), p. 39.
54 Richards, Anthony. 'From Terrorism to "Radicalization" to "Extremism": Counterterrorism Imperative or Loss of Focus?' *International Affairs*, 91, no. 2 (2015), p. 376.
55 Ibid., p. 371.
56 Alimi, Eitan Y., Charles Demetriou and Lorenzo Bosi. *The Dynamics of Radicalization: A Relational and Comparative Perspective* (Oxford: Oxford University Press, 2015), p. vi.
57 Busher, Joel, Donald Holbrook and Graham Macklin. 'The Internal Brakes on Violent Escalation: A Typology', *Behavioral Sciences of Terrorism and Political Aggression*, 11, no.1 (2019), p. 21.
58 Tilly, Charles and Sidney Tarrow. *Contentious Politics* (Colorado: Paradigm Publishers, 2007), p. 4.
59 Ibid., p. 11.
60 Ibid., p. 12.
61 Ibid., p. 16.
62 Ibid., pp. 16–17.
63 Zald, Mayer N. and Bert Useem. 'Movement and Countermovement Interaction: Mobilization, Tactics, and State Involvement', in *Social Movements in an Organizational Society*, Edited by Mayer N. Zald and John D. McCarthy (Oxford: Transaction Books, 1987). pp. 247–248.
64 Ibid., p. 248.
65 Della Porta, Donatella. *Social Movements, Political Violence, and the State: A Comparative Analysis of Italy and Germany* (Cambridge: Cambridge University Press, 1995), p. 154.
66 Ibid., p. 154.
67 Ibid., p. 155.
68 McCauley, Clark and Sophia Moskalenko. 'Mechanisms of Political Radicalization', *Terrorism and Political Violence*, 20, no. 3 (2008), pp. 426–428.
69 Ibid., p. 427.
70 Ibid., p. 427.
71 Alimi, Y. Eitan, Charles Demetriou and Lorenzo Bosi. *The Dynamics of Radicalization: A Relational and Comparative Perspective* (Oxford: Oxford University Press, 2015), p. 46.
72 Bloom, Mia. *Dying to Kill: The Allure of Suicide Terror* (New York: Columbia University Press, 2005).
73 Della Porta, Donatella. *Clandestine Political Violence* (Cambridge: Cambridge University Press, 2013), p. 76.
74 Ibid., p. 108.
75 Meyer, David S. and Staggenborg, Suzanne. 'Movements, Countermovements, and the Structure of Political Opportunity', *American Journal of Sociology*, 101, no. 6 (1996), p. 1633.
76 Ibid., p. 1650.
77 Della Porta, Donatella. *Social Movements, Political Violence, and the State: A Comparative Analysis of Italy and Germany* (Cambridge: Cambridge University Press, 1995), p. 85 & p. 26.

78 Ibid., p. 107.
79 Della Porta, Donatella. *Clandestine Political Violence* (Cambridge: Cambridge University Press, 2013), p. 33.
80 Dooley, Brian. *Black and Green: The Fight for Civil Rights in Northern Ireland & Black America* (London: Pluto Press, 1998), p. 4.
81 McCauley, Clark and Sophia Moskalenko. *Friction: How Radicalization Happens to Them and Us* (Oxford: Oxford University Press, 2011), p. 426.
82 Ibid., p. 426.
83 Ibid., p. 427.
84 McCauley, Clark and Sophia Moskalenko. 'Mechanisms of Political Radicalization: Pathways Toward Terrorism', *Terrorism and Political Violence*, 20, no. 3 (2008), p. 417.
85 Moloney, Ed. *Voices From the Grave* (London: Faber and Faber, 2010), p. 47.
86 Gutmann, Amy. *Identity in Democracy* (Princeton: Princeton University Press, 2003), p. 89.
87 Ibid., p. 91.
88 Anderson, Elizabeth. 'Sen, Ethics and Democracy', *Feminist Economics*, 9, no. 2–3 (2011), pp. 242–244.
89 Moore, Gavin, Neophytos Loizides, Nukhet A. Sandal and Alexandros Lordos. 'Winning Peace Frames: Intra-Ethnic Outbidding in Northern Ireland and Cyprus', *West European Politics*, 37, no. 1 (2014), p. 159.
90 De Fazio, Gianluca. 2013 'The Radicalization of Contention in Northern Ireland, 1968–1972: A Relational Perspective', *Mobilization: An International Quarterly*, 18, no. 4 (2013), p. 477.
91 Rhodes, James. 'The "Trouble" with the "White Working Class": Whiteness, Class and "Groupism"', *Identities: Global Studies in Culture and Power*, 19, no. 4 (2012), p. 488.
92 Thomas, Paul, Joel Busher, Graham Macklin, Michelle Rogerson and Kris Christmann. 'Hopes and Fears: Community Cohesion and the "White Working Class" in One of the "Failed Spaces" of Multiculturalism', *Sociology: The Journal of the British Sociological Association* (2017), pp. 4–5.
93 Rogaly, Ben and Becky Taylor. 'Moving Representations of the "Indigenous White Working Class"', in *Who Cares about the White Working Class?* Edited by Kjartan Páll Sveinsson (London: Runnymede, 2009), pp. 51–52.
94 Gillborn, David. 'The White Working Class, Racism and Respectability: Victims, Degenerates and Interest-Convergence', *British Journal of Educational Studies*, 58, no. 1 (2010), pp. 3–4.
95 Ibid., p. 14.
96 Ibid., p. 17.
97 Ibid., p. 12.
98 Ibid., p. 20.
99 Lawler, Steph. 'White like Them: Whiteness and Anachronistic Space in Representations of the English White Working Class', *Ethnicities*, 12, no. 4 (2012), p. 409.
100 Ibid., pp. 410–411.
101 Rhodes, James. 'The "Trouble" with the "White Working Class": Whiteness, Class and "Groupism"', *Identities: Global Studies in Culture and Power*, 19, no. 4 (2012), p. 487.
102 Thomas, Paul, Joel Busher, Graham Macklin, Michelle Rogerson and Kris Christmann. 'Hopes and Fears: Community Cohesion and the "White Working Class" in One of the "Failed Spaces" of Multiculturalism', *Sociology: The Journal of the British Sociological Association*, 52, no. 2 (2017), p. 5.

103 Rhodes, James. 'The "Trouble" with the "White Working Class": Whiteness, Class and "Groupism"', *Identities: Global Studies in Culture and Power*, 19, no. 4 (2012), pp. 489–490.
104 Ibid., pp. 489–490.
105 Ibid., pp. 489–490.
106 Ibid., p. 490.
107 Ibid., p. 490.
108 Ibid., p. 490.

2

FASCISTS AND ANTI-FASCISTS, 1920–1940

Introduction

In the 1930s, a movement-countermovement (M/CM) contest developed between fascists and anti-fascists in Britain. The conflict between the far right and the far left led to tens of thousands of people being mobilised on the streets of Britain, as well as many instances of large-scale political violence and public disorder. This chapter will explore these events to examine whether or not cumulative extremism developed between these groups; in Roger Eatwell's terms, if and how 'one form of extremism [fascism]' fed off and magnified 'other forms [militant anti-fascism; communism].'[1] The key questions here, then, are to what extent did the activities of the fascists and anti-fascists affect the levels of mobilisation and the radicalisation of their opponents.

1920–1932

The embryonic rumblings of the fascist/anti-fascist contest which would take place in the 1930s occurred a decade earlier. The earliest expressions of British fascism were in the late 1910s and early 1920s, with the formation of groups such as the British Fascisti (later the British Fascists) and the Britons.[2] While in reality these groups were more ultra-conservative or proto-fascist in character, with relatively unsophisticated political programs and philosophies, they were nevertheless broadly speaking both anti-Semitic and hostile towards the left and organised labour in general.[3] Accordingly, a number of small-scale skirmishes occurred between the British far left and the incipient British fascist movement. In 1925, the British Fascisti provocatively kidnapped the leading Communist Party of Great Britain (CPGB) activist Harry Pollitt; an act which understandably alarmed the communists.[4] In response to the fascist threat the CPGB organised a 'Workers' Defence Corps', which later became known as the 'Labour League of Ex-Servicemen'. After a group of more hard-line activists split from the British Fascisti and formed the National Fascisti, there was a series of low-key tit-for-tat encounters between the CPGB and National Fascisti. Meetings were disrupted and small fights occurred between the two groups. This back and forth culminated in the hijacking at gunpoint of a van carrying issues of the pro-Labour *Daily Herald* by four members of the National Fascisti. However, lack of funds, widespread disinterest, and internal disputes meant that the British fascist movement failed to achieve serious momentum in the 1920s, and as it ebbed into insignificance so did the tactical response from the left.[5]

Robert Skidelsky has argued that the later conflict between the BUF and its opponents can be thought of as 'an interactive chain of provocation and counter-provocation that probably has its roots in the New Party.'[6] Although this description is arguably unfair in ascribing equal measures of blame to the two sides, it is correct in assessing that some of the seeds for the later conflict were sown right from the beginning of the New Party. Oswald Mosley, who had been a Labour party member, formed the New Party (NP) with a small number of rebellious Independent Labour Party (ILP) MPs that resigned with him – as well as a smaller number of other MPs – in February 1931. Right from the very beginning, and throughout the party's short life, New Party meetings were plagued by left-wing disruption. Much of this opposition, especially towards the end of the NP's life, came from the Communist Party. As Mosley's burgeoning fascism came to the fore, the far left mobilised in opposition. Importantly, the communists employed physical force opposition, violently disrupting several New Party meetings and viciously attacking NP speakers with weapons.[7] Perhaps unsurprisingly, Mosley felt the need to train stewards to become a 'defence force'. Even after the New Party had been wound down, its 'youth movement', NUPA, carried on holding meetings and events which were often characterised by violence and disorder. Indeed, in the later days of the New Party/NUPA the pattern of provocation, disruption and violence between Mosley's 'Biff Boys' and communists was well established. Before long, 'the Communists and NUPA were inter-reliant and constituted the main audience at the other's meetings, with the result that a tradition was born'.[8]

However, initially the main source of the opposition to the NP was not so much born out of movement-countermovement interactive escalation, but rather came from the electoral threat it posed to the Labour Party. Not only had Mosley enticed several MPs away from Labour when forming the NP, but there was also a concern that the entire ILP could defect and join Mosley. Furthermore, the Labour party, being a minority government in an economic crisis, was in a particularly vulnerable position.[9] Labour responded to this threat by organising large high-profile meetings in the constituencies of the former Labour MPs, by utilising the local Labour-friendly press into spreading anti-NP propaganda, and by mobilising the rank-and-file at New Party meetings. These tactics meant that 'the New Party fell on stony ground', and their message failed to win over their target audience of working class Labour supporters.[10] It soon became clear that Labour's attempt to marginalise the New Party had been successful – although in the short-term it may have been something of a pyrrhic victory. The NP suffered a disappointing by-election defeat at Ashton-under-Lyne in what should have been a very fertile constituency for them in April 1931, but Labour also lost out to the Conservatives who gained the seat from them. As the electoral threat from the NP waned, so did Labour's opposition to them.[11]

John Strachey later claimed that Mosley's ideological radicalisation to fascism can be pinpointed to this one specific event; when a large mob of Labour supporters in Ashton-under-Lyne hurled vicious abuse at Mosley for splitting the anti-Tory vote and, in their eyes, handing the constituency to the Tories. As Nigel Copsey has argued, this is certainly a reductionist position; however, the hostile reaction the New Party received from Labour supporters, coupled with the way the Labour Party successfully managed to marginalise them in their target constituencies, undoubtedly contributed to the conditions in which 'Mosley finally embraced fascism'.[12] Nevertheless, it is important to note that during this time the M/CM contest was beginning to demonstrate processes of CE, in that the violence experienced by New Party members contributed to their tactical radicalisation; specifically, the use of stewards to physically police events and the desensitisation towards, and socialisation in, political violence occurred partly due to the physical-force opposition they were subjected to at the hands of the communists. It is also equally important to describe the limits of this process. While some degree of socialisation to violence occurred through the antagonists' interactions, this only affected a small pool of activists. Further, the level of violence never exceeded small-scale non-lethal scuffles, so in terms of intensity and scale, this dynamic, while present, was low-key.

1932–1935

Oswald Mosley formed the British Union of Fascists in October 1932.[13] Between its inception and the spring of 1933 the BUF began growing rapidly, and so caught the attention of the Home Office (HO). In a report to the latter, MI5 linked the rising fortunes of continental fascism to their British counterparts, noting that since

> the advent of the Hitler government in Germany, the British Movement seems to have increased its activities and its meetings have been more numerous. At least 16 branches of various sections of the movement exist in London and these hold regular meetings.[14]

The Home Office later gained intelligence showing that 'Mosley was in receipt of a substantial subvention from Mussolini'.[15]

Indeed, international events were to be the impetus for the initial growth of both the fascist and anti-fascist movements, rather than any interactions between the two. This is evidenced by the way that the levels of anti-fascist activity against Mosley's activists were lower in the early stages of the BUF's life than they had been throughout all of the NP's, but increased dramatically after news about the Reichstag fire, Hitler's ascension, and reports of Nazi mistreatment of Jews, anti-fascists and workers came to light.[16] The international involvement in, or transnational aspect of, contentious episodes can influence M/CM contests in direct and indirect ways. In terms of the latter, it may produce what is referred to in the literature on ethnic conflict and civil war as a 'demonstration effect', whereby a contentious episode in one country may help 'activists elsewhere to develop new strategies... [and] can also prompt new calculations regarding the chances of success and the likely costs.'[17] In this instance, it certainly seems that the BUF felt that the successes of European fascists were an indication of the potential for their own success while anti-fascists had the possible consequences of their failure to resist fascism thrown into sharp relief. In terms of the former, a transnational movement can form 'solidarity networks' with their counterparts in other countries who can then help them by 'mobilizing material resources'.[18] Here the 'substantial subvention from Mussolini' which the Home Office referred to can only have helped the BUF in their efforts to build a domestic fascist movement.

The British left was largely divided into two camps over the best way to tackle fascism, one moderate or 'legal' and one 'radical'.[19] The most prominent left-wing anti-fascist group was the Moscow influenced Communist Party of Great Britain (CPGB). Having witnessed the Nazi power grab in Germany in the early 1930s, which had been made easier by the fractured relationship between German communists and social democrats, Moscow urged the CPGB to approach 'the Labour Party, trade unions and the Co-operative Party in March 1933 with a proposal for joint activity in a "United Front Against Fascism"'.[20] However, of the groups invited into the United Front, only the more radical ILP was prepared to work with the CPGB against the BUF. The reformist Labour Party and Trades Union Congress (TUC) were convinced that a strong democratic system was the best antidote to fascism, whereas direct action would just feed extremism of the left and right. They discouraged 'extra-legal' activities, arguing that militancy from the left could act as a 'recruiting sergeant' for the BUF. Instead, Labour and the TUC preferred to tackle fascists through parliament, and by running educational campaigns.[21] However, Labour did take the threat of international fascism seriously, and gave its official support to the boycott of German goods which had been organised by various members of the British labour movement and Jewish community.[22]

Undeterred by the rejection from the leaders of the mainstream labour movement, the communists went about the business of opposing the fascists head-on. BUF meetings faced organised violent disruption from the CPGB in Manchester, Leeds, Southampton, Durham, Stockton, Oxford and London.[23] Communists also laid siege to the BUF branch in Walworth and attacked the BUF's HQ.[24] Throughout the year, radical tactics were being employed with increasing frequency. The Metropolitan Police counted 28 'disorders' involving the BUF in 1933.[25] It should be borne in mind, though, that this did not necessarily represent a dramatic radicalisation of the CPGB, as 'Communist disruption long predated the establishment of the BUF. Throughout the 1920s they had targeted Labour politicians as much as Conservative ones.'[26] Further, apart from the formation of the Fascist Defence Force in 1932, the aggressive actions of the communists were not reciprocated by the BUF, who rarely, if ever, disrupted their enemies' meetings throughout this period.

Indeed, in its early life the BUF was much more extreme and violent in its within-movement, rather than M/CM, interactions. Often this was down to rivalry, but the groups' relationship to their European counterparts was also a contributing factor. The first major inter-fascist clash occurred in 1933. At this time, in a bid to strengthen good relations with Italy – and also to distance itself from the more extreme events in Nazi Germany – Mosley tried to clampdown on the anti-Semitism in the BUF.[27] However, on 20 July, members of the British Fascists happened to pass the BUF's headquarters in Chelsea while chanting anti-Semitic slogans and wearing black shirts. A BUF Staff Officer, Mr Piercy, observed the BF and stated that 'these chaps are getting us a bad name, we had better see what we can do'.[28] It seems likely that Mr Piercy then conferred with Mosley, before ordering a large BUF contingent of around 40 members to storm the British Fascists' HQ. The Blackshirts smashed the windows of the HQ to gain access, then spent about ten minutes doing 'as much damage as possible'. They caused approximately £300 worth of damage and assaulted several of the BF present there.[29]

This incident was the first in a series of clashes within the British fascist movement across 1933, as Mosley attempted to either extinguish or control the rival fascist groups. Not long after this, on 2 October members of the British Fascists and the BUF would clash again in Sloane Street, London.[30] A little over a week later, on 12 October 1933, 'a group of men clad in uniform and purporting to act on behalf of Sir Oswald Mosley's British Union of Fascists' attempted to raid the HQ of the Imperial Fascist League (IFL).[31] Reporting on the incident, the British Fascists showed solidarity with their fascist fellow travellers, and claimed that the BUF were in fact controlled by communists and Jews:

> We offer our sympathies and expressions of common solidarity to our friends of the Imperial Fascist League… The Jew and the Communist driven into their last ditches, are attempting to save the day by subsidising and directing so-called Fascist organisations in order that they may discredit the Fascist ideal.[32]

The IFL, for their part, also frequently attacked the BUF as being under Jewish influence in their journal, *The Fascist*, calling them 'The British Jewnion of Fascists' and 'Kosher Fascists'.[33] Towards the end of 1933, Mosley changed tack and sought to court the National Socialist German Workers' Party (NSDAP).

However, he was spurned when the NSDAP stated that they felt it improper to favour one British fascist group over another while they were in conflict. In response, Mosley ordered his Blackshirts to close down the feud. In a bid to do just this, on Sunday 24 November 1933 around 50 Blackshirts viciously attacked an Imperial Fascist League meeting in Trinity Hall, Great Portland Street. The Hall was severely damaged in the ensuing fight, which one newspaper described as 'the biggest fight that had ever been seen at a London meeting.'[34] This intra-fascist feud is worth noting because it represents one of the few times the BUF aggressively and pro-actively pursued a strategy of political violence, rather than engaging in excessive violence at their own meetings or provoking it with demonstrations and marches.[35]

Paralleling the division within the labour movement, the Anglo-Jewish community's response to the rise of fascism was manifested in both a radical and moderate form. Of the former, several organisations were created to coordinate direct action against the fascists. The League of Jewish Youth and the Jewish United Defence Association both attracted young Jews eager to tackle fascism and anti-Semitism head-on.[36] The United Jewish Protest Committee managed to mobilise thousands of Jews and Jewish allies in a march from Stepney Green to Hyde Park on 20 July 1933 'as a protest against the persecution of Jews in Germany.'[37] Further, there was a boycott of German goods organised by Jews and sections of the British left. The response from the traditional community leadership, the Board of Deputies of British Jews (BoD), however, was much more muted. They worried that Jewish direct action in Britain would play into the hands of the BUF, and first and foremost encouraged Jews to stay away from Fascist meetings and demonstrations, and to avoid violence at all costs. Further, they were concerned that the boycott against German goods could endanger the lives of their coreligionists in that country. They publicly distanced themselves from the movement, although many of them sympathised with it privately.[38]

The state also began taking a keen interest in the BUF. As early as 1931 the Home Office had requested that the police provide them with details of all disturbances between conflicting political groups, under which instructions they provided information on the BUF's clashes for its entire existence.[39] More specifically, at a conference called by the Home Office in November 1933, and attended by representatives from MI5 and Special Branch, it was decided to start collecting intelligence on Mosley's organisation just as they did on the CPGB (although the latter organisation ranked higher in their assessment of the threat from the two groups).[40] As a direct result of this Special Branch was increased in size by around 50%.[41] There was also more direct interventions by the state into the BUF's activities. Throughout 1933 some BUF paper sellers were arrested for breaching the peace after they provocatively marched through Jewish areas, even though they were technically obeying the letter of the law[42] (Lord Trenchard, the Commissioner for the Metropolitan Police at the time, 'recognized the problem of patrolling the borderline of the excesses of freedom of speech, and the injustice of punishing those provoked rather than the provokers').[43] Further, the police sometimes worked behind the scenes to prevent potentially violent circumstances developing, such as when they

> forestalled a BUF rally at White City on 5 August 1934 by persuading General Critchley, Chairman of the White City Board, to demand so high a bond for the safety of the hall that Sir Oswald would have to decline the booking.[44]

From early 1934 the BUF was growing at a fairly astonishing rate.[45] Special Branch noted that their rapidly increasing membership – 1,400 new recruits had enrolled during the week ending 21 January 1934 at the HQ alone – was partly down to the very favourable publicity they received in the *Daily Mail*, *Evening News* and *Sunday Dispatch*.[46] The press magnate Lord Rothermere, seeing a promising anti-communist force in Mosley and his organisation, had thrown his weight behind the BUF's cause. Having this kind of explicit media support is a rare and valuable thing for a social movement organisation. Generally speaking, how 'the media frames movement protest is an unknown outcome for a movement. Decisions about framing depend on several factors, some of which lie outside the control of movement actors.'[47] In an M/CM conflict opposing movements will compete to have their 'issue frames' presented through the media, thereby drawing positive attention to their cause. In order to facilitate this, movements usually have to embed their narrative within more 'dominant frames' which are already established within the media so as to make them 'newsworthy': '[t]o be labelled "not newsworthy" is to lose the framing contest within the mass media'.[48] However, with three major newspapers openly supporting them, the BUF could have their 'issue frames' presented in a much more controlled manner; further, they were able to spread their narrative to a far greater number of people than they otherwise would have been had they only their own publications to rely on.

The results of this were dramatic in terms of growth in support. However, the rapid fascist mobilisation also generated a concomitant anti-fascist mobilisation. On 23 April 1934, around 5,000 people marched through London from Aldgate to Victoria Park in a rally against fascism, and as a response to Mosley's threat to march through the East End. Special Branch considered this to be:

> a demonstration of some significance… the speakers, who represented all shades of Left opinion, were uncompromisingly hostile to Fascism, and especially to any attempt of British Fascism to make headway in the East End of London. Speakers were trying to impress both moderate Trade Union and Jewish opinion with a view to moulding a solid united front against fascism.[49]

Indeed, throughout 1934 they were locked in a cycle of mobilisation and counter-mobilisation, with the fascists holding – or attempting to hold – meetings and events, and the communists disrupting these or holding counter-demonstrations. In January the *Blackshirt* noted that the BUF were facing organised opposition from 'reds' in Dover who regularly attempted to break up their meetings there; and in Manchester, the BUF's area HQ was allegedly raided and vandalised, with an attempt at arson being foiled by the arrival of the police.[50]

In February, a meeting in Kilburn was disrupted by communists who threw vegetables and bottles at the speaker.[51] Similar problems faced the BUF throughout the first half of the year in Plymouth, Portsmouth, Bristol, London, Newcastle, and Edinburgh.[52] As well as this local-level, small-scale agitation there were a number of much bigger events in 1934 for which larger numbers of activists were mobilised on both sides. The first of these was to be at the Olympia exhibition centre in London, where the BUF announced they were to hold a rally on 7 June. The CPGB called for a counter-demonstration to the event, and encouraged its members to obtain free tickets by posing as fascists or fascist sympathisers.[53] On the day of the event there were roughly 1,000 anti-fascists and 2,000 Blackshirts, 1,000 of whom then acted as stewards during the meeting. Inside the building, as the CPGB had planned, a large number of communists had managed to gain entry and managed to successfully disrupt the event for about an hour – from around 8:40 until about 9:45 pm. The Blackshirts dealt with the anti-fascist hecklers violently, and many of them were bleeding from the face as they left.[54]

On trying to explain the violent events at Olympia, Lewis has argued that it is necessary to examine the actions of the CP and the BUF in the period leading up to the meeting. After announcing its plans to oppose the Blackshirts, the communists publicly made plans to mobilise as many workers as possible for their demonstration:

> These preparations have been frequently commented upon, but the BUF's attitude to them has received little attention. The party was certainly aware of the possibility of trouble and boasted that those attempting to disrupt the meeting would be '... put outside, swiftly, efficiently, and with minimum of noise'...
>
> It would appear, then, that for the BUF and its opponents the Olympia meeting had taken on the appearance of a showdown long before the evening of 7 June. Both sides had prepared for a violent confrontation and then proceeded to act in such a manner as to produce it.[55]

Lewis is probably correct, but perhaps underestimates specifically the provocative effect the *Daily Worker* had on the leaders of the BUF. Every day in the week running up to the event, the Communist Party did their best to rile up their supporters through the pages of the *Daily Worker*. As well as accusing Mosley of trying to set up a regime in the style of Hitler (1 June); and the Blackshirts of defeating a strike (2 June); crucially they linked the Olympia counter-demo to a violent anti-fascist demonstration which had just occurred in Paris, in a long glowing report about the latter.[56] After describing how Parisian anti-fascists had pelted their enemies with missiles, before overturning cars and slashing their tyres, the Daily Worker commented that:

> The anti-Fascist action of the workers of Paris precedes the great counter-demonstration against Mosley at Olympia tomorrow night. The past few weeks have witnessed a gathering storm among the working-class against Fascism, and Mosley's challenge to London workers tomorrow will be replied to by thousands of workers participating in the Communist counter-demonstration.[57]

The next day, the day of the meeting, they reported on the incident again, describing how the 'fascist thugs' had been routed by the workers, who had pelted them and the police with stones, before beating and stripping the fascists.[58] It is highly likely that the violent treatment of the communists by the BUF was a considered and pre-decided response to the *Daily Workers'* provocative coverage in the run up to the event; especially their linking the violence in Paris with their own demonstration at Olympia. An MI5 report written shortly after the meeting stated that:

> …but the point which has been generally ignored is that British Union of Fascist leaders were well aware of these writings and of the elaborate plans of the Communist party of Great Britain to break up their meeting. To them it clearly amounted to an incitement to violence which justified drastic action.[59]

This argument was reinforced by Mosley himself, who told the *Manchester Guardian* that: '[f]or over three weeks certain communists and socialist papers have published incitements to their readers to attack this meeting.'[60]

The immediate effect of the violent events at Olympia was to mobilise large numbers of people, boosting membership both for the CPGB and the BUF.

> In fact, both the British Union of Fascists and the Communist Party of Great Britain were delighted with the results of Olympia. Each felt that it had given a great impulse to their movement. Both look[ed] forward to the next big meeting for the same reason.[61]

However, the boon given to the BUF by the events in June were short-lived. The biggest blow struck to the fascists came not (directly) from the anti-fascists, but from the removal of Rothermere's support in the wake of the violent events in Olympia, coupled with the alarming news of the events of the Night of Long Knives in Germany. The BUF's support began to drain away at the same impressive rate with which it had flowed to it during the first half of the year. Whether or not the communists knew that the BUF had fallen on hard times, they continued their agitation of local BUF groups. Two weeks after Olympia, Mosley cancelled a planned BUF meeting on Newcastle Town Moor, as there was a high risk of violence from communists and there was likely to be women and children present due to a carnival, which had been organised there at the same time.[62]

The next large-scale mobilisation of fascist and anti-fascist forces was to be in Hyde Park, London, on 9 September 1934. There was a sizable anti-fascist counter-demonstration planned, which Moscow was supplying the Communist Party £2,000 with in order to make sure it was a success.[63] Fortunately for the CPGB, events in Germany and Austria had seen 'considerable repercussions' in Britain, and 'the general feeling among the working classes [was] very hostile towards fascism.'[64] Once again international developments, rather than M/CM interactions, acted as a motivational agent. Not only were 'material resources' mobilised by the international communist movement, but the actions of the continental fascists had once more provided an arresting example of the potential costs of failure to oppose the BUF.[65] Consequently, many trade union branches decided to take part in the counter-demonstration, especially ones from the East End of London.[66]

On 9 September, the BUF held a meeting with around 3,000 members in attendance, across five platforms in Hyde Park. In a different area, the anti-fascists' counter-demo had mobilised around 5,600 activists, with 20 speakers on four platforms. There was also something in the region of 60,000 people in attendance at the Park, and Special Branch observed that the general feeling of the crowd was one of antipathy towards the fascists. However, despite this hostile sentiment, and the large crowds assembled, the event was generally an uneventful one. Eighteen people were arrested for insulting behaviour and obstructing the police, and around six people had to be taken to hospital but compared to Olympia this was an orderly event.[67] Part of the reason for this was that, following the shocking scenes at Olympia, the state was very keen to ensure that order was maintained at this event. At the same time, there was an awareness that a denial of any one group's right to demonstrate could generate more support for them:

> The Commissioner…proposed that the police should take steps to clear a path through the crowd for the Fascist procession to their meeting place. The Commissioner said that he would take similar action if any attempt were made by political opponents to prevent a May Day gathering in Hyde Park.
> …On consideration, the Secretary of State agreed with the Commissioner's proposal [because if] the Fascists were prevented by their political opponents from holding an open air meeting in Hyde Park, strength would be given to their claim that it was not possible to obtain free speech in this country…[68]

This even-handed approach by the state, what Thurlow refers to as 'hard-nosed liberalism towards extremism', was no doubt an important factor in the M/CM contest not escalating further than it did.[69] Where a state intervenes in a ham-fisted manner, either by ignoring a group's legitimate grievances or by unfairly repressing one group and not another, this can both incense a movement's activists and radicalise them to some degree as well as inadvertently helping a movement gain support by making them seem sympathetic and unfairly downtrodden. Another reason for the relative quiet at Hyde Park was a shift in the CPGB's attitude, who were now making a concerted effort to conduct themselves in a responsible way to win over wider support from the labour movement. Consequently, all the anti-fascist speakers at Hyde Park 'emphasised that the counter-demonstration had not been organised as a display of violence, but to show a mass working-class opposition to fascism and all it stands for.'[70]

After the event at Hyde Park, the CPGB's analysis of fascism, and by extension Mosley and the BUF, shifted. In late 1934, their 'social fascist' analysis had led them to the conclusion that 'finance capitalism backed the National Government as the main weapon of "fascisation".'[71] Yet while capitalists were able to exert their dominance over the working class through their control of the state, the CPGB reasoned, they also financed the BUF as an 'auxiliary irregular force' in the eventuality that this should prove insufficient.[72] Anti-fascism, then, could not involve 'bourgeois democracy', given that it was every bit as much a threat as the BUF. By extension, the reformist Labour Party was not considered to be part of the antifascist struggle, committed as they were to the extant political architecture of Britain.[73] However, following the 7th World Congress of the Communist International (Comintern) in 1935, their perspective changed. Here the theoretical line was developed that fascism was in fact 'the last stage of capitalism: the substitution of one form of class domination (bourgeois democracy) with another – the open terrorist dictatorship of the "most reactionary elements" of finance capital.'[74] Given what was at stake, the Comintern endorsed the development of broad anti-fascist 'popular front' coalitions with socialists, social democrats, liberals and even conservatives.[75]

Lewis Young has argued that this new imperative from the Comintern allowed the CPGB to reframe their conflict against the fascists as not only being along the lines of democracy (themselves and their allies) versus fascism (the BUF), but also as being a part of a much larger struggle involving most of Europe. This was a shrewd strategy, allowing them to paint themselves as defenders of British values and the fascists as a dangerous foreign import: 'the BUF … was held up by the CPGB as an antithesis to the "British" way of life. Although "Britishness" was never specifically defined in this analysis, the CPGB in its Popular Front phase broadly understood it to be about a commitment to the principles of democracy and the ideals of liberty, tolerance, and moderation.'[76] This allowed them to once again start making overtures to the Labour Party and the broader labour movement (and also necessitated attempting to distance themselves from political violence and public disorder). As ever, the Labour Party leadership were unwavering in their rebuffing of the CPGB's advances, but nevertheless the communists did manage to forge productive relationships with other significant actors in the British labour movement such as the Independent Labour Party and the Socialist League (itself a group operating within the left of the Labour Party).[77] Perhaps most importantly, with the Popular Front strategy 'the party was aiming its message at a much wider constituency and anti-fascism was therefore open to all.'[78] Going forward the CPGB managed to gather a lot of support and mobilise a significant number of people for the anti-fascist cause, forming an important bulwark against fascism's growth.

The mainstream leadership of the labour movement and Anglo-Jewry continued to act as moderating forces, encouraging their community members to avoid the anti-fascist mobilisations. Both groups had indirect institutional and legal means of tackling fascism. Labour argued for further legislation to restrict 'extremism', while using its power to deny the BUF access to local authority premises where and when they could.[79] The Board of Deputies – some of whom were extremely influential – were also able to pursue avenues of resistance which were not open to working-class radical groups. So, on 31 October 1934, the president of the Board Neville Laski had a meeting with Geoffrey Lloyd MP, the Parliamentary Private Secretary to Stanley Baldwin, to discuss the BUF threat. While the option of Stanley Baldwin writing a letter to the press about the British Union of Fascists was considered, they decided that 'it would be a mistake to give Mosley the opportunity of further advertisement... [as] Fascism in this country was a rapidly dying movement'.[80] However, they left open the possibility of Baldwin mentioning Mosley and the 'Jewish Question' in a speech he was to be giving in Scotland soon. Lloyd also asked Laski to furnish him, in his capacity as Baldwin's secretary, with regular 'reports and news of more than minor interest relative to the Jewish community', so that he could pass the information on to Baldwin.

In early 1935 the security services observed that the BUF was in sharp decline. They were haemorrhaging members, branches were closing and the sales of their newspapers were dropping. The withdrawal of Rothermere's support, the increasingly extreme actions of the NSDAP in Germany, and the skilful manipulation of events by their enemies had taken its toll on the BUF. A letter from Special Branch to sir Vernon Kell, Director General of MI5, stated that matters were being made worse by the radical left, as 'some of the undesirable elements at the Fascist meetings from the Communist and other extreme political organisations are preventing responsible and substantial persons from joining.'[81]

Between 1932 and 1935, the M/CM dynamic between the opposing sides was not being significantly shaped by CE. Tactical use of violence and disruption was very one-sided; with the generally consistent disruption of BUF events by the left-wing being largely unreciprocated. Further, a significant motivating factor for this opposition came from factors outside the country. Surprisingly, after Olympia when BUF membership plummeted and their activity declined, Cullen has shown that at the local level communists pursued an increasingly aggressive strategy against the fascists. In 1934, of 89 BUF meetings recorded by the police, 14 of them (16%) were disrupted by communists; in 1935, communists disrupted 17 out of 53 meetings (32%) recorded, which further suggests that the intensity of communist anti-fascist opposition was not strongly tied to the actions of the BUF.[82] The concept of how opposing movements are 'coupled' is a useful conceptual tool for understanding why CE was not developing in this period between the fascists and anti-fascists. M/CM conflicts are 'loosely coupled' to the degree that they mobilise and demobilise at different rates and do not react quickly to developments in their opponents' strategies and contentious repertoires.[83] Conversely, the more that a movement's tactics and choice of 'battlefields' are influenced by an opposing movement, the more 'tightly coupled' the conflict is.[84] Further, opposing movements are often asymmetrically coupled; that is, one movement is more tightly coupled to its opponents than vice versa.[85] Clearly between 1932 and 1935, the anti-fascists were asymmetrically coupled to the fascists, who did very little in terms of pro-actively challenging their far-left opponents.

However, it is the case that in 1934, the actions of the BUF – as opposed to other factors – did provoke large-scale mobilisations of militant anti-fascists. Further, it seems that the violence at Olympia on the part of the fascists was born out of provocation from communist propaganda. While this is a case of extreme narrative provoking extreme behaviour, it also demonstrates that the opposing groups' strategies were coevolving even if to a limited degree, rather than the entire episode being a wholly asymmetric or one-sided affair. Finally, the public clash between the two sides on 7 June did also produce a short-lived spike in support for both the fascists and communists.

1936–1940

To reverse the BUF's ailing fortunes, Mosley attempted to capitalise on what pre-existing anti-Semitic sentiment there was in Britain at that time.[86] The main focus of this strategy, and the area that experienced the most violence as a result, was London's East End.[87] Mosley's first big action in 1936 was to hold a meeting at the Albert Hall on Sunday 22 March. On 25 March, Vernon Kell wrote to Sir Russell Scott at the Home Office about the BUF meeting, noting that 'the vehemence of Mosley's attack on the Jews greatly exceeded that of his previous utterances on this subject', and felt that the 'reason for Mosley's taking this line perhaps is that anti-Jewish propaganda has been effective in recent months in the East End of London.'[88] Once again, in the lead up to the meeting, the *Daily Worker* 'did all in its power to link the events in Germany with Mosley's efforts.'[89]

Mosley's anti-Semitic campaign had indeed found fertile ground in the East End of London, among the extant communal strife between Irish Catholics and Anglo-Jews, and Bethnal Green had become their London stronghold.[90] By the same token, the CPGB also managed to make political capital out of this situation by positioning itself as the main opponent of fascism in the area, and so attracted a large Jewish membership base. However, the Communist Party was not the only militant organisation facing the BUF. On 26 July, the left-wing

Jewish Labour Council (JLC) organised a conference which was attended by representatives of over 80 Jewish working-class organisations.[91] The delegates at this conference founded the Jewish People's Council Against Fascism and Anti-Semitism (JPC). Formed partially in response to the perceived inaction on the part of the BoD, the JPC's analysis of fascism and anti-Semitism was that the two were inseparable, and one could not be tackled without also tackling the other.[92] They quickly went about organising meetings, distributing leaflets and lobbying the government to introduce legislation banning incitement to racial hatred.[93]

Around the same time, the Board of Deputies began to debate the need for a 'Jewish Defence Scheme'.[94] At a meeting on 19 July, the Board decided to form a Co-ordinating Committee to 'unify and direct activities in defence of the Jewish Community against attacks made upon it.'[95] Importantly, the Board continued to make use of their connections to the state and political elites. The same month that the two Jewish defence bodies were formed, Neville Laski met with the Home Secretary John Simon, at the House of Commons. Laski stated that the BUF meetings had gone beyond free speech and were firmly in the sphere of 'direct incitement to breaches of the peace.'[96] He requested of the Home Secretary that

> special officers should be detailed to attend those meetings, with authority to arrest speakers using provocative and inciting language against Jews, and…to appoint plain clothes officers from outside the districts where meetings were held to mingle with the crowd for the purpose of preventing disorder.

It seems that as a direct result of this meeting Simon redoubled his anti-fascist measures, sending as many police as he could to Jewish areas in the East End and emphasising that police should intervene if anyone used grossly provocative anti-Semitic language.[97]

The militant anti-fascist groups continued to oppose the Blackshirts more directly, although there was some degree of dissonance between attitudes towards violence at the leadership and rank and file levels. After Mosley announced that he intended to lead a march through East London, the leaders of the Communist Party called on workers to attend a Young Communist League (YCL) meeting at Trafalgar Square to raise funds for the Spanish Civil War before heading to an East End anti-fascist meeting later in the evening after Mosley's had finished.[98] They were keen to avoid any disorder and by extension any public relations disasters. However, the local rank and file were determined to oppose Mosley head-on. Indeed, there was such a strong resolve to oppose Mosley among the people of the East End in general that Joe Jacobs, the Stepney Branch secretary, felt that the CP would be 'finished' in the region if they did not get directly involved.[99] After the level of commitment to this strategy became clear the party leadership decided it would be wise to throw their weight behind the local membership's plans; however, the *Daily Worker*'s coverage of the event was lacklustre in comparison to previous promotional campaigns for large anti-fascist mobilisations.[100] The JPC also mobilised its members to oppose Mosley on 4 October, and organised an unsuccessful petition to the Home Office to have the BUF's march banned.[101]

The events at Cable Street on 4 October 1936 have been extensively covered elsewhere, and do not need repeating.[102] All that needs to be conveyed here is that, faced with a vast crowd of around 100,000 militant anti-fascists throughout East London, and scenes of violent disorder between police and anti-fascists, the Commissioner of Police, Sir Philip Game, decided to divert Mosley's men away from the East End.[103] However, Lewis' claim that Cable Street 'was a momentous victory for the forces of anti-fascism', while not totally inaccurate, does need some revision.[104] As with Olympia, the sizeable mobilisation and scenes of disorder acted as a 'recruiting sergeant', with the BUF's local membership briefly surging by around 2,000 new recruits. Further Mosley was subsequently able to hold several large meetings in the East End with enthusiastic crowds estimated to be several thousand in size, and 'the display of pro-fascist sentiments on the streets surprised a number of experienced observers'.[105] Perhaps more worryingly, a few days later on 11 October, the Mile End Road in the East End was the scene of a pogrom, with around 100 people vandalising Jewish shops and attacking Jews. It was the opinion of MI5 that the BUF managed to whip up significant tensions in the East End, albeit tensions which they then entirely failed to capitalise on:

> The Fascists instead of keeping the situation at boiling point have allowed it to subside again during the latter part of October and November.
>
> It is not clear how far this failure to keep up the temperature is to be attributed to Mosley's incapacity to take advantage of a situation of this kind, or how far it is to be attributed to the final announcement that fresh legislation would be adopted to deal with the situation which he had created.[106]

The legislation mentioned by the Security Services was the Public Order Act (POA), which was rushed through parliament in December that year. This piece of legislation had three main strands: 'the prohibition of political uniforms, the outlawing of paramilitary organisations and the regulation and control of public processions and assemblies.'[107] There has been mixed assessments of the value, impact and efficacy of the Public Order Act by historians. Of those who see it in a favourable light, Thurlow has argued that in giving it the ability to ban political uniforms and marches, the POA allowed the Home Office to control violence in much of the East End after July 1937.[108] Similarly, Anderson has claimed that the

> purpose [of the POA] was not so much to meet a threat to the government as to control the disturbances that had rocked the East End. The act was fairly successful in this purpose, but its critics were right; the Fascists could be controlled, but so could everyone else.[109]

Anderson went further, specifically stating that 'the amount and intensity of public disorder did decline [since the passage of the POA], and the threat of prosecution under the provisions of the Public Order Act was no doubt a major deterrent.'[110]

Others have not treated the legislation so kindly. Lewis has argued that the government exploited the conflict between fascists and anti-fascists, and under the guise of attempting to maintain public order actually increased 'its arsenal of repressive measures.'[111] This was demonstrated by the way in which the Act was used to curb militant left wing activities, such as happened when police arrested activists seemingly without cause at an industrial dispute in Harworth Colliery during the spring of 1937. Lewis claims that not only did the state aim the POA at the Left more than at fascists, but that the POA was a dismal failure in terms of its aim to prevent the fascists using anti-Semitic language:

> [...] the police continued to apply section five of the Public Order Act primarily against the left... The moral, it seemed, was that anti-Semitism was a good deal more acceptable as far as the police were concerned than was republicanism...
>
> There was no evidence to suggest that the record of police action improved. Between August 1936 and December 1938 the BUF held a total of 2,108 meetings in east London. Yet despite the BUF's pursuance of vigorous anti-Semitic propaganda fascist speakers were cautioned on only 16 occasions. In all there were only seven prosecutions and three convictions.[112]

From the other end of the political spectrum, Richard Bellamy, the former BUF Director of Propaganda, has claimed that the POA was 'aimed solely at Mosley's Movement,' and that the act of handing control of the maintenance of order at outside meetings exclusively to the police had the effect of repressing the movement, as meetings would be shut down prematurely at 'the first sign of rowdiness'.[113]

Firstly, Lewis' claim that the attempt to curb anti-Semitic language through the Act failed needs addressing. Importantly, Lewis argues that the BUF maintained its use of 'vigorous anti-Semitic propaganda' during this time. The POA did grant the police greater powers in preventing offensive racist language, if that language was likely to lead to a breach of the peace, and Figure 2.1 demonstrates that, while there were two waves of arrests for anti-Semitic language across 1937 and 1938, the second wave was smaller and both were smaller than the peak of arrests in August 1936.[114] This suggests that either the police's attitude towards anti-Semitic language became increasingly relaxed throughout this period, or, more plausibly, that the fascist speakers began to, on the whole, self-censor themselves due to concerns over the POA. This latter theory is given more weight by the regular reports made by police on cases of 'Jew Baiting' in the East End, where they frequently noted that the BUF speakers carefully avoided using language that would land them afoul of the POA.[115]

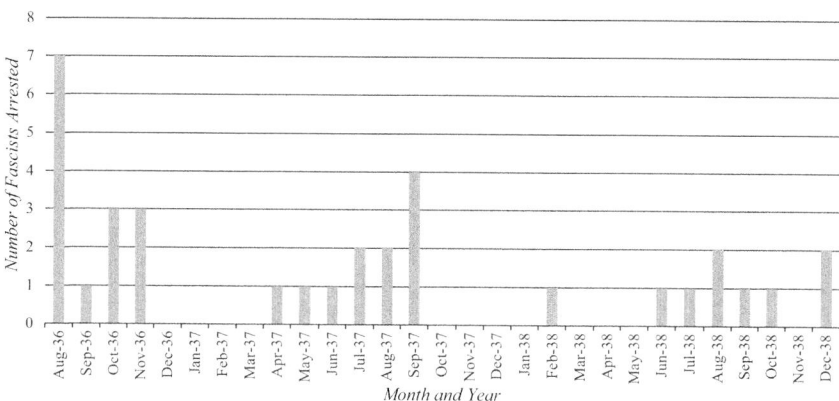

FIGURE 2.1 Fascists arrested or cautioned for anti-semitic language (Source: Metropolitan Police Records MEPO 2/3043.)

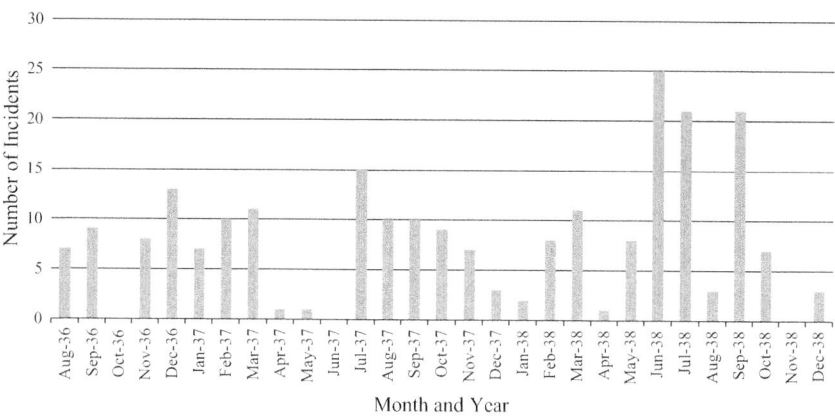

FIGURE 2.2 Alleged cases of assaults, insults and vandalism against Jews (Source: Metropolitan Police records MEPO 2/3043.)

However, while general verbal expressions of anti-Semitism were curbed, Figure 2.2 indicates that other more direct expressions of anti-semitism – alleged cases of assaults and insults committed against individual Jews, as well as cases of vandalism of Jewish buildings and anonymous anti-Semitic letters posted to Jews – increased. If anything, it seems that as the anti-Semitic language of fascist public speakers decreased, more serious anti-Semitic acts increased, suggesting that the POA may have channelled anti-Semitic hostility into the wrong direction; although, as we shall see, this could have had more to do with the increasing hostilities between fascists and anti-fascists in the East End during this time than it did with the POA.

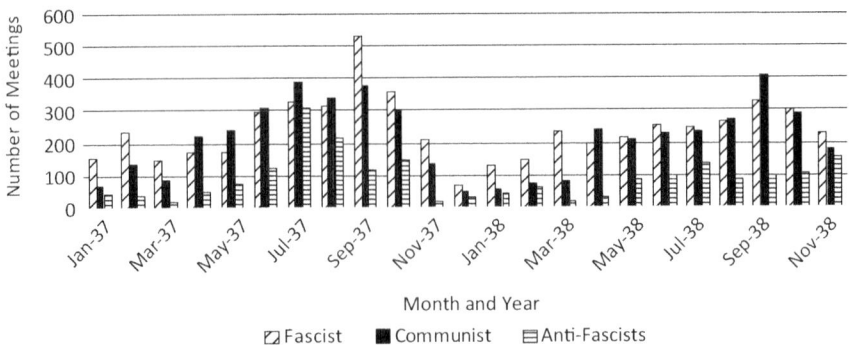

FIGURE 2.3 Number of fascist, communist, and anti-fascist meetings that police attended (Source: Metropolitan Police Records MEPO 2/3043.)

Secondly, careful examination of Metropolitan Police records from the time cast serious doubt on the claim that the POA was 'successful' in controlling 'the disturbances that had rocked the East End.'[116]

Figure 2.3 demonstrates that, there was a general decline in the recorded number of meetings held by the opposing groups across 1937 and 1938 (fascists held 443 less meetings in 1938 than 1937, communists held 383 less, and anti-fascists held 254 less).[117] However, there were two large waves of activity following the introduction of the POA. Further, the picture painted by the data here suggests that the mobilisation of the two movements was quite closely linked. This is obviously largely due to external factors; the reasons for there being peaks of activity in the summer and troughs at Christmas do not need to be expanded on here. Nonetheless, the similarities in the levels of activity between the two sides are striking. The peak of the two sides' activity, in terms of the number of open air meetings being held, was in September 1937, although there was still a serious level of activity going right through to the end of 1938. More importantly though, Figure 2.4 suggests that the Public Order Act failed to lessen the intensity of the conflict between the opposing movements, as measured by the numbers of arrests of fascists and anti-fascists for disorder and violence.

After an initial lull in arrests in January 1937, there was a general *increase* in the numbers of activists being arrested for violence or causing disorder, with the most intense prolonged period being from February 1938 to November 1938. Indeed, far from curbing the escalation between the belligerent political groups, this period of time is particularly interesting as at this point the BUF, who previously had made much of their claim to be a law-abiding party who never attacked their opponents' meetings, began to actually go on the offensive and aggressively confront their enemies. Of course, these data only show the number of arrests, and so is not necessarily an entirely accurate reflection of the increasingly radical behaviour of those involved.

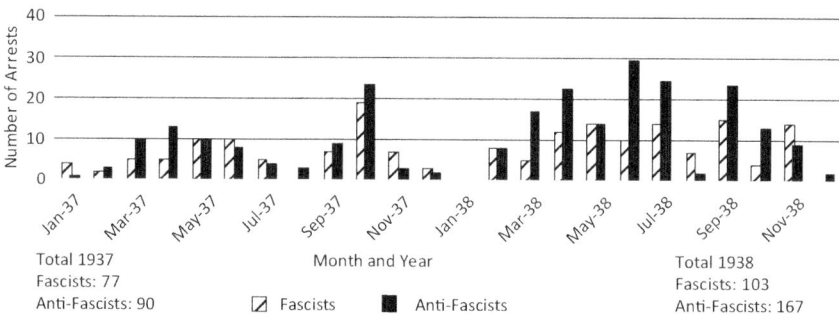

Total 1937
Fascists: 77
Anti-Fascists: 90

Month and Year

Total 1938
Fascists: 103
Anti-Fascists: 167

☑ Fascists   ■ Anti-Fascists

FIGURE 2.4 Number of arrests of fascists and anti-fascists for disorder and violence discounting arrests at Trafalgar Square and Bermondsey (Source: Metropolitan Police Records MEPO 2/3043.)

However, the argument presented here is supported by the observations of police officers at the time who reported that fascists had begun to adopt

> the tactics of their opponents and attend rival meetings in force, to heckle and generally interrupt the speakers. Police have had to order the closure of meetings on a number of occasions, and have also found it necessary to separate the opposing parties at meetings and to disperse antagonistic groups to prevent disorder.[118]

From around May 1937, when the fascists started copying their opponent's' tactics by openly trying to disrupt the anti-fascists' meetings, there was a qualitative shift in the nature of the conflict between fascists and anti-fascists – instead of just a series of spikes of activity, such as followed Cable Street and Olympia, from 1937 to 1938 there was a mutually-sustaining cycle of violence, provocation and disorder between the groups. So, despite the intervention by the state, this period is the only point at which the M/CM dynamic seems to have taken on the shape of CE.

Interestingly, this dynamic happened counter to the aims of the main organisations involved. At the national level, partly because of the POA, the leadership of both sides of the M/CM contest were trying to prevent their rank-and-file from engaging in extremist behaviour. With regard to the BUF, Webber has suggested that the Public Order Act (POA) forced it to become more restrained and to embrace a more 'respectable', middle-class, fascism.[119] Certainly, by 1938 the Board noted that the BUF had started shifting its focus to 'indoor gatherings at which addresses have been delivered' in a bid to 'appeal to a more intelligent section of the people'[120] and the Metropolitan Police noted that fascist leaders that year were attempting to discourage their members from attending their opponents' meetings (as were the anti-fascist leaders).[121] Further, that year the BUF published a new 'Constitution and Rules' for its members. In this, the leadership clearly stated that all 'members on all occasions must obey the law of the land, and in particular they must observe the provisions of the Public Order Act, 1936'.[122]

As already stated, much of the anti-fascist movement had already been trying to pursue legal and moderate methods, and the POA was yet another incentive to carry on this path. The CPGB were still attempting to present themselves as a respectable party so as to win over the wider labour movement, and after the outbreak of the Spanish Civil War in July 1936 had tended to 'devote themselves, principally, to matters connected with events in Spain and to international, rather than national anti-Fascist propaganda.'[123] On top of this, the party was acutely aware that militant actions could possibly lead to prosecution under the POA.[124] The JPC, representing the more radical wing of the Anglo-Jewish anti-fascist movement, had in fact been in talks with the Board over the possibility of placing itself under the more moderate group's control since towards the end of 1936 (although for the time being their respective differences over the tactical solution to fascism were too great), and after the violent anti-Semitic reaction to the events on October 4, 1936 were growing much more moderate in their approach.[125] The talks between the JPC and the Board over the reins of communal defence being placed in the latter's sole possession continued, and by 1939 the JPC had agreed entirely to the Board's conditions for this – although with the outbreak of war that year the JPC instead dissolved itself.[126]

That radical mobilisation at the grassroots level was a countervailing trend to the increasingly moderate stance of the organisations in question is demonstrated by the BUF's march to Bermondsey in October 1937. Having been prevented from marching through the East End again, this time because of the POA, Mosley instead was allowed to march his men from Westminster to Bermondsey. He was met with a large-scale mobilisation of around 2,000 anti-fascists at nearby Borough underground station, of whom roughly 75% were Jewish.[127] However, this impressive turnout happened despite the JPC taking a 'neutral stance on Jewish involvement in the counter-demonstration, neither advocating nor discouraging it.'[128] Furthermore, in September 1937 the number of meetings held by fascists and anti-fascists 'exceeded any previous month and these...have tended to be more disorderly and consequently necessitated the presence of more police';[129] this was all occurring just a few months after the CPGB had issued a statement instructing members not to involve themselves in violent confrontations, and after the JPC had released publications warning its supporters not to disrupt BUF meetings and to generally avoid direct confrontation with fascists.[130]

It seems that the contest between fascists and anti-fascists unleashed pre-existing communal hostilities which had been simmering for a while. Elaine Smith argues that, even before the BUF existed, some 'of the strongest manifestations of hostility towards Jews emanated from the other major ethnic group in the East End, namely the Irish Catholics... Hostility to the Jews was most clearly in evidence over housing, work, and political issues.'[131] Once the BUF and CPGB had politicised these issues further, and ignited the tensions by making political capital out of them, they were difficult for the movement organisations to control. This case reveals an important aspect of the development of CE: the relationship between social movements and the social bases from which they attempt to draw support. Social movement organisations will try to frame their campaigns in such a way that their aims and objectives appear to align with the broader interests of larger social groups (for example, the labour movement, or even an entire ethnic group). The greater the extent to which a group manages to do this, the more likely they are to draw support from that community. By the same token, if their aims and objectives are perceived as threatening an extant group, the likelihood of them generating a countermovement increases; and the greater the threat they pose the more radical the response is likely to be. As Fadaee has observed, if a 'given movement is perceived to threaten the dominant values of a group or of a society in general, then the formation of an influential countermovement gains high probability.'[132]

In 1939, as war was drawing closer, MI5 noted that:

> This failure of the BUF to make headway is due to various causes. The main cause is probably to be found in the foreign policy of Hitler and Mussolini. It is hardly necessary to labour this point. The various acts of aggression committed by Germany and Italy in recent years have given rise to a general feeling in this country that the Axis is aiming at world domination and the destruction of the British Empire. By openly identifying itself with the German and Italian cause the BUF is running counter to this strong current of British public opinion.[133]

Britain joined the war against the Axis on 3 September 1939. On that day, the windows of the BUF's shop in Pitfield Street were smashed by 'persons unknown'. The next day the BUF emptied the shop, closed it, and boarded up the windows.[134] In October, Philip Game wrote to Laski to say that the BUF 'have no public support at present worth talking about,' and that there 'is a very great body of unanimity indeed in our participation in the war.' Furthermore, the 'same applies equally to the Communist element at the other extreme. The number of political meetings of all sorts in September dropped almost 75%.'[135] In the summer of 1940, in 'view of the obvious danger to the state presented by the British Union of Fascists it was banned… and its principal leaders and organisers were arrested' and interned under Defence Regulation 18b.[136]

Conclusion

Figure 2.5 suggests that, at the national level, and in very broad terms, the fortunes of the BUF and the CPGB were in some way linked.[137] After the initial astonishing rise and dramatic drop in the BUF's membership over 1934 and 1935,

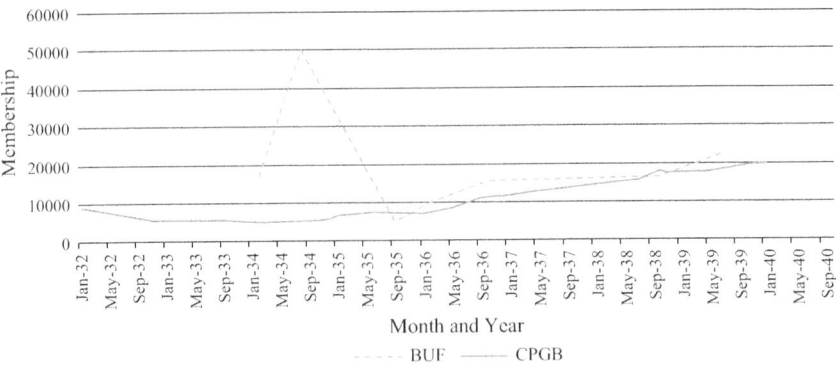

FIGURE 2.5 Membership of the Communist Party of Great Britain and the British Union of Fascists 1932–1940 (Source: See endnote 137.)

largely due to Rothermere's media empire giving and then withdrawing its support, coupled with the actions of the NSDAP in Germany, the BUF and the CPGB both enjoyed a similarly steady rise in membership up until 1939. While this was partly because both parties were benefiting from the same volatile social and political conditions, it is also no doubt true that the conflict between the two groups was mutually beneficial. The benefit to the BUF after Olympia and Cable Street has already been mentioned, and as MI5 noted: 'Perhaps the most unfortunate effect of the growth of the British Union of Fascists hitherto has been the fillip which it has given to the Communist movement', however they did add that 'this must be attributed, to a great extent, to the propaganda and the policy directed from Moscow. In the coordination of its "anti-fascist" policy Moscow has been unusually fortunate and remarkably adept at seizing an opportunity.'[138] Once more, the transnational nature of this M/CM contest was hugely important in how it developed; the actions of the European fascists indicated the costs in allowing the domestic movement to grow unimpeded, and thus hindered the BUF's progress by mobilising people against them, while Moscow maintained 'solidarity networks' with the CPGB and aided their efforts.

Looking more closely at the case-study, it is clear that there were very different patterns of interaction between the opposing movements in the periods from 1932–1935 and 1936–1940. In the first period, after events in Germany and Italy mobilised the anti-fascists and, to a lesser extent, the fascists, the general pattern of interaction between the CPGB and BUF was one of fairly consistent disruption of fascist events by communists – which did not give rise to a concomitant escalation in tactics from the BUF – interspersed with several larger spikes of mobilisation and demobilisation on both sides. While both sides benefited in terms of recruitment from their feuding (if only in the short term), there was little in the way of mutual radicalisation occurring. Olympia was the outlier here, where the CPGB seem to have provoked the BUF into employing violent tactics, which then contributed to the BUF's decline over the rest of this period.

However between 1936 and 1939 a different pattern emerges, at least in the East End of London. Here, from 1937, the BUF began to adopt the tactics of their enemies; the two movements became both more closely and more symmetrically coupled. Fascists were arrested at communist meetings, and there was an increase in arrests for violence and disorder by both parties, with a particularly prolonged feud seeming to run from January to December 1938. They became locked in a cycle of violent mobilisation against each other. Even after the state intervened and introduced the POA, M/CM interactions still became more intense. Further, while the POA did seem to quell fascist public speakers' use of anti-Semitic language somewhat, there was also a rise in the number of reports of anti-Semitic incidents of violence and abuse in the streets. This raises the question as to whether the M/CM dynamic led to an ideological radicalisation of the BUF; that is, whether the conflict between movement and countermovement provoked 'an ascent towards the top of the "narrative pyramid"' towards anti-Semitism'.[139]

There is a long-running debate between historians over the causes of the BUF's shift to anti-Semitism, and broadly speaking there are two approaches to this problem: 'the traditional scapegoat theories which have cast the Jew as the innocent victim of fascist aggression, and the more revisionist analyses which have explained the conflict in terms of the interaction between fascists and Jews'.[140] Interactionist approaches posit that because of various actions taken by the Anglo-Jewish community, from the Boycott of German goods to active anti-fascist activities, a portion of the blame for the BUF's anti-Semitism must rest on their shoulders. Writing in this tradition, Robert Skidelsky claimed that the BUF had no anti-Semitic policy for the first two years of its existence, and this only changed because of 'the attitude of the Jews themselves, so they must take some of the blame for what subsequently happened.'[141] Specifically, from 'the earliest days' of the BUF, groups of Jews were breaking up BUF meetings.[142] Skidelsky thus explained the BUF's anti-Semitism in terms of a reaction to Jewish attacks on the fascists movement. Similarly, Holmes argues that Anglo-Jewry became radicalised by events in Germany which led to them opposing Mosley in Britain,

> with Jewish anti-fascists engaging in the disruption of BUF meetings and doing what they could generally to defeat the Fascists. In turn, this strengthened the anti-Semitic sentiment in the BUF. It was through this interacting combination of circumstances that, after 1934, anti-Semitism within Mosley's movement began to flower more profusely....[143]

Scapegoat theories, on the other hand, stress how the BUF's ailing fortunes after 1934, coupled with the improving economy, led to the BUF making political capital out of anti-Semitism in a bid to gain more supporters and reinvigorate the movement. Lewis, for instance, argues that the decision to adopt a policy of anti-Semitism was merely a politically expedient one for Mosley, who was faced with internal pressure from high-ranking hard-line Blackshirts as well as the need for an 'alien but flexible stereotyped enemy' to focus BUF propaganda on as economic recovery rendered the Party's economic arguments less relevant.[144] Likewise, Daniel Tilles points out that, given that 'those Jews who were involved in active opposition to the BUF represented a small minority of the British anti-fascist movement and an even smaller fraction of Anglo-Jewry' that it is implausible to state that Jewish opposition affected the BUF's ideological stance. Rather, 'Jewish opposition – imagined or real – merely provided a useful pre-text for changes in policy that were implemented for other reasons.' Elsewhere, David Rosenberg has cited BUF defector Charles Wegg-Prosser as saying that he 'believed that antisemitism was a tool of convenience in Mosley's hands, utilised very cautiously at first, and only after previous "crusades" had fallen flat.'[145]

The interactionists' claim that the, actually tiny, number of Jews involved in the anti-fascist movement up until 1936 could have provoked a shift in pol-icy seems hugely unlikely. According to the police records, only ten Jews were arrested for disrupting meetings out of the 142 BUF meetings that the police recorded over 1934 and 1935. What's more, this was split rather evenly with six arrests in 1934 and four in 1935, indicating that there was not a growing threat from militant anti-fascist Jews.[146] In contrast however, Figure 2.5 demonstrates that the BUF's membership had plummeted to its lowest point by October 1935, adding weight to the political expediency argument. This argument is further supported by Tilles' convincing demonstration, through a thorough quantitative investigation of the BUF's publications as well as analysis of other documentary sources, that anti-Semitism was a major aspect of the BUF's ideology from its inception.[147]

One factor which seems to escape attention, though, is that within-movement competition between the fascist groups could have also contributed somewhat to the BUF making anti-Semitism a more prominent aspect of their programme. Indeed, it seems possible that part of the reason for the anti-Semitic turn of the BUF from 1934 was competition with the Imperial Fascist League over favour from the NSDAP. In October 1935, MI5 noted that Otto Bene, the Director of Britain for the NSDAP's Foreign Policy Office, regarded Mosley 'with some contempt for as being financed from Jewish sources.'[148] By contrast, the Nazi party was looking on the Imperial Fascist League very favourably. Despite the League's modest membership (of around 1,000), following an official invitation from the Nazis they sent four representatives to Nuremberg in September 1935. It is possible that the BUF felt that the IFL were 'out-bidding' them in terms of the anti-Semitic content of their program and were reaping the benefits. Indeed, MI5 hypothesised that Mosley's increased hostility to the Jews might be due to German influence.[149] This view was reinforced a year later when MI5 received a report from 'a particularly secret source' that claimed 'There is some reason to suspect that by including Jews in his attacks he (Mosley) hopes to receive financial support from the Germans.' MI5 also stated that the BUF's anti-Semitism had been exacerbated because of allegations from Arnold Leese, leader of the IFL, that Mosley was being 'soft on Judaism'.[150]

From 1936, it also seems unlikely that CE led to an increase in anti-Semitic belief at the local level in the East End. Rather, it seems probable that the fascists exploited pre-existing hostility to Jews; it is certainly significant that in October 1936, when the BUF was enjoying a massive surge in popularity following the events at Cable Street, the Police Commissioner stated that

> Though I doubt if the Fascists have made a single convert to Fascism, they have crystallized the ever present jealousy and dislike of the Jews in and around the predominantly Jewish districts of the East End, and have undoubtedly swelled the number of their apparent supporters.[151]

However, in politicising the division between the Jewish and Irish Catholic populations in the East End in the context of a violent feud with the CPGB, who were themselves benefiting from the politicisation of this issue, the M/CM contest did seem to channel this sentiment into a more violent and extreme direction. Indeed, the presence of the pre-existing ethnic strife in the area seems to be a major factor in explaining why processes of CE shaped the tactical escalation in the M/CM contest in the East End from 1936, but not before that or elsewhere. Other noteworthy characteristics of this area, namely the relatively high levels of overpopulation and poverty, were no doubt other major contributing factors.[152]

However, as Macklin and Busher have argued, 'If we do not analyse and theorise why these interactions *sometimes do not* escalate towards violence and *sometimes do not* lead to greater societal polarisation, it is likely that CE will become a rather blunt analytical instrument.'[153] In the contest between fascists and anti-fascists, there was strong pressures acting on the movements to not engage in 'extremist' behaviour right from the beginning. The most obvious factor was the presence of a stable high-capacity and legitimate state authority. In such contexts, groups are much more likely to pursue democratic methods of campaigning because the potential costs to violent mobilisation are extremely high, just as the chances of such methods working are extremely low.[154] Further, the even-handed way in which the state apparatus was used to protect the freedom of speech of fascists and communists without allowing serious disorder to arise no doubt facilitated a more peaceful M/CM contest.

Indeed, the policing of the conflict was no doubt one of the major reasons that the situation did not escalate further than it did. As mentioned, the state began collecting intelligence on both the CPGB and the BUF right from the beginning of this episode, as well as intervening occasionally. In the second half of the decade, though, its interventions became much weightier. One of the most important strategies employed by the state in this respect, from 1937 onwards, was the mobilisation of large numbers of extra police officers across the East End to prohibit violent clashes from escalating. As Thurlow has noted,

> such tactics worked; although Jewish radicals, communists and much of the community in the East End of London distrusted police impartiality, blanket saturation by the police of all potential disturbances, together with the restrictions imposed by the Public Order Act, and the banning of all marches and demonstrations in the East End after July 1937, effectively kept the lid on the seething confrontation between fascists and antifascists in the area.[155]

This goes some way in explaining why there were no fatalities due to any of the clashes between fascists and anti-fascists in this period.

A further source of moderation on the contest came from within the wider social-movements themselves. As mentioned above, both the British Left and Anglo-Jewish communities were largely dominated by the Labour Party and the Board of Deputies, who were unwavering in their denouncement of extra-legal tactics. These organisations were effective champions for the interests of Anglo-Jews and British workers in the conflict against the fascists. For instance, the Home Secretary regularly accepted deputations and reports from the Board of Deputies over the BUF's anti-Semitic campaign, and it seems likely that the Board even influenced the government's actions this way; further, several members of the Board were in fact MPs.[156] Similarly, the Labour Party used their political clout to help usher in the Public Order Act, and deny the BUF the use of public authorities buildings. Indeed, Copsey has argued that in the late 1930s the efforts of Labour controlled councils to deny the BUF venues for their meetings and events 'probably proved more damaging to the BUF than any remaining physical opposition by anti-fascists.'[157] Furthermore, in 1934 the Home Secretary also accepted a deputation from the National Joint Council of the Labour Party, the parliamentary Labour Party and the Trades Union Congress over the 'justifiable anger' of members of the labour movement who were reacting to fascist provocation by forming militant anti-fascist groups.[158] Because these organisations could affect real change, the rank-and-file of their movements were more likely to listen to their advice and engage in legal forms of campaigning. This, then, became the path of least resistance. As Holmes points out, 'group violence often occurs when conflict has not been resolved through nonviolent and institutional channels'; the moderate organisations provided this channel relatively successfully for much of the M/CM conflict.[159]

However, in the East End after 1936, many people felt their interests were not being adequately defended by the Board and/or Labour, and so adopted more radical means – as these were the only means they felt were left for them to utilise. Thus, as H. Solomon, the Secretary of the BoD, noted:

> I have been asked on several occasions 'what is the Board of Deputies doing about it?' The Jewish People's Council are holding meetings and,

therefore, local residents want to know why we are not doing the same and they will accept no explanation or excuse. However the feeling of indignation in the East End is spontaneous and to my mind it would not be fair to lay the blame for this on any organisation.

However wise it may be to tell the people to 'stay away', they simply will not do so. They are not being whipped up. The opposition last Sunday in Stepney Green, for example, consisted chiefly of housewives from the neighbouring buildings and not of members of any particular political organisation or association. It is only fair to state this.[160]

Nevertheless, partly because of the moderating effect these organisations had on the wider communities which they represented, even the more radical organisations spent much of the conflict pursuing non-violent tactics. Where activists did engage in violence, it was as a result of local feeling over-riding directives from the party leadership. The aforementioned overpopulation, poverty and communal antagonisms in the East End led to a greater dissonance between local feeling and party/communal leadership than elsewhere, which contributed to the cycle of violence which occurred here.

Eventually, just as they had sparked it off, international factors extinguished the conflict. As the war with the fascist powers seemed increasingly likely, the BUF's popularity plummeted. When the leaders were interned after war finally broke out, the BUF really did collapse, and with it so did the movement-countermovement contest.

Notes

1 Eatwell, Roger. 'Community Cohesion and Cumulative Extremism in Contemporary Britain', *Political Quarterly*, 77, no. 2 (2006), p. 205.
2 Thurlow, Richard. *Fascism in Britain: From Oswald Mosley's Blackshirts to the National Front* (London: I.B. Tauris Publishers, 1998).
3 Anderson, Gerald. *Fascists, Communists, and the National Government* (London: University of Missouri Press, 1983); Thurlow, Richard. *Fascism in Britain: From Oswald Mosley's Blackshirts to the National Front* (London: I.B. Tauris Publishers, 1998).
4 Copsey, Nigel. *Anti-Fascism in Britain* (London: Macmillan Press Ltd, 2000), p. 4.
5 Ibid., pp. 6–7.
6 Skidelsky, Robert. 'Reflections on Mosley and British Fascism', in *British Fascism: Essays on the Radical Right in Interwar Britain*, Edited by Kenneth Lunn and Richard C. Thurlow (London: Croom Helm, 1980), pp. 84–87.
7 *The Times*, Monday, 21 September 1932; *Western Daily Press*, Monday, 19 October 1931.
8 Dorril, Stephen. *Blackshirt: Sir Oswald Mosley and British Fascism* (London: Penguin, 2007), p. 190.
9 Copsey, Nigel. 'Opposition to the New Party: An Incipient Anti-Fascism or a Defence Against "Mosleyitis"?', *Contemporary British History*, 23, no. 4 (2009), pp. 461–475.
10 Ibid., p. 13.
11 Ibid., p. 13.
12 Ibid.; Worley, Matthew. 'What Was the New Party? Sir Oswald Mosley and Associated Responses to the "Crisis", 1931–1932', *History*, 92, no. 305 (2007), pp. 39–63.
13 Dorril, p. 217.

14 See the National Archives (NA) NA: HO 45/25384 Home Office: Registered Papers. Registered Papers, 1920 onwards. DISTURBANCES: British Union of Fascists: Reports on meetings and activities.

15 Ibid.

16 Copsey, Nigel. *Anti-Fascism in Britain* (London: Macmillan Press Ltd, 2000).

17 Saideman, Stephen M. and R. William Ayres. 'Determining the Causes of Irredentism: Logit Analyses of Minorities at Risk Data from the 1980s and 1990s', *The Journal of Politics*, 62, no. 4 (2000), pp. 1129–1130.

18 Zarnett, David. 'Transnationalized Domestic Contention: Explaining the Varying Levels of Western Solidarity Given to the Kurds and Palestinians', in *Contentious Politics in the Middle East: Popular Resistance and Marginalized Activism beyond the Arab Uprisings*, Edited by Fawaz A. Gerges (New York: Palgrave Macmillan, 2015), pp. 197–202.

19 Copsey, *Anti-Fascism*, p. 3.

20 Ibid., p. 15; *Daily Worker*, Saturday, 6 May 1933, p. 2.

21 Hodgson, Keith. *Fighting Fascism: The British Left and the Rise of Fascism, 1919–39* (Manchester: Manchester University Press: 2010).

22 Copsey, *Anti-Fascism*, p. 19.

23 *Daily Worker*, Tuesday, 14 March 1933; *Daily Worker*, Wednesday, 11 October 1933; *The Blackshirt*, No. 10, 1 July 1933; *The Blackshirt*, No. 14, July 29 1933; *The Blackshirt*, No. 21, 16 September 1933.

24 *The Blackshirt*, No. 5, 17 April 1933.

25 NA: MEPO 2/10646 Reports and Correspondence About Fascist Activities.

26 Pugh, Martin. *'Hurrah for the Blackshirts!' Fascists and Fascism in Britain Between the Wars* (London: Pimlico, 2005), p. 148.

27 Dorril, Stephen. *Blackshirt: Sir Oswald Mosley and British Fascism* (London: Penguin, 2007), p. 244; Tilles, Daniel. *British Fascist Anti-Semitism and Jewish Responses 1932–40* (London: Bloomsbury, 2015), p. 102.

28 NA: MEPO 3/1256 Metropolitan Police: Office of the Commissioner: Correspondence and Papers, Special Series.

29 Ibid.

30 NA: MEPO 2/10646.

31 *British Fascism*, 'Stop Press!', Extra Autumn Issue, 1933, p. 2.

32 Ibid., p. 2.

33 NA: MEPO 2/10646.

34 Dorril, *Blackshirt*, p. 262; *Edinburgh Evening News*, Saturday, 25 November 1933, p. 7.

35 *The Blackshirt*, No. 39, 19 January 1934; Jacobs, Joe. *Out of the Ghetto: My Youth in the East End, Communism & Fascism 1913–1939* (London: Janet Simon, 1978), p. 97.

36 Tilles, Daniel. *British Fascist Anti-Semitism and Jewish Responses 1932–40* (London: Bloomsbury, 2015), p. 105.

37 *The Times*, Wednesday, 19 July 1933; p. 14.

38 See London Metropolitan Archives (LMA) LMA: ACC/312/A/26: Minutes of Meetings of Board of Deputies of British Jews, 1932–33.

39 Thurlow, Richard. 'State Management of the British Union of Fascists in the 1930s', in *The Failure of British Fascism The Far Right and the Fight for Political Recognition*, Edited by Mike Cronin (Basingstoke: Macmillan, 1996), p. 40.

40 Thurlow, Richard. 'The Straw that Broke the Camel's Back: Public Order, Civil Liberties and the Battle of Cable Street', *Jewish Culture and History*, 1, no. 2 (1998), p. 76.

41 Thurlow, Richard. 'State Management of the British Union of Fascists in the 1930s', in *The Failure of British Fascism The Far Right and the Fight for Political Recognition*, Edited by Mike Cronin (Basingstoke: Macmillan, 1996), p. 40.

42 Stevenson, John. 'The BUF, The Metropolitan Police and Public Order', in *British Fascism: Essays on the Radical Right in Inter-War Britain*, Edited by Kenneth Lunn and Richard C. Thurlow (Oxon: Routledge, 1980), p. 140.

43 Thurlow, Richard. 'State Management of the British Union of Fascists in the 1930s', in *The Failure of British Fascism The Far Right and the Fight for Political Recognition*, Edited by Mike Cronin (Basingstoke: Macmillan, 1996), pp. 40–41.

44 Stevenson, John. 'The BUF, The Metropolitan Police and Public Order', in *British Fascism: Essays on the Radical Right in Inter-War Britain*, Edited by Kenneth Lunn and Richard C. Thurlow (Oxon: Routledge, 1980), pp. 145–146.

45 NA: MEPO 2/10646 Reports and Correspondence About Fascist Activities.

46 Ibid.

47 Baylor, Tim. 'Media Framing of Movement Protest: The Case of American Indian Protest', *The Social Science Journal*, 33, no. 3 (1996), p. 241.

48 Ryan, Charlotte. *Prime Time Activism: Media Strategies for Grassroots Organizing* (Boston: South End Press, 1991), p. 76.

49 NA: HO 45/25383.

50 *The Blackshirt*,No. 39, 19 January 1934.

51 *The Blackshirt*, No. 41, 2 February 1934.

52 *The Blackshirt*, No. 46, 9 March 1934; *The Blackshirt*, No. 47, 16 March 1934; *The Blackshirt*, No. 50, April 6 1934; *The Blackshirt*, No. 53, 27 April 1934; *The Blackshirt*, No. 55, 11 May 1934.

53 NA: HO 144/20140: 3 March 1934–11 June 1934 DISTURBANCES Activities of the British Union of Fascists.

54 Ibid.

55 Lewis, *Illusions of Grandeur*, p. 120.

56 *Daily Worker*, Monday, 1 June 1931; *Daily Worker*, Tuesday, 2 June 1931.

57 *Daily Worker*, Thursday, 6 June 1931.

58 *Daily Worker*, Friday, 7 June 1931.

59 NA: KV3/58 Activities of the British Fascist Organisation in UK.

60 *The Manchester Guardian*, 9 June 1934, p. 13.

61 NA: KV3/58.

62 *The Blackshirt*, No. 61, 22 June 1934.

63 NA: HO 45/25383 Disturbances: Anti-fascist activities; anti-fascist demonstrations and activities directed against meeting of the British Union of Fascists in Hyde Park on 9 September 1934.

64 Ibid.

65 Saideman, Stephen M. and R. William Ayres. 'Determining the Causes of Irredentism: Logit Analyses of Minorities at Risk Data from the 1980s and 1990s', *The Journal of Politics*, 62, no. 4 (2000), pp. 1129–1130; Zarnett, David. 'Transnationalized Domestic Contention: Explaining the Varying Levels of Western Solidarity Given to the Kurds and Palestinians', in *Contentious Politics in the Middle East: Popular Resistance and Marginalized Activism beyond the Arab Uprisings*, Edited by Fawaz A. Gerges (New York: Palgrave Macmillan, 2015), pp. 197–202.

66 NA: HO 45/25383 DISTURBANCES.

67 Ibid.

68 Ibid.

69 Thurlow, Richard. *The Secret State: British Internal Security in the Twentieth Century* (Oxford: Blackwell, 1994), p. 10.

70 NA: HO 45/25383 DISTURBANCES.

71 Copsey, Nigel. *Anti-Fascism in Britain*, 2nd ed. (Oxon: Routledge, 2017), p. 27.

72 Young, Lewis. 'Fascism for the British Audience: The Communist Party of Great Britain's Analysis of Fascism in Theory and Practice', *Fascism*, 3, no. 2 (2014), p. 108.

73 Copsey, Nigel. *Anti-Fascism in Britain*, 2nd ed. (Oxon: Routledge, 2017), p. 28.

74 Ibid., p. 43.

75 Hodgson, Keith. *Fighting Fascism: The British Left and the Rise of Fascism, 1919–39* (Manchester: Manchester University Press, 2010), p. 146.

76 Young, Lewis. 'Fascism for the British Audience: The Communist Party of Great Britain's Analysis of Fascism in Theory and Practice', *Fascism*, 3, no. 2 (2014), p. 108.

77 Corthorn, Paul. *In the Shadow of the Dictators: The British Left in the 1930s* (London: I.B. Taurus, 2006), pp. 108–109.

78 Hodgson, Keith. *Fighting Fascism: The British Left and the Rise of Fascism, 1919–39* (Manchester: Manchester University Press, 2010), p. 148.

79 Ibid., p. 141.

80 LMA: ACC/3121/E3/96: Growth of Fascist Activities and the Authorities' Response.

81 NA: KV3/59 Activities of the British Fascist Organisation in UK.

82 Cullen, Stephen. 'Political Violence: The Case of the British Union of Fascists', *Journal of Contemporary History*, 28, no. 2 (1993), pp. 245–267.

83 Zald, N. Mayer and Useem Bert. 'Movement and Countermovement Interaction: Mobilization, Tactics, and State Involvement', in *Social Movements in an Organizational Society: Collected Essays*, Edited by Mayer N. Zald and John D. McCarthy (London: Transaction Publishers, 1984), p. 251.

84 David S. Meyer and Suzanne Staggenborg. 'Movements, Countermovements, and the Structure of Political Opportunity', *American Journal of Sociology*, 101, no. 6 (1996), pp. 1628–1660.

85 Busher, Joel and Graham Macklin. 'Interpreting "Cumulative Extremism": Six Proposals for Enhancing Conceptual Clarity', *Terrorism and Political Violence*, 27, no. 5 (2014).

86 Pugh, Martin, *Hurrah*, p. 220.

87 Thurlow, Richard. *Fascism in Britain: From Oswald Mosley's Blackshirts to the National Front* (London: I.B. Tauris Publishers, 1998), p. 77.

88 Ibid., p. 77.

89 Jacobs, Joe. *Out of the Ghetto: My Youth in the East End, Communism & Fascism 1913–1939* (London: Janet Simon, 1978), p. 198.

90 NA: MEPO 2/3043 1936–1939: 'Jew Baiting' Incidents: Action to be Taken by Police; with Memo by Sir John Simon; Smith, R. Elaine. 'Jews and Politics in the East End of London, 1918–1939', in *The Making of Modern Anglo-Jewry*, Edited by David Cesarani (Oxford: Basil Blackwell, 1990), p. 54.

91 Tilles, *British Fascist*, p. 136.

92 Smith, R. Elaine. 'Jews and Politics in the East End of London, 1918–1939', in *The Making of Modern Anglo-Jewry*, Edited by David Cesarani (Oxford: Basil Blackwell, 1990), p. 159.

93 Endelman, Todd M. *The Jews of Britain, 1656 to 2000* (London: University of California Press, 2002).

94 *The Jewish Chronicle*, 29 May 1936.

95 LMA: ACC/3121/A/28: Minute Book of Board of Deputies of British Jews, 1935–1936.

96 LMA: ACC/3121/E3/96: Growth of Fascist Activities and the Authorities' Response.

97 Tilles, *British Fascist*, p. 119.

98 *Daily Worker*, 30 September 1936.

99 Jacobs, *Ghetto*, p. 238.

100 Ibid., p. 238.

101 *The Blackshirt*, No. 198, 26 September 1934; *The Blackshirt*, No. 199, 3 October 1934; PRO: MEPO 2/3043 1936–1939: "Jew Baiting" Incidents.

102 Jacobs, Joe. *Out of the Ghetto: My Youth in the East End, Communism & Fascism 1913–1939* (London: Janet Simon, 1978).

103 PRO: MEPO 2/3043 1936–1939: "Jew Baiting" Incidents.

104 Lewis, S. David. *Illusions of Grandeur: Mosley, Fascism and British Society, 1931–81* (Manchester: Manchester University Press, 1987), p. 125.

105 NA: KV3/59; PRO: MEPO 2/3043.

106 NA: KV3/59.

107 Thurlow, Richard. *The Secret State: British Internal Security in the Twentieth Century* (Oxford: Blackwell, 1994), p. 201.

108 Ibid., p. 203.

109 Anderson, Gerald. *Fascists, Communists, and the National Government* (London: University of Missouri Press, 1983).

110 Ibid., p. 202.

111 Lewis, *Illusions*, p. 159.

112 Ibid., pp. 172–173.

113 Bellamy, Richard. *We Marched with Mosley: The Authorised History of the British Union of Fascists* (London: Black House Publishing, 2013), p. 121.

114 NA: MEPO 2/3043.

115 Ibid.

116 Anderson, Gerald. *Fascists, Communists, and the National Government* (London: University of Missouri Press, 1983).

117 NA: MEPO 2/3043.

118 PRO: MEPO 2/3043.

119 Webber, Gerald C. 'Patterns of Membership and Support for the British Union of Fascists', *Journal of Contemporary History*, 19, no. 4 (1984), p. 597.

120 LMA: ACC/3121/A/30: Minutes Book of Board of Deputies of British Jews, 1938 –1940.

121 NA: MEPO 2/3043.

122 Copsey, Nigel. *Anti-Fascism in Britain*, 2nd ed. (Oxon: Routledge, 2017), p. 58.

123 NA: MEPO 2/3043.

124 Copsey, *Anti-Fascism*, pp. 69–70.

125 Tilles, *British Fascist*, pp. 160–162.

126 Ibid., p. 176.

127 Copsey, *Anti-Fascism*, p. 71.

128 Tilles, *British Fascist*, p. 162.

129 PRO: MEPO 2/3043.

130 Copsey, *Anti-Fascism*, p. 162.

131 Smith, R. Elaine. 'Jews and Politics in the East End of London, 1918–1939', in *The Making of Modern Anglo-Jewry*, Edited by David Cesarani (Oxford: Basil Blackwell, 1990), p. 54.

132 Fadaee, Simin. 'Social Movements, Counter-movements, and Their Dynamic Interplay', in *Women's Movements and Countermovements: The Quest for Gender Equality in Southeast Asia and the Middle East*, Edited by Claudia Derichs and Dana Fennert (Newcastle: Cambridge Scholars Publishing, 2014), p. 19.

133 NA: KV4/140 Control of British Unions of Fascists General.

134 LMA: ACC/3121/E/3/247 Fascists: Meetings and Attacks on Jews 1938–39.

135 Ibid.

136 NA: KV4/140 Control of British Unions of Fascists General.

137 Sources for data: G. C. Webber, 'Patterns of membership and support for British Union of Fascists', *Journal of Contemporary History*, 19 (1984), pp. 576–606 & Thorpe, Andrew, 'The Membership of the Communist Party of Great Britain, 1920–1945', *The Historical Journal*, 43, no. 3 (2000), pp. 777–800. The data for BUF membership is based on a combination of MI5 intelligence, BUF sources and educated guess work. However, as Thurlow suggests 'Although some of the assumptions behind these figures are questionable, the basic pattern is the most plausible that has been suggested.' *Secret State*, p. 192. The CPGB figures come from the Party's own censuses, held at the Russian Centre for the Preservation of Contemporary Historical Documents (formerly the archive of the Institute of Marxism-Leninism) in Moscow and so should be fairly reliable.

138 NA: KV3/59.

139 Busher, Joel and Graham Macklin, 'Interpreting "Cumulative Extremism": Six Proposals for Enhancing Conceptual Clarity', *Terrorism and Political Violence*, 27, no. 5 (2014), p. 4.

140 Lewis, *Illusions*, p. 95.

141 Skidelsky, Robert. *Oswald Mosley* (London: Macmillan, 1981), p. 381.

142 Ibid., p. 381. It should be noted that the evidence put forward for this claim, that is, the testimony of A. K. Chesterton and Oswald Mosley, should be viewed sceptically.

143 Holmes, Colin. 'Anti-Semitism and the BUF', in *British Fascism: Essays on the Radical Right in Interwar Britain*, Edited by Kenneth Lunn and Richard C. Thurlow (London: Croom Helm, 1980), pp. 120–122.

144 Lewis, *Illusions*, p. 101.

145 Rosenberg, David. *Battle for the East End: Jewish Responses to Fascism in the 1930s* (Nottingham: Five Leaves, 2011), p. 102.

146 Cullen, Stephen. 'Political Violence: The Case of the British Union of Fascists', *Journal of Contemporary History*, 28, no. 2 (1993), pp. 245–267.

147 Tilles, Daniel. *British Fascist Anti-Semitism and Jewish Responses 1932–40* (London: Bloomsbury, 2015), Chapter 2 & p. 187.

148 NA: KV3/59.

149 Ibid.

150 Barnes, James and Patience Barnes. *Nazi's in Pre-War London 1930–1939* (Brighton: Sussex Academy Press, 2005).

151 PRO: MEPO 2/3043.

152 Anderson, Gerald. *Fascists, Communists, and the National Government* (London: University of Missouri Press, 1983), p. 139.

153 Busher, Joel and Macklin, Graham. 'Interpreting "Cumulative Extremism": Six Proposals for Enhancing Conceptual Clarity', *Terrorism and Political Violence*, 27, no. 5 (2014), p. 3.

154 Tilly, Charles. *The Politics of Collective Violence* (Cambridge: Cambridge University Press, 2003).

155 Thurlow, Richard. 'The Straw that Broke the Camel's Back: Public Order, Civil Liberties and the Battle of Cable Street', *Jewish Culture and History*, 1, no. 2 (1998), p. 78.

156 LMA: ACC/3121/E3/96.

157 Copsey, Nigel. *Anti-Fascism in Britain*, 2nd ed. (Oxon: Routledge, 2017), p. 65.

158 Thurlow, *Fascism in Britain*, p. 72.

159 Holmes, Colin. *Anti–Semitism in British Society, 1876–1939.* (London: Edward Arnold, 1979).

160 LMA: ACC/3121/E/3/247.

3

FASCISTS AND ANTI-FASCISTS IN THE 1970s[1]

Introduction

From 1967 to 1979 another movement–countermovement contest (M/CM) developed between fascists and anti-fascists in Britain. The main groups involved in this competition were organisations of the far right, such as the National Front (NF) and the British Movement (BM), and those of the far left such as the International Socialists/Socialist Workers' Party (IS/SWP) and International Marxist Group (IMG). In between these contenders were the social groups who they were either competing over or trying to radicalise for their own political ends, such as the working class and British minority communities. While these interactions were occurring, they were further altered by the actions of the state and the media, who played vital roles in escalating and de-escalating the contest. In revisiting this period, this chapter will assess the extent to which this M/CM contest generated processes of cumulative extremism (CE) leading to tactical escalations between the opposing social movements.

1967–1975

Following the triumph of the Allies in the Second World War and the revelations of the atrocities committed by the Nazis, fascism was widely seen as an horrific and alien ideology in Britain. Accordingly, attempts to mobilise by the far right (such as former members of the British Union of Fascists) were small scale – as was the anti-fascist response. Far right organisations such as the British League of Ex-Servicemen and Oswald Mosley's Union Movement did face opposition from anti-fascist groups including the Association of Jewish Ex-Servicemen, the 43 Group and the 62 Group in the twenty years following the Second World War – but these were nowhere near the scale of mobilisations experienced during the interwar period. As Copsey notes, 'the scope for fascist growth was so limited in Britain during this period that even without the existence of an organised anti-fascist opposition, fascism would have struggled to find popular appeal.'[2]

Indeed it was not until February 1967, when the National Front was founded, that this situation began to change.[3] Nevertheless, this change did not occur rapidly, and for the first few years of the nascent organisation's existence very little of consequence happened. While there were certainly violent skirmishes between the NF and their opponents, these tended to be localised, often spontaneous, and always small-scale, with only a handful of people from each side involved.[4]

There were two major events during the later part of the 1960s and the beginning of the 1970s that helped pave the way for the NF's subsequent growth. The first was the 'Rivers of Blood' speech given by renegade Tory MP Enoch Powell on 20 April 1968. Powell's speech emotively described a near-apocalyptic vision of the UK, its ruin brought about by continued non-white immigration. It provoked dramatic displays of public support. The day after the speech, striking dockers marched from East London to Parliament in support of Powell, and there was a string of other strikes around the country with similar motives for the following week.[5] Further, many scholars argue that Powell's speech, as well as his subsequent anti-immigration campaigning over the next few years, 'effectively dissolved the Conservative and Labour parties' racial consensus'.[6] Whether or not this is true he certainly went some way towards politicising the issues of race and immigration, which in turn helped to legitimise racist arguments and by extension the organisations who espoused them.

The second occurred in August 1972, when the Conservative government allowed thousands of Ugandan Asian refugees who had been exiled by Idi Amin to enter the country. As the 'immigration' issue was thrust once more into the forefront of public discourse, the NF leadership acted with impressive speed to capitalise on the opportunity: within '24 hours of the first alarming headlines from Uganda, the NF had organized a 100-strong picket of Downing St. in the afternoon of 14 August, followed by the delivery of a petition of protest by John Tyndall [chairman of the NF] to Number 10 that evening.'[7] The NF's subsequent anti-immigration campaign was successful. Over the last four months of 1972 the Front gained over 800 new members, and their annual Remembrance Day march that year drew 1,500 activists, twice as many as in 1971.[8] Martin Webster, National Activities Organiser of the National Front, later remarked that the organisation's real beginnings lay with the arrival of the Ugandan Asian immigrants.[9]

The following year the National Front's good luck continued, as they gained their best parliamentary result with 16.2% of the vote in a Parliamentary by-election in West Bromwich and had also reportedly grown their membership to 14,000.[10] Buoyed by their successes, the NF confidently announced that they would be fielding 54 candidates in the February 1974 general election.[11] As the NF went from strength to strength there was an attendant growth in anti-fascist activities. From 1973 onwards, spurred into action by the advances made by the NF, many local anti-fascist organisations were formed.[12] Indeed, 'the more successful [the NF] became, in local elections, the more Left-wing and liberal bodies throughout the country recognised the threat and began to mobilise against it. The obvious weapon for them to use, in leaflets and in speeches, was the political histories of Tyndall and Webster.'[13] Tyndall and Webster had both previously been members of the openly Nazi National Socialist Movement (NSM), and incriminating photos of them from those days had landed in the hands of their enemies. However, the NF's plans to field 54 candidates in the February 1974 election, and the five minutes of free radio and TV broadcasting time this entitled them to, was an even stronger motivational influence on the growing anti-fascist movement.[14]

From 1974, there was an intensification in the M/CM relationship, in terms of both the size of anti-fascist mobilisations and the commitment to confrontational tactics. On 21 May 1974, between 300 and 400 anti-fascists attempted to break up a National Front meeting at Oxford Town Hall, where Martin Webster was speaking.[15] In Canterbury on the 8 June, students at an NF meeting 'scuffled' with police while attempting to interrupt the proceedings. Around 300 students marched through the streets in protest at the NF meeting, and NF stewards later attacked this counter-demo with staves, badly injuring some of them, after which two people were arrested.[16]

A week later, on 15 June, the mounting tensions between the fascists and the left erupted in the biggest clash between fascists, anti-fascists and the police seen in the UK since the interwar period. The NF had organised a protest march culminating in a meeting in Conway Hall, London, and a corresponding counter-demonstration had been called by the anti-imperialist organisation, Liberation, with the backing of a broad cross-section of the labour movement.[17] It was arranged with the police that both groups would be allowed to march to Red Lion Square, where the NF would hold their meeting in Conway Hall; a small number of anti-fascists would have a meeting in another room of the building which they would access via a side entrance, and the rest of the counter-demonstrators would hold their protest outside. These plans were, however, thrown into disarray by the International Marxist Group's (IMG) efforts (enacted with the aid of the International Socialists (IS)) to deny the NF access to the hall by forming 'a mass picket at the main entrance' and refusing the police's orders to disperse.[18]

The incident provoked two short but intense waves of fighting between the activists and the police, during which time the student Kevin Gately was fatally wounded.[19] Walker has argued that towards the end of the fracas the police made an unnecessary push through the crowd, an action which 'led to individual acts of police violence against demonstrators and… gave the far left permanent ammunition in its long arguments against the police as the physical weapon of the establishment.'[20] Indeed, as we shall see, interactions between the police and the far left continued to escalate from this point.

In the findings of the official enquiry into the disorder at Red Lion Square, Lord Scarman 'largely absolved the police of any wrongdoing'[21] while stating that the IMG 'initiated the disorder' and thus 'bear a heavy moral responsibility for the violence and injuries which followed.'[22] It should be noted, though, that many of the people present at the event strongly disagreed with Scarman's conclusions. The CPGB, while admonishing the IMG's actions for playing 'into the hands of all those in the key positions of establishment ... aimed at destroying our basic democratic rights', stated clearly that there was 'absolutely no reason why the police could not have contained the situation peacefully *at all times*'.[23] Similarly, the President of the National Union of Students, John Randall, stated to the *Morning Star* that 'Kevin Gately died as a direct result of police violence'.[24]

The NF came through the situation unscathed, however, having conducted their march in a relatively orderly fashion while obeying any instructions from the police. More than one commentator posited that the incident, which had essentially been a fight between anti-fascists and police, hugely backfired, bringing only sympathy and support to the NF. Walker argued that it was the NF who 'emerged as the innocent victims of political violence, the left who emerged as the instigators', while Clutterbuck claimed that the publicity the Front gained in this incident caused a 'substantially increased vote... at the next general election'.[25] However, Taylor has dismissed these claims, demonstrating that although the NF did fare better in a number of constituencies, overall their total average share of the vote decreased marginally, leading him to conclude that in all probability 'the events at Red Lion Square neither helped nor hindered the NF in October 1974.'[26]

Red Lion Square was a major fillip to the anti-fascist movement, causing a spike in M/CM mobilisations. NF marches were opposed by large anti-fascist mobilisations in Leicester in August 1974, and in Hyde Park the following month. In Leicester a large group of around 6,000 anti-fascists peacefully opposed around 1,500 NF marchers, and in Hyde Park 7,000 anti-fascists occupied the NF's planned route, forcing the police to divert their march. At a meeting following the latter incident, NF member Walter Barton declared: 'It's time to turn our young men loose on the Reds.'[27] Indeed, between 1972 and 1974 the growing violent opposition to NF activities had provoked the development of a defence strategy, whereby groups of men would be positioned around any NF march ready to link arms and repel attacks. 'These "defence groups" had become, by the 1974 Remembrance Day parade, an organised body of tough young militants who bore the name of the 'Honour Guard'.[28] The interactions between the far right and their enemies were beginning to take on the shape of CE: the achievements and actions of the far right invigorated and fuelled the anti-fascist movement, whose militancy and radicalism in turn provoked the formation of marshal bodies and aggressive attitudes and tactics amongst the fascists.

The NF polled relatively well in the October 1974 election, receiving 112,000 votes.[29] However, with the election over, the need to appear internally united disappeared. Consequently, throughout 1975, as the leadership fought over the reins of the Front, the grassroots members orchestrated a series of violent attacks on left-wing and anti-fascist targets. In August 1975, a group of between

30 and 40 NF members and Loyalists attacked a meeting organised by Northern Ireland Civil Rights Association (NICRA) in Liverpool. They assaulted the speaker and other attendees with chairs, hospitalising one person and severely injuring several others.[30] In November 1975, a National Council of Civil Liberties (NCCL) sponsored event at Manchester Polytechnic, at which Northern Irish politician and activist Bernadette Devlin was scheduled to speak, was attacked by a large group of NF and BM activists.[31] Six people were badly hurt, with one man requiring nineteen stitches after a fascist smashed a bottle into his face.[32]

The anti-fascists, for their part, maintained constant pressure on the NF. In March 1975, an NF demonstration in Islington, North London, was opposed by around 6,000 anti-fascists. On 6 September, the National Front held a 'March Against Muggers' event through East London, which faced heavy opposition from assorted left-wing activists. Had it not been for a heavy police presence there might have been large-scale fighting between the two groups.[33] The next month the Front's AGM in Chelsea Town Hall faced opposition from an IS and IMG-organised counter-demo with roughly 1,000 anti-fascists present.[34] It seems that the relationship between the opposing social movements was providing some succour to both sides; the more they opposed each other, the more they provided motivation. On the other hand, while their clashes may have been generating support for one or both sides – alongside other factors, such as the influx of refugees and Powell's intervention – they did not have a significant radicalising effect beyond activists engaging in casual street-brawls.

A key theoretical point can be made with regard to the foregoing discussion; namely that the issues of race and class were central to the escalation of this episode. Firstly, both the fascists and the far left were competing over the constituency of the white working class. This shaped the tactics of both groups: the NF attempted to co-opt left wing tactics, like the short lived Trade Unions Against Immigration (TRU-AIM),[35] and the far left used displays of militant opposition against the Front and the police to demonstrate that they were the true revolutionary force of the working class.

The issue of race was just as key in shaping the tactics and areas of operation of the opposing groups. The fascists hoped to exacerbate existing racial social divisions between white and non-white communities to start a 'race war' and divide the labour movement, an aim which was greatly helped by the arrival of the Ugandan Asians. This was the reason so many of their later marches were through immigrant communities like the East End of London. The far left hoped to recruit minority communities to aid their revolutionary struggle and to prevent the division of the working class. This analysis is strengthened by the fact that the NF polled noticeably better in the October 1974 election in constituencies in London which were both working class and contained a higher proportion of non-white residents.[36] From this perspective, it seems clear that this conflict was not one fuelled by cumulative extremism, at least not largely speaking, in that it was not the 'extremism' of one group fuelling the 'extremism' of another. Rather the relationship the opposing movements had with third party groups which shaped the escalation and de-escalation of the conflict. This reinforces Busher's and Macklin's argument that to understand why and how CE may or may not develop it is necessary to pay attention to the 'multiple pathways of influence' that exist between the 'multiple actors' involved in a contest.[37]

Throughout 1975, a rift had been growing between two camps within the Front, the 'populists' and the 'neo-Nazis', and in November it came to a head, resulting in the populists seceding from the Front to form the National Party (NP). Although the NP was never as successful in terms of total vote share or membership size as the NF (although they were to win two council seats in Blackburn), they did rob their erstwhile colleagues of a number of their most experienced organisers and activists, roughly 2,000 of their members (around one fifth of the total), as well as the financial backing of the prominent benefactor Gordon Marshall/Brown, and thereby did do some serious damage to the NF.[38] The magazine *Campaign Against Racism and Fascism* (*CARF*) later argued that by successfully labelling them as Nazis, 'the NF split in 1975 can in part be attributed to' the anti-fascist movement.[39]

This demonstrates two factors which can inhibit a social movement's momentum and thus interrupt processes of CE from developing. In the first instance, as social movements mobilise they attempt to advance 'collective action frames'; that is, 'the interpretive packages that activists develop to mobilize potential adherents and constituents'.[40] These processes then become the 'subject of intense contestation between collective actors representing the movement, the state, and any existing counter movements.'[41] These 'framing contests' are important because how 'successfully groups frame their identities for the public thus affects their ability to recruit members and supporters, gain a public hearing, make alliances with other groups, and defuse opposition.'[42] Further, social movement organisations that are engaged in an M/CM conflict are not only attempting to frame their own identities and grievances, but also their enemies'. By highlighting the openly Nazi past of the leaders of the NF the anti-fascist movement was very successful in framing them as racists and fascists, thus impeding their ability to gain mass appeal and generate more support. The second factor is the degree of internal unity a social movement organisation can maintain: the less cohesive a social movement organisation is the greater the difficulty it will often have in sustaining mass-mobilisations of its members. While this is something which often has more to do with the internal political and social chemistry of an organisation or movement than any external factors, divisions can be created, exacerbated and exploited by countermovements – as is demonstrated here.

1976–1977

The events at Red Lion Square notwithstanding, the relations between the various groups embroiled in this M/CM contest only really began to heat up during 1976. Anti-fascists clashed with NF members who were walking to an assembly point for a march on 28 February, during a by-election in Coventry. During the fracas, Andrew Fountaine, John Tyndall and Martin Webster were all assaulted, with Tyndall receiving a brick to the side of his face.[43] Two months later, on 24 April, the BM held a 'Patriots' March' in London on the same day that the NF held one in Bradford, an area with a large Asian community. The BM event was heavily policed, and the hundreds of fascists and anti-fascists were kept separate as the BM marched towards Trafalgar Square. However as they entered the Square, the anti-fascists briefly broke through the police lines and exchanged blows with the BM before being forced back again by the police.[44]

The NF marched through Bradford 'deliberately provoking a violent confrontation with Asian youth'.[45] Indeed, young people from minority communities had now begun to engage in the anti-fascist actions with gusto; a development that the NF had no doubt been hoping for, as it leant 'empirical credibility' to the framing devices in their propaganda which painted their enemies as fundamentally un-British and lawless troublemakers.[46] Six hundred NF members faced off against between 3 and 4,000 counter-demonstrators, and as the day wound on groups of young anti-fascists clashed with both the police and the NF. A police riot van was pushed onto its side and a patrol car was turned over; counter-demonstrators also hurled missiles at the police and the fascists.[47] This could not have been a better outcome for the NF: ostensibly violent minority-community and left-wing hooligans attacking the forces of law and order.

Mirroring events in 1972, the NF's fortunes were once again improved by a highly publicised wave of refugees arriving in Britain. The regime in Malawi had expelled its Asian population, many of whom were British passport holders. As the first immigrants arrived in Britain, the mainstream press published highly inflammatory headlines: *The Sun* ran the headline 'Scandal of £600-a-Week Immigrants: Giant Bill for Two Families Who Live in a 4-Star Hotel' on 4 May, with the *Mirror* running the line 'New Flood of Asians into Britain'.[48]

This development was a spark which ignited 'the long hot summer of 1976', in which the NF experienced a period of growth while community tensions were increasingly strained.[49] On 4 June 1976, 10 year old Gurdip Singh Chaggar was killed in what has been widely seen as a racially motivated attack. Chagger's death provoked a huge reaction from within the local community, while community leaders did their best to rein in the expressions of anger from amongst the Asian youth: 'When the murder took place there was on the one hand a massive reaction amongst the Asian community of insecurity, of anger; there was also a reaction amongst many sections of white people fearful of the possible counter-violence by young Asians.'[50] It is highly likely that this was exactly what both the NF and BM were hoping would happen.

The communal leadership of the Asian community struggled to pacify their youth:

> The leaders of the Indian Workers' Association [IWA] were in some difficulty to cope with the rising tide of feeling amongst the Asian community… For instance, several hundred young Asian lads went to an already scheduled

IWA meeting on the Sunday two days after the murder, and effectively took it over. In a spontaneous way they initiated a demonstration to the local police station and it was left to one or two of our comrades to go with them to try to contain any wild activity. The IWA leadership did not go with them.[51]

The group marched to the police station, blocking the roads around the building. The police's first action was to arrest two of the protesters, one of whom had been with Chaggar when he was murdered. The Youth group proceeded to engage in a sit-in, and ultimately the police released the people that had been arrested. The day after this the Southall Youth Movement (SYM) was formed.[52] It is worth quoting Ramamurthy here:

> For Mohsin Zulfiqar, the protests in Southall 'really gave us the basis that direct action [does bring] positive results, hence our own ability to challenge the National Front by saying that we're prepared to fight against you physically, not just have demonstrations and pickets and so on['].... The authority of individuals in SYM was accepted 'because some of them had reputations as good fighters and organisers against racism in the schools – particularly in the fights with skinhead gangs several years ago...'[53]

The SYM went about ensuring that their *modus operandi* was one of self-defence, rather than aggressive campaigns of political violence. A peaceful march was held in Southall, attended by around 7,000 people. A meeting was also held at the local Sikh temple on the Wednesday five days after the murder, with between 150 and 200 attendees. The IWA, other local immigrant organisations, religious groups, trades unions, Labour and the Communist Party of Great Britain (CPGB), were all represented. At this meeting it was agreed that a demonstration should be held, so as not to create a political vacuum, but it was also widely agreed that the issue of communal 'self-defence' should be avoided, as it was just likely to lead to further 'violence and division in the community'.[54] So, despite hate crime and fascist provocation, there were still influential and moderate communal voices helping to prevent non-white communities from becoming radicalised to the point of using organised violence.

The same month as Chaggar's death, Community Relations officers in Blackburn released a dossier detailing more than 30 attacks carried out on Asian families and their properties. The officers argued that the blame for these attacks lay with the local National Party (an NF splinter group) and their provocative activities.[55] On the 15 July a group of NF members attacked a West Indian club in Bradford, injuring several people.[56] The murder, rising incidence of racist attacks, the growth of the fascist movement and hostility from the police and media all combined to provoke a growing militant attitude amongst black and Asian youth. Militant immigrant groups in London, Leicester, Blackburn and Birmingham, supported by the Institute of Race Relations, developed self-defence groups within their communities: 'The young Asian militants wanted direct action to protect themselves against racist attacks by individuals and discrimination by the authorities, rather than relying on the State.'[57] The SYM, and the other Asian Youth Movements (AYM) that followed, were organised and militant in their own way but were not provoked into being aggressive by their right wing antagonists.[58]

Drawing a *direct* causal link between the fascist parties' activities and the high incidence of racist attacks, and, by extension, ethnic minority militancy, is impossible. However, as Taylor suggests, the 'existence of widespread support for racism as demonstrated by electoral support for the NF was, it could be argued, an indication to those contemplating such attacks on coloured people that such violence was, if not necessarily socially acceptable, at least more likely to be condoned than other types of violence.'[59] This suggestion is lent further weight when one considers that former NF chairman Kingsley Read made a speech following Chaggar's death in which he stated 'One down – a million to go'.[60] That exacerbating conflict across racial lines was one of the NF's main strategies is lent further credence when one considers that as early as February 1976 the Association of Jewish Ex-Servicemen (AJEX) observed that 'Webster's idea of direct action is to provoke a Race War'.[61] In short, cumulative extremism was Webster's explicit aim. Further, across the month that Chaggar died, it 'seems likely that... the NF received over a thousand enquiries for membership.'[62]

The first major confrontation of 1977 happened at Wood Green in London on 23 April 1977. Around 1,500 NF members gathered at Ducketts Common to march to Palmers Green, and were opposed by around 3,000 anti-fascists from the IMG, Socialist Workers' Party (formerly the IS), the Labour Party, the IWA, and anarchist groups. The more militant sections of the opposition, led by the SWP, broke away from the peaceful counter-demo and laid an ambush for the NF. Notably, ethnic minority groups had clearly been radicalised by the provocative tactics of the fascists, and a large number of local youths from the Cypriot and West Indian communities joined in the militant opposition to the Front. As the NF march neared them, the anti-fascists launched a barrage of missiles at the fascists. In the ensuing fighting 81 people were arrested, and one anti-racist was stabbed.[63]

The following month the local elections were held, and once again the NF's results were the source of serious concern for the left. This was particularly true of their performance in London, where they received 119,063 votes. When a group of young black people, later dubbed the Lewisham 21, were arrested during early morning raids for suspicion of 'conspiring with each other and persons unknown to rob persons unknown', and their cause was taken up by community and left-wing activists, the NF were presented with an ideal target: ostensibly law-breaking British black people being defended by both their community and the left.[64] Accordingly, on 17 June 1977 a meeting of the Defence Committee for the Lewisham 21 (later the Lewisham 24) was attacked by NF members who beat one of the women present unconscious. The SWP, who were heavily involved in the Lewisham 21 Defence Committee, decided it was necessary to escalate the situation and go on the offensive. Central Committee member John Deason organised a group of stewards to defend not only the activities of the Defence Committee, but all the SWP's operations. These groups of stewards became known as the 'Squads':[65] 'Officially sanctioned by the SWP leadership, [the Squads] were tightly organised groups of anti-fascists whose job was to attack NF initiatives, as well as defend anti-fascist events.'[66]

The next time the NF attacked the Defence Committee's stall they were ambushed by a Squad who viciously fought them off.[67] This development served to escalate hostilities in the region for a while. The next month, on 2 July, a group of around 200 National Front members again violently attacked the Defence Committee who had organised a rally in Lewisham. The police arrested 50 people, 23 anti-fascists and 27 fascists.[68] The high number of anti-fascists arrested, mainly for defending themselves, reinforced the view that the police were a racist organisation.[69] Shortly afterwards, almost certainly in an attempt to further inflame communal tensions, the NF announced that they would hold an 'Anti-Mugging' march from New Cross to Lewisham.

The day of the march was 13 August 1977. As the Front gathered to march through South London, two different groups of anti-fascists prepared their response. The first, organised by the All Lewisham Campaign Against Racism and Fascism (ALCARAF), was a peaceful affair orchestrated to avoid the NF's march altogether. The second, largely coordinated by the SWP, had every intention of physically opposing the NF.[70] Around 3,000 militant anti-fascists, many armed with blunt instruments and knives, waited on the NF's route at Clifton Rise, and as the fascists approached them the anti-fascists hurled a barrage of missiles at their enemies.[71] A strong police presence managed to maintain control of the situation for a while, but eventually some determined anti-fascists broke through their line to attack the NF close up, splitting their march in two.[72] This led to vicious fighting between the two sides and the police.

The first main point to be made about the riot in Lewisham is that it seems likely that at least some of the people involved in the fighting enjoyed the thrill of the experience itself, over and above the ideological commitment to defeating their enemies. One anarchist present at the day stated:

> A Nazi leapt out yelling, "COME ON THEN, YOU RED BASTARD!" We struggled, me slamming him with a lump of wood… I had that glorious novocaine feeling above my upper lip. Pure adrenaline, pure violence.[73]

Similarly, Steve Tilzey of the SWP who was also in the thick of the conflict described how it 'was a real buzz, and I felt as if I had been part of something really special.'[74] Yet another anti-fascist recounted that 'We were at Clifton Rise when the march got split in two by a wedge of anti-fascists. We charged through and threw things at the retreating fascists. It was absolute chaos but incredibly, incredibly exhilarating.'[75] This all points to the way that highly emotionally charged situations can socialise groups of people into becoming desensitised to violence, and thus perhaps lead to increasingly militant viewpoints. Further, the intense emotions experienced at events such as this can help to maintain certain activists' commitment to the movement; as demonstrated, some activists enjoy these confrontations and actively seek them out.

The police eventually managed to divert the NF members down side streets to the pre-arranged meeting held by John Tyndall. The militant anti-fascists, their numbers now swelled by local black and Asian youths, pressed forward into Lewisham.[76] Here the main conflict was between the militant anti-fascists and the police, as the former pushed forward in an attempt to attack the police station. As the remaining anti-fascists marched past the Lewisham clock tower and the police's numbers having thinned, the militants hurled smoke bombs and other missiles at the remainder of them. The second point to be made about the day's events was the escalation in policing tactics. As the anti-fascists continued towards the police station, they were met with a novel site:

> Down from where we'd just come, across the wide road, slowly advancing, a line of police with riot shields. It looked spooky, fascinating even, the whole scene made menacing by blackened skies and the distant plume of smoke.[77]

It was the first time that the UK police used riot gear and tactics outside of Northern Ireland, demonstrating a mutually radicalising effect between the forces of law and order and militant social movements. In their work on 'spirals of violence' between movements and countermovements, Busher and Macklin argue that 'contest escalation often occurred at the intersection with other more violent contests', pointing out that fascists and anti-fascists in Britain who were also politically invested in the Irish Troubles sometimes borrowed the more deadly tactics of the conflict there, with one English anti-fascist even detonating a bomb in London.[78] Here it seems that there is evidence that the police, or state apparatuses in general, are prone to this pattern as well, as the British state took tactics it had developed in the far more bloody conflict in Northern Ireland and used them in the streets of the capital. The sight of riot police would become a much more common occurrence at political demonstrations as the years passed.

Shortly after the riot police arrived, the anti-fascists' plan to storm the police station was thrown into disarray by the arrival of even more Special Patrol Group (SPG) officers, and so most of the militants took the opportunity to retreat rather than being arrested. Shortly after the events, Steve Redford wrote in *CARF* magazine that:

> The tactics adopted by the police at New Cross and later in the day in Lewisham High Street both appalled and astounded me... I am not one of those who believes that the police are a fascist force – not yet anyway – but their actions on August 13 can only strengthen the position of those who do argue this line.[79]

The popular narrative amongst the left, which had taken root after Kevin Gately's death, that the major concern of the police was to suppress the forces of the revolutionary left, was gaining traction. However, it should be noted that this narrative did not find acceptance among the general population. The actions of the (overwhelmingly Protestant) Royal Ulster Constabulary (RUC) in Northern Ireland during the Troubles were often interpreted by virtually the whole Catholic community as unfairly repressive, and thus had a radicalising influence on the wider community as well as activists.[80] This is largely because the RUC were widely perceived as being biased and on more than one occasion they unnecessarily employed extreme methods. By contrast, when anti-fascists faced the police in Britain they were often the instigators of violence (even if the police did then react disproportionately harshly), and as such were not widely perceived as the victims among the broader British population. Thus, their inter-actions with the police, while possibly radicalising already committed activists, did not draw in others into the conflict. The exception to this observation were the black and Asian communities, whose daily experiences of institutional rac-ism often led to them viewing the police in much the same way that Catholics in Northern Ireland viewed the RUC.

Which brings us to the third and final noteworthy aspect of the 'Battle of Lewisham': the involvement of minority community members. As Martin Lux noted:

> …knots of young blacks and Asians fought the cops… On the other side of the road a dozen beefy middle aged blacks emerged from a minicab firm, some wearing crash helmets, others carrying bin lids like shields. All were tooled up.[81]

This was something the far left recognised and tried to capitalise on. As Tim Potter from the SWP argued: 'It was they [the 'young West Indians'] who gave Lewisham its special character. Traditionally alienated from the revolutionary left, they assembled in the thousands to stop the Front. We must learn what produced that situation and how the strength and militancy of black youth can become a central component in the mass struggle against the fascists and racists in Britain.'[82] As already noted, both the far left and the far right were trying to radicalise minority communities, in a similar fashion to how both sides were competing for the hearts and minds of the working class. The far left wanted non-white com-munities to join their revolutionary cadres, while the fascists wanted to provoke a race war. Indeed, it was widely felt by many on the left that Lewisham was, in particular, a turning point in the M/CM contest: 'Lewisham was important since it marks the first point in the clash between these movements; the radicalisation of parts of the black community, a growing fascist movement, attracting attention from the press, and the police adopting a policy of confrontation.'[83]

The events at Lewisham did demonstrate an increasing involvement of black and Asian youth in the anti-fascist and anti-state struggle, though this had started long before Lewisham. It stretched back from at least as early as Bradford in April 1976 and continued to grow through the events following Chaggar's murder, the formation of the Southall and Asian Youth Movements, and the Cypriot and West Indian involvement at the clash at Wood Green. While there was often friction between the minority community activists and the far left, they did increasingly work together against their common enemies of the state and the far right.[84] It also needs to be taken into account that the police's actions were often as much a driving force of Asian and black radicalisation as the far right.[85]

In November 1977 the Anti-Nazi League was formally launched by Paul Holborow, Peter Hain and Ernie Roberts.[86] The League's objectives were 'to organise on the widest possible scale against the propaganda and activities of the Nazis in Britain today.'[87] The formation of the ANL was the result of a confluence of different factors. Firstly, 'the highly publicized electoral advances of the National Front in the 1977 Greater London Council elections…convinced many left activists, and specifically those within the SWP, to create a broad-based, umbrella movement to combat the Front,'[88] as it was felt that the SWP was too small to 'stem the tide'.[89] Secondly, the SWP were aware that they alienated themselves from the rest of the labour movement with their aggressive tactics and wanted a specifically anti-fascist organisation to carry on their work without catching the flack for this, demonstrating that the need on the part of a social movement organisation to win votes and garner support from a wider movement may act as moderating force. Thirdly, and perhaps most importantly, the ANL was a response to what many felt was a lacklustre attempt on the part of Labour to fight the NF.[90] The ANL was the first national body entirely dedicated to anti-fascism.[91]

1978–1979

In 1978 the ANL joined forces with Rock Against Racism (RAR). RAR had been founded between August and December in 1976, by the photographer Red Saunders and others, in response to racist comments made by Eric Clapton, David Bowie and Rod Stewart.[92] In the battle for the loyalty and support of the working class, as well as British youth in general, music scenes were a key battlefield, and RAR was a fairly successful initiative in this endeavour. Dave Renton has written widely on this cultural war fought between the far left and far right over parts of the British music scene from the 1970s onwards after the event of punk rock in 1976:

> The quick demise of bands like the Sex Pistols created a space that was partly filled by a revived skinhead subculture, with which the National Front attempted to connect… The people who organized Rock Against Racism deliberately endorsed the rougher music of bands like the UK Subs or Jimmy Pursey's Sham 69… Sham 69 gave anti-racists a route into the minds of young skinheads. In adopting this street music, Rock Against Racism grabbed it out of the hands of white racists.[93]

This is an important aspect of this episode. For the most part, the 'battle lines', or conflict cleavage, between the far right and far left were non-ascriptive (e.g. ideological) rather than ascriptive (e.g. ethnic). Both sides wanted to recruit British youth and the working class to their cause, and so had to be cautious in their application of violence. When violence was used, it was against members of the minority communities or against committed activists – this necessarily limited the number of people who would be drawn into the conflict. Whereas republicans and loyalists in Northern Ireland detonated bombs which killed Catholics and Protestants not actively involved in the Troubles, thereby creating an impetus for others to join through a drive for revenge or protection, a similar use of mass violence would have gained nothing for the NF or the SWP – indeed, if anything it would have delivered a propaganda victory to their enemies.

Rather, their efforts were somewhat channelled in this less violent direction. Just one year after the establishment of Rock Against Racism, 'the National Front adopted the Socialist Workers Party's method of recruiting members through music… [and launched] Rock Against Communism (RAC) as a national movement in direct response to the NF's opponents'.[94] NF member Eddy Morrison also developed a publication called '*The Punk Front*, which promoted neo-Nazi bands and prominently featured the NF logo. Morrison explained later that "straightforward participation in parliamentary democratic politics is not enough", and setting up "social clubs" for youth recruitment was important for shaping society.'[95] Generally speaking, when an M/CM conflict is structured this way, with two opposing movements competing for support from the same social group, there is a lower probability of the conflict escalating to include the use of sustained lethal violence than if both opposing movements were attempting to draw support from separate and distinct communities.

On 4 May 1978, local elections were held, and the results seemed to show that the NF had lost support.[96] However, on the night of the local elections, a 25 year old Bengali called Altab Ali was murdered by three teenage boys as he walked home from where he worked in the East End of London. Even if Ali's murderers were not members of the NF, many observers felt that following their poor performance at the election in May the party's tactics changed, with Stan Taylor arguing that they embarked on a campaign of violence and provocation in the East End.[97] The Bethnal Green and Stepney Trades Council argued:

> The relatively poor showing of the National Front in the local Council elections, on the same night that Altab Ali was stabbed to death, seemed to signal a marked change of tactics by racist groups … [toward] a much more overtly provocative posturing, their members becoming openly involved in the serious mass outrages which have shocked the East End in recent months.[98]

Racial attacks on immigrants in the East End were becoming increasingly common, especially towards the Bengali community. It was also strongly felt by many that the

Metropolitan Police's attitude towards these events tended to be at best indifferent, at worst openly hostile to the victims.[99]

Soon after Ali's murder, around 7,000 people, largely from the Bengali community, and organised by the Federation of Bangladesh Youth Organisations, marched behind his coffin to Hyde Park in a protest against racist violence.[100] The next month, on 12 June, around 150 white youths 'went on a "racialist rampage" in Brick Lane in Hackney during which they smashed the property of Bengalis and attacked them with stones, bricks and bottles'.[101] A 55-year-old man was knocked unconscious due to the group throwing rocks through his shop window: 'This was by far the biggest group to have threatened the Asian community in [the] area, and heralded a new and frightening escalation of racial incitement. Some Asians and anti-racists fought off the attackers, it was perhaps ten minutes before the police arrived.'[102]

On 25 June another Bengali, Ishaque Ali, was murdered in Hackney, East London. The murders provoked days of protests, which culminated in the full-scale occupation and shutting-down of Brick Lane.[103] Another result of racist attacks was the development of a hardened cadre of Bengali men eager to defend their community from their fascist antagonists:

> Now, however, a new attitude is developing among the young men of the Asian community in the East End. The ability to fight, the martial arts, the language of 'self defence' and an aggressive self-awareness has taken over from the gentler approach of their elders.[104]

Once again, the police's reaction, or lack thereof, towards black and Asian murders acted as a radicalising agent: 'we went to the police and the police took the attitude that, "What can we do?"…and there was the time when we said "Right if you can't defend us, then we will have to defend ourselves… Police indifference was an experience that was witnessed again and again".'[105]

After June the escalating tactics of the far right were becoming more obvious. Attacks on members of the black and Asian communities were increasing. A 'whole series of arson attempts were made on the Immigrants Advice Bureau and on the Asian premises in its vicinity in Hanbury Street.'[106] Further, a black man was stabbed by two white youths in Mile End Road.[107] In early July a group of Bengali workers were leaving their shift at a bottling plant in East London when they were attacked by around 30 white men armed with bottles and bricks. Eight of the Bengalis were hospitalised over the attack. The police issued a statement claiming this was a fight over a car, despite the Bengali men emphatically stating that it was an unprovoked racist attack.[108] Around this time a man named Fred Challis and three accomplices were jailed for admitting to 300 racially motivated attacks in Tower Hamlets, as well as the murder of a homeless man. Challis smashed the man's face in with a gas cylinder, before scrawling 'NF rules OK' on the wall in blood; Challis was not actually a member of the NF but felt that the party would appreciate this act.[109]

Taylor has argued that these developments cannot be 'divorced from the presence of the NF in the East End of London, both indirectly in that racism was given a "legitimate" outlet, and directly insofar as it was alleged that not only were NF members involved in violence but that the NF's leadership was turning a blind eye to such behaviour.'[110] His arguments were given some weight by Granada TV's *World In Action* series which aired an investigation of the NF in July 1978. The programme included the alleged testimony from an undercover Special Branch operative who claimed that the systematic use of violence to terrorise political opponents and ethnic minorities was at least tacitly accepted by the national leadership.[111] The same month, on 15 July, three of the largest British Asian community organisations – the Standing Conference of Pakistani Organisations in Britain, the IWA, and the Federation of Bangladeshi Associations – all asserted the need for Asian 'self-defence' groups, and encouraged their members to join the ANL. This was a clear sign of the growing militancy within the Asian community, who had formerly been affiliated with the much more moderate Joint Committee Against Racialism (JCAR).[112]

Meanwhile, the more militant elements of the anti-fascist movement were continuing their aggressive campaign against the National Front. Towards the end of 1978, the SWP Squad in Manchester successfully had the local NF's football team, the 'Lillywhites', removed from the football league.[113] Subsequently they attacked NF members in Manchester city centre, disrupting their paper-selling activities.[114] At the same time, some NF members began looking for more extreme means to use against their political foes. At the end of 1978, two prominent NF members were imprisoned for possession of explosives. James Tierney from Devon, and Newcastle branch 'Security Officer' Alan Birtley both received three years for the offenses. Birtley admitted in court that several members of his branch were capable of making explosives and they had intended on using them against their opponents.[115] On 19 and 20 January 1979 at their Annual General Meeting, the NF's John Tyndall said that it 'hasn't been the National Front that's been obliterated. The obliteration has been of the red mobs who declared war against the National Front – the red mobs whose members, as they nurse their scars and bruises, are now perhaps wiser than before.'[116]

Nevertheless, despite these relatively small isolated incidents, the national picture tended to be much less violent. The ANL had not only gained thousands of supporters (very few of whom were streetfighters), but an impressive roster of celebrity sponsors including the comedian Dave Allen, the authors Iris Murdoch and Melvyn Bragg, and football managers Terry Venables and Brian Clough. Peter Hain considered that part of the ANL's success was the result of 'a decision by the SWP which agreed to moderate its politics, toning down the street violence which had proved counter-productive at Lewisham'.[117] Whether or not this is true, when measured against the universe of possible instances of violence occurring – given the tens of thousands of people mobilised by the ANL – it must be considered a moderate movement. Indeed, in 1978 the ANL and RAR held carnivals in May and September in London with as many as

100,000 and 150,000 people attending respectively, as well as one in Manchester with as many as 35,000 attendees, all of which were peaceful affairs. More militant anti-fascists who were active at the time even criticised the ANL for being too moderate, arguing that it channelled 'healthy street violence into acceptable modes of protest, alternative consumerism and the deadly embrace of Labour; the Trots gleefully scooping up any detritus'.[118]

Part of the reason that the ANL achieved vast mobilisations with only limited radicalisation may be down to what Busher, Holbrook and Macklin refer to as the 'internal brakes on violent escalation'. In particular, the brake which they have termed 'identification of non- or less violent strategies of action as being as or more effective than more violent alternatives.'[119] One of the ANL's chief concerns was attracting young people 'who, according to several studies, were disproportionately represented within the ranks of the National Front. The carnivals provided the Anti-Nazi League with a platform to influence this constituency.'[120] Whereas there was a strategic logic in having squads of activists acting as a defence force for events, violent attacks on the NF did not attract vast numbers of young people to their cause the way their music and cultural events did: '[ANL's] alliance with RAR, the enormously successful Carnivals fused together a mass cultural movement, expressed through music, and a political campaign and gave us a bridge to tens of thousands of people, particularly the young'.[121] Moreover, it seems that one of the sub-mechanisms of this 'brake' identified by Busher *et al.* also has some explanatory power in terms of the lack of violence displayed in this episode: what they refer to as 'expressions of scepticism about their ability to beat their opponents in a violent struggle' was no doubt present in the minds of some anti-fascists.[122] One former militant SWP member who was involved in violent clashes with the NF argued that 'The people who come on anti-racism demonstrations are working, they've got families. We can't train people for violence in the way fascists can. Their thugs will always be better than our thugs.'[123]

However, there was to be one last large-scale fracas of the decade. On 23 April 1979, in Ealing, the NF booked a meeting at Southall Town Hall. This action faced opposition from both the IWA and the ANL. The former suggested closing down local business on that particular day in protest and encouraged people to ignore the event, while the latter suggested a more confrontational approach.[124] Activists from the SYM, ANL and other anti-fascist groups congregated around the Southall Town Hall prior to the NF meeting. As the counter-demo grew, around 3,000 police, including the now notorious SPG, horses, dogs and a helicopter descended onto the area.[125] The police

> split the demonstrators into distinct groups thereby preventing the possibility of a peaceful sit-down protest. Serious disturbances between police and demonstrators then followed at various locations. Missiles were thrown at police from the Anti-fascist side, including flares, smoke-bombs and a petrol bomb, which was hurled at a police coach…[126]

At some point during this chaos the activist Blair Peach was killed due to a blow to the head, widely believed to have come from an SPG officer.[127] Copsey has highlighted the fact that having refused to run an official inquiry into Peach's death, many felt that the State had absolved the police of all guilt, the result being that 'the actions of the police at Southall represented a crucial moment in the anti-fascist struggle, with the state now replacing the NF as the main adversary.'[128]

On 3 May 1979 the general election was held, and the National Front 'captured two British electoral records: that for the largest number of candidates (303) put up by an insurgent party since 1918… and that for the smallest average share of the total vote per candidate (1.6%)'.[129] Indeed, the NF's results were disastrously low, with a 'drop in the NF vote which varied between 25% and 75% in the constituencies which were contested in both 1974 and May 1979'.[130] Although over 190,000 people voted for them, this result nonetheless effectively sounded the death knell for the NF as a serious political force.[131] After their failure, the NF descended into both sectarian in-fighting and more vicious street-fighting against the left; It also saw a fault line widen within the ANL and SWP, with some of those urging the need for violent anti-fascist means being expelled from the SWP.[132]

In answering the question as to why the NF fared so badly in the election, Messina argues that '[c]onsiderable credit must be given to the efforts of the Anti-Nazi League. By making the NF the issue in its campaign, the ANL focused public attention on the National Front in a manner that diminished its appeal as an electoral alternative.'[133] Similarly, David Renton posits that 'at a time when politics was shifting to the right, when the generation of Left activists was moving largely towards cynicism, and when racist ideas were becoming more acceptable… the Anti-Nazi League succeeded in its aim of isolating the National Front, which had acted as the main carrier of organised racism in Britain.'[134] Even Martin Lux, an ardent critic of the ANL, stated that in 1979 there had 'been a change, albeit slight, in working class racism and support for fascists such as the NF… [partly because of] the ANL which for all its faults and limitations had provided an alternative to the hideous racism so sadly the norm in the sixties and throughout most of the seventies.'[135]

However, it is easy to overstate the impact the ANL had over the NF. The membership of the National Front had in fact peaked between 1973/4 with around 14,000 members, well before the ANL was launched.[136] Further, in a *World in Action* television interview with Margaret Thatcher, the future Prime Minister claimed that whites in England felt 'swamped' by other cultures, indicating to the electorate that Conservative policy on immigration would become more harsh, thereby stealing the NF's unique selling point.[137] Moreover, as Copsey has argued, it 'may well have been the case… that hostility from the mainstream media impeded the National Front more than the activities of opposition groups. Certainly this was the view of the National Front, who after the 1979 general election identified the media and not the ANL as its 'number one enemy".[138]

So, it seems that although the ANL almost certainly significantly contributed to a culture of anti-racism, the NF would likely have fared poorly in the 1979 election and then gone into decline without their intervention.

Conclusion

As with any contentious episode, the group actors in this case study were all involved in a process of 'coevolution'.[139] The interactions between the two movements and the state did lead to some degree of escalation in terms of each of their 'collective action repertoires':[140] the SWP's Squads and the NF's Honour Guard, martial bodies who used violence for defensive and offensive purposes; the Bengali groups trained in martial arts and the SYM and AYMs, who were organised to defend themselves and their communities with more skill; and the introduction of the riot police by the state, measures which had been developed through interaction with the lethal paramilitaries of Northern Ireland and which were then employed to quell the rising militancy of the far left in Britain. Yet even though there is evidence of each of these groups being radicalised to some extent, these processes were limited, and clearly affected them at different rates and to different extents.

The fascists and the far-left anti-fascists coevolved in a much more closely symbiotic, or tightly and symmetrically 'coupled', fashion. Both the Squads and the Honour Guard were formed because of interactions between the two movements, and the actions of one (such as protests or carnivals) was highly likely to provoke a response from the other. However, despite many large-scale mobilisations, several of which descended into relatively serious cases of public disorder, the levels of violence employed by both movements remained relatively stable across this case study, while gradual escalations (increases in attacks on the enemy's events for instance) occurred more-or-less evenly on both sides. Walker has addressed the question as to why the fascists' and anti-fascists' conflict during this period did not escalate further:

> The real cause of their hostility was that they both saw themselves as revolutionaries against the liberal capitalism of the British state. They each desired passionately to win the allegiance of the working class, and to destroy their opponents…
>
> The passionate vocabulary of the Left, and the equally passionate speeches of Tyndall and Webster suggested that they were unsuccessful rivals for the support of the same social groups – neither Tyndall nor the Trotskyists had made any real headway within the mass of the British Labour Movement, and until they did the violence of which they spoke was unlikely to materialize…[141]

This is an astute observation, which accurately describes how the escalation of the conflict was, at least in part, contingent on the success of one or the other group in gaining hegemonic dominance over the social group whom they both sought to court. Further, as stated above, the competition over a social base had a limiting effect on the levels of violence employed, in that groups were obviously less likely to use violence indiscriminately for fear of alienating their target constituency.

The minority communities and the social movement organisations which sprang from them, however, were much more reluctant to engage directly with the far right. Unlike the fascists and anti-fascists, they were not engaged in a struggle for ideological dominance of the working class but rather were concerned with 'self-defence' and campaigning for 'black rights on a variety of levels'.[142] While they were organised in opposition to the fascists – indeed, they arguably had a much more pressing motivation to do so than the far left – they were also motivated by tackling racism and improving the lot of their communities. For them to organise with an eye to being aggressively involved in large-scale violent conflicts, as the far left and far right did, would have been a counterproductive move that may well have reinforced racism at the local and state levels while possibly bringing about repressive measures from the state and impeding their efforts to 'promote the cause of equal rights and social and economic opportunities.'[143]

It is likely that both the National Front and the SWP would have been pleased with a more militant and confrontational attitude developing amongst the British minority communities. The far left were interested in how 'the strength and militancy of black youth can become a central component in the mass struggle against the fascists and racists in Britain.'[144] For their part, the NF wanted the social boundaries between white and non-white communities to become more pronounced and for animosity to develop across them. As Joe Pearce, editor of the Young National Front magazine *Bulldog*, explained:

> The strategy was simple. We had to stir up enmity and hatred between black and white youths, thereby making multiculturalism untenable and a race war inevitable. The newly formed Young National Front... would become an army of race warriors, a new Sturmabteilung, the stormtroopers of the New Order.[145]

This is very similar to McCauley's concept of 'JuJitsu Politics'. McCauley writes that a group may intentionally provoke an enemy into attacking their target constituency so that in response they will be radicalised into joining them. McCauley cites the actions of the terrorists involved in the 9/11 attacks on America as being an example of this strategy, in that their ultimate goal was to provoke counterattacks from the US in order to radicalise parts of global Muslim population (which, to a greater or lesser extent, it did).[146]

Obviously this theoretical concept needs some revision if it is to be applied to this case study. Whereas for Al-Qaeda this was a 'weapon of the weak' in their war against an overwhelmingly superior force, for the NF it was an attempt to mobilise the majority population and the state against minority communities. Actions such as their 'Anti-Muggers March' through Lewisham and their physical attacks on groups like the Lewisham 21 Defence Campaign were intended to radicalise the black and Asian communities so as to foster communal animosity. The ultimate hope was that the white British population would come to see the National Front as the best channel through which to express their group interests. However, these groups that the NF attempted to provoke were typically moti-vated by a 'desire to be accepted as equal citizens and to belong in Britain', and had little interest in fighting a war on the streets.[147] The NF employed similar tactics toward the far left. As Taylor and Layton-Henry observed, by the second half of 1977 they had begun to rely on 'the now traditional strategy of provoking their Left wing opponents… to generate the publicity they needed for a good result.'[148] Here, at least, it did seem the tactic produced some support for them. They garnered both media attention and, it seems, votes through their clashes with the far left; although it is not clear the extent to which their association with violence was ultimately off-putting to the electorate.

As has been demonstrated, the development of collective action frames by the fascists and anti-fascists had a significant impact on the extent to which both movements were capable of generating and mobilising supporters. In the first instance, political developments such as Powell's 'Rivers of Blood' speech and the large influx of Ugandan refugees in 1972 created conditions which were condu-cive to National Front narratives of racial competition. However, the anti-fascists' 'counterframes' that painted the National Front as fascists and their policies as racist, which were lent empirical credibility by images documenting the explicitly neo-Nazi past of Tyndall and Webster, gave them the upper hand in the 'framing contest' and seriously hindered the NF's progress.[149] Interestingly, the National Front both benefited from and was damaged by the media's involvement with these framing processes. The incendiary headlines that were published by the tabloid press following the arrival of the Malawi Asian refugees in 1976 created fertile soil for the NF's xenophobic ideology, yet by the same token the media's explicit hostility towards the fascists was one of their greatest barriers to success.

Notes

1 This chapter was previously published as: Carter, Alexander J. 'The Dog that Didn't Bark? Assessing the Development of Cumulative Extremism between Fascists and Anti-fascists in the 1970s', in *Tomorrow Belongs to US: The British Far Right since 1967*, Edited by Nigel Copsey and Matthew Worley (Routledge: London, 2018), pp. 90–112.

2 Copsey, Nigel. *Anti-Fascism in Britain* (Oxon: Routledge, 2017), p. 105.

3 Taylor, Stan. 'The National Front: Anatomy of a Political Movement', in *Racism and Political Action in Britain*, Edited by Robert Miles and Annie Phizacklea (London: Routledge & Kegan Paul Ltd, 1979), p. 124; LMA: ACC/3121/C6/1/6: Jewish Defence Committee Minutes, 7 October 1965 to 5 May 1969.

4 ACC/3121/C6/1/2: Jewish Defence Committee Minutes, 10 June 1969 to 4 December 1972; Hill, Ray and Andrew Bell. *The Other Face of Terror: Inside Europe's Neo-Nazi Network* (London: Grafton Books,1988), p. 36; Walker, Martin. *The National Front* (Glasgow: Fontana Paperbacks, 1977), p. 92.

5 Lindorp, Fred. 'Racism and the Working Class: Strikes in Support of Enoch Powell in 1968', *Labour History Review*, 66, no. 1 (Spring 2001), pp. 79–100.
6 Messina, Anthony M. *Race and Party Competition in Britain* (Oxford: Oxford University Press, 1989), p. 106; also see Trilling, Daniel. *Bloody Nasty People: The Rise of Britain's Far Right* (London: Verso, 2013), pp. 36–37.
7 Walker, Martin. *The National Front* (Glasgow: Fontana Paperbacks, 1977), p. 135.
8 Ibid., p. 138.
9 *Campaign Against Racism and Fascism*, April 1978.
10 Miles, Robert and Annie Phizacklea. *White Man's Country: Racism in British Politics* (London: Pluto Press, 1984), p. 122.
11 Copsey, Nigel. *Anti-Fascism in Britain* (London: Macmillan Press Ltd, 2000), p. 119.
12 *Campaign Against Racism and Fascism*, April 1978.
13 Journalists had obtained pictures of John Tyndall and Martin Webster wearing Nazi uniforms in the early 1960s; Walker, Martin. *The National Front* (Glasgow: Fontana Paperbacks, 1977), p. 148.
14 Copsey, Nigel. *Anti-Fascism in Britain* (London: Macmillan Press Ltd, 2000), p. 119.
15 AJEX Defence Bulletin, No. 1, 1 July 1974, p. 1.
16 Ibid., p. 1.
17 Copsey, Nigel. *Anti-Fascism in Britain* (London: Macmillan Press Ltd, 2000), p. 119.
18 Copsey, Nigel. *Anti-Fascism in Britain*, 2nd ed. (Oxon: Routledge, 2017), p. 116.
19 Scarman, Leslie. *The Red Lion Square Disorders of 15 June 1974* (London: HMSO, 1975).
20 Walker, Martin. *The National Front* (Glasgow: Fontana Paperbacks, 1977), pp. 162–163.
21 Smith, Evan. 'A Bulwark Diminished? The Communist Party, the SWP and Anti-Fascism in the 1970s', *Socialist History Journal*, 35 (2009), p. 65.
22 Scarman, Leslie. *The Red Lion Square Disorders of 15 June 1974* (London: HMSO, 1975), p. 43.
23 Smith, Evan. 'A Bulwark Diminished? The Communist Party, the SWP and Anti-Fascism in the 1970s', *Socialist History Journal*, 35 (2009), p. 65.
24 *Morning Star*, 18 June 1974.
25 Clutterbuck, R. *Britain in Agony* (London: Faber & Faber, 1978), p. 163; Walker, Martin. *The National Front* (Glasgow: Fontana Paperbacks, 1977), p. 163.
26 Taylor, Stan. 'Race, Extremism and Violence in Contemporary British Politics', *New Community*, 7, no. 1 (1978), p. 59.
27 Walker, Martin. *The National Front* (Glasgow: Fontana Paperbacks, 1977), p. 163.
28 Ibid., p. 163.
29 Taylor, Stan. *The National Front in English Politics* (London: Macmillan Press Ltd, 1982), p. 36.
30 SCH/01/Res/SLI/02/001: Box 1: Pre–Magazine Cuttings and Bombing, 1964–1975: Personal Correspondence to Maurice Ludmer.
31 'British Tidings', *Bulletin of British Movement*, No. 51 November 1975.
32 Hann, Dave and Steve Tilzey. *No Retreat: The Secret War Between Britain's Anti-Fascists and the Far Right* (Lytham: Milo Books, 2003), p. 21.
33 Lux, Martin. *Anti-Fascist* (London: Phoenix Press, 2006) Chapter 10; Kenneth, Leech. *Brick Lane, 1978: The Events and Their Significance* (London: Stepney Books, 1994), p. 12.
34 Copsey, Nigel. *Anti-Fascism in Britain* (London: Macmillan Press Ltd, 2000), pp. 122–123.
35 Walker, Martin. *The National Front* (Glasgow: Fontana Paperbacks, 1977); Taylor, Stan. *The National Front in English Politics* (London: Macmillan Press Ltd, 1982).
36 Husbands, Christopher T. *Racial Exclusionism and the City: The Urban Support of the National Front* (London: George Allen and Unwin, 1983), p. 39.
37 Busher, Joel and Graham Macklin. 'Interpreting "Cumulative Extremism": Six Proposals for Enhancing Conceptual Clarity', *Terrorism and Political Violence*, 27, no. 5 (2014), p. 893.

38 Walker, Martin. *The National Front* (Glasgow: Fontana Paperbacks, 1977); Taylor, Stan. *The National Front in English Politics* (London: Macmillan Press Ltd, 1982), p. 44.

39 *Campaign Against Racism and Fascism*, April 1978 p. 15.

40 Polletta, Francesca and James M. Jasper. 'Collective Identity and Social Movements', *Annual Review of Sociology*, 27 (2001), p. 291.

41 McAdam, Doug, John D. McCarthy and Mayer N. Zald. 'Introduction: Opportunities, Mobilizing Structures, and Framing Processes – Towards a Synthetic, Comparative Perspective on Social Movements', in *Comparative Perspectives on Social Movements: Political Opportunities, Mobilizing Structures, and Cultural Framings*, Edited by Doug McAdam, John D. McCarthy and Mayer N. Zald (Cambridge: Cambridge University Press, 1996), p. 16.

42 Polletta, Francesca and James M. Jasper. 'Collective Identity and Social Movements', *Annual Review of Sociology*, 27 (2001), p. 295.

43 *Spearhead*, No. 92, March 1976.

44 Lux, Martin. *Anti-Fascist* (London: Phoenix Press, 2006), p. 41.

45 Farrar, Max 'Social Movements and the Struggle Over "Race"', in *Democracy and Participation: Popular Protest and New Social Movements*, Edited by Malcolm J. Todd, and Gary Taylor (London: Merlin Press, 2004), p. 8.

46 Benford, Robert D. and David A. Snow 'Framing Processes and Social Movements: An Overview and Assessment', *Annual Review of Sociology*, 26 (2000), pp. 611–639.

47 *The Telegraph and Argus*, 24 April 2014.

48 *Campaign Against Racism and Fascism*, Issue 1, May 1977; Taylor, Stan. *The National Front in English Politics* (London: Macmillan Press Ltd, 1982).

49 *Campaign Against Racism and Fascism*, April 1978.

50 *Comment: Communist Fortnightly Review*, 10 July 1976, p. 213.

51 Ibid., p. 212.

52 Ramamurthy, Anandi. *Black Star: Britain's Asian Youth Movements* (London: Pluto Press, 2013), p. 26.

53 Ibid., p. 27.

54 *Comment: Communist Fortnightly Review*, 10 July 1976, p. 213.

55 Walker, Martin. *The National Front* (Glasgow: Fontana Paperbacks, 1977), p. 199; Hann, Dave. *Physical Resistance: A Hundred Years of Anti-Fascism* (Alresford: Zero Books, 2013), p. 253.

56 *Campaign Against Racism and Fascism*, Issue 8, October 1977.

57 Smith, Evan. 'Conflicting Narratives of Black Youth Rebellion in Modern Britain', *Ethnicity and Race in a Changing World*, 2, no. 1 (2010), p. 20.

58 Ramamurthy, Anandi. 'The politics of Britain's Asian Youth Movements', *Race & Class*, 48, no. 38 (2006), p. 38.

59 Taylor, Stan. *The National Front in English Politics* (London: Macmillan Press Ltd, 1982), p. 111.

60 Ibid., p. 111.

61 *AJEX Defence Bulletin*, Vol. 2, No. 1, February 1976, p. 3.

62 Walker, Martin. *The National Front* (Glasgow: Fontana Paperbacks, 1977), p. 199.

63 *Campaign Against Racism and Fascism*, Issue 7, August/September 1977; Hann, Dave. *Physical Resistance: A Hundred Years of Anti-Fascism* (Alresford: Zero Books, 2013), p. 263.

64 Bogues, Tony. 'Black Youth in Revolt', *International Socialism*, 1, no. 102 (1977), p. 12.

65 Anon. *Anti-Nazi League: A Critical Examination 1977–81/2 and 1992–95* (London: The Colin Roach Centre, 1995), p. 4; Hann, Dave. *Physical Resistance: A Hundred Years of Anti-Fascism* (Alresford: Zero Books, 2013), p. 265.

66 Birchill, Sean. *Beating the Fascists: The Untold Story of Anti-Fascist Action* (London: Freedom Press, 2010), p. 36.

67 Hann, Dave. *Physical Resistance: A Hundred Years of Anti-Fascism* (Alresford: Zero Books, 2013), p. 265.
68 *Campaign Against Racism and Fascism*, August/September 1978; Hann, Dave. *Physical Resistance: A Hundred Years of Anti-Fascism* (Alresford: Zero Books, 2013), p. 287.
69 *Campaign Against Racism and Fascism*, August/September 1978; Potter, Tim, 'Lessons of Lewisham', *International Socialism*, 1, no. 101 (1977), p. 19.
70 Hann, Dave and Steve Tilzey. *No Retreat: The Secret War Between Britain's Anti-Fascists and the Far Right* (Lytham: Milo Books, 2003); Copsey, Nigel. *Anti-Fascism in Britain* (London: Macmillan Press Ltd, 2000).
71 Copsey, Nigel. *Anti-Fascism in Britain* (London: Macmillan Press Ltd, 2000); Hann, Dave and Steve Tilzey. *No Retreat: The Secret War Between Britain's Anti-Fascists and the Far Right* (Lytham: Milo Books, 2003).
72 Anon. *Anti-Nazi League: A Critical Examination 1977–81/2 and 1992–95* (London: Colin Roach Centre, 1995), pp. 11–12.
73 Lux, Martin. *Anti-Fascist* (London: Phoenix Press, 2006), Chapter 18.
74 Hann, Dave and Steve Tilzey. *No Retreat: The Secret War Between Britain's Anti-Fascists and the Far Right* (Lytham: Milo Books, 2003), p. 10.
75 Hann, Dave. *Physical Resistance: A Hundred Years of Anti-Fascism* (Alresford: Zero Books, 2013), p. 268.
76 Lux, Martin. *Anti-Fascist* (London: Phoenix Press, 2006), Chapter 18.
77 Ibid., p. 65.
78 Busher, Joel and Graham Macklin. 'The Missing Spirals of Violence: Four Waves of Movement–Countermovement Contest in Post-war Britain', *Behavioral Sciences of Terrorism and Political Aggression*, 7, no. 1 (2015), p. 60.
79 *Campaign Against Racism and Fascism*, Issue 1, May 1977, p. 10.
80 Carter, A. J. 'Cumulative Extremism: Escalation of Movement–Countermovement Dynamics in Northern Ireland between 1967 and 1972', *Behavioral Sciences of Terrorism and Political Aggression*, 9, no. 1 (2017), pp. 41–42.
81 Lux, Martin. *Anti-Fascist* (London: Phoenix Press, 2006), p. 63.
82 Potter, Tim. 'Lessons of Lewisham', *International Socialism*, 1, no. 101 (1977), p. 19.
83 Ibid., p. 19.
84 Smith, Evan. 'Conflicting Narratives of Black Youth Rebellion in Modern Britain', *Ethnicity and Race in a Changing World*, 2, no. 1 (2010); Ramamurthy, Anandi. *Black Star: Britain's Asian Youth Movements* (London: Pluto Press, 2013).
85 Bethnal Green and Stepney Trades Council. *Blood on the Streets A Report* (London: Bethnal Green and Stepney Trades Council, 1978), pp. 7–8.
86 Renton, David. *When We Touched the Sky* (Cheltenham: New Clarion Press, 2006), p. 77.
87 *Anti-Nazi League Founding Statement*, November 1977.
88 Messina, Anthony M. *Race and Party Competition in Britain* (Oxford: Oxford University Press, 1989), pp. 110–111.
89 Renton, David. *When We Touched the Sky* (Cheltenham: New Clarion Press, 2006), p. 77.
90 Ibid., p. 77.
91 Copsey, Nigel. *Anti-Fascism in Britain* (London: Macmillan Press Ltd, 2000), p. 131.
92 Hann, Dave. *Physical Resistance: A Hundred Years of Anti-Fascism* (Alresford: Zero Books, 2013), p. 259.
93 Renton, David. *When We Touched the Sky* (Cheltenham: New Clarion Press, 2006), pp. 36–38.
94 Shaffer, Ryan. 'The Soundtrack of Neo-fascism: Youth and Music in the National Front', *Patterns of Prejudice*, 47, no. 4–5 (2013), p. 467.
95 Ibid., p. 467.
96 Taylor, Stan. *The National Front in English Politics* (London: Macmillan Press Ltd, 1982), p. 152.

97 Ibid., p. 155.
98 Bethnal Green and Stepney Trades Council. *Blood on the Streets: A Report* (London: Bethnal Green and Stepney Trades Council, 1978), p. 32.
99 Ibid., p. 9.
100 Ramamurthy, Anandi. 'The Politics of Britain's Asian Youth Movements', *Race and Class*, 48, no. 38 (2006), p. 286.
101 Taylor, Stan. *The National Front in English Politics* (London: Macmillan Press Ltd, 1982), pp. 155–156.
102 Bethnal Green and Stepney Trades Council. *Blood on the Streets: A Report* (London: Bethnal Green and Stepney Trades Council, 1978), p. 41.
103 Hann, Dave. *Physical Resistance: A Hundred Years of Anti-Fascism* (Alresford: Zero Books, 2013), p. 286.
104 *Campaign Against Racism and Fascism*, August/September 1978, p. 15.
105 Ramamurthy, Anandi. *Black Star: Britain's Asian Youth Movements* (London: Pluto Press, 2013), p. 46.
106 Bethnal Green and Stepney Trades Council. *Blood on the Streets: A Report* (London: Bethnal Green and Stepney Trades Council, 1978), p. 42.
107 Ibid., p. 42.
108 Ibid., p. 43.
109 Ibid., p. 44.
110 Taylor, Stan. *The National Front in English Politics* (London: Macmillan Press Ltd, 1982), p. 156.
111 *YJAR Mag: Young Jews Against Racialism*, No. 1, April 1979.
112 Taylor, Stan. *The National Front in English Politics* (London: Macmillan Press Ltd, 1982), p. 156.
113 Hann and Tilzey, *No Retreat*, p. 35.
114 Ibid., pp. 40–48.
115 *Action Briefing*, Association of Jewish Ex–Servicemen & Women, no. 11, May 1979, p. 7.
116 *Campaign Against Racism and Fascism*, Issue 8, 1979, p. 8.
117 Renton, David. *Never Again: Rock Against Racism and the Anti-Nazi League 1976–1982* (Oxon: Routledge, 2019), p. 91.
118 Lux, Martin. *Anti-Fascist* (London: Phoenix Press, 2006), p. 71.
119 Busher, Joel, Donald Holbrook and Graham Macklin. 'The Internal Brakes on Violent Escalation: A Typology', *Behavioral Sciences of Terrorism and Political Aggression*, 11, no. 1 (2019), p. 8.
120 Messina, Anthony. M. *Race and Party Competition in Britain* (Oxford: Oxford University Press, 1989), p. 119; Also see Taylor, Stan. 'Racism and Youth', New Society, 3rd August 1978 for one such study.
121 *Big Flame*, 'The Past Against Our Future: Fighting Racism and Fascism', no. 14, 1980 p. 36.
122 Busher, Joel, Donald Holbrook and Graham Macklin. 'The Internal Brakes on Violent Escalation: A Typology', *Behavioral Sciences of Terrorism and Political Aggression*, 11, no. 1 (2019), p. 8.
123 Renton, David. *Never Again: Rock Against Racism and the Anti-Nazi League 1976–1982* (Oxon: Routledge, 2019), p. 164.
124 Copsey, Nigel. *Anti-Fascism in Britain* (London: Macmillan Press Ltd, 2000), p. 148.
125 Fryer, Peter. *Staying Power: The History of Black People in Britain* (Pluto Press: London, 1984), p. 397.
126 Copsey, Nigel. *Anti-Fascism in Britain* (London: Macmillan Press Ltd, 2000), p. 149.
127 Ibid., p. 149.
128 Ibid., p. 149.
129 Taylor, Stan. 'The Far Right Fragments', *New Society*, 26 August 1981.
130 *Spearhead*, No. 128, May/June 1979, p. 18.

131 Copsey, Nigel. *Anti-Fascism in Britain* (London: Macmillan Press Ltd, 2000), p. 150.
132 Anon. *Anti-Nazi League: A Critical Examination 1977–81/2 and 1992–95* (The Colin Roach Centre: London, 1995), pp. 11–12.
133 Messina, Anthony M. *Race and Party Competition in Britain* (Oxford: Oxford University Press, 1989), pp. 122–123.
134 Renton, David. *This Rough Game: Fascism and Anti-Fascism* (Gloucester: Sutton Publishing, 2001), p. 181.
135 Lux, Martin. *Anti-Fascist* (London: Phoenix Press, 2006), p. 89.
136 Taylor, Stan. *The National Front in English Politics* (London: Macmillan Press Ltd, 1982), p. 102.
137 Ibid., p. 146.
138 Copsey, Nigel. *Anti-Fascism in Britain* (London: Macmillan Press Ltd, 2000), p. 115.
139 Oliver, Pamela E. and Daniel J. Myers, 'The Coevolution of Social Movements', *Mobilization*, 8, no. 1 (2002), p. 2.
140 Beckwith, Karen. 'Hinges in Collective Action: Strategic Innovation in The Pittston Coal Strike', *Mobilization: An International Quarterly*, 5, no. 2 (2000), p. 179.
141 Walker, Martin. *The National Front* (Glasgow: Fontana Paperbacks, 1977), p. 173.
142 Ramamurthy, Anandi. *Black Star: Britain's Asian Youth Movements* (London: Pluto Press, 2013), p. 28.
143 Ibid., p. 40.
144 Potter, Tim. 'Lessons of Lewisham', *International Socialism*, 1, no. 101 (1977), p. 19.
145 Pearce, Joseph. *Race with the Devil: My Journey from Racial Hatred to Rational Love* (Charlotte: Saint Benedict Press, 2013), p. 62.
146 McCauley, Clark. 'JuJitsu Politics: Terrorism and Responses to Terrorism', in *Collateral Damage: The Psychological Consequences of America's War on Terrorism*, Edited by Paul R. Kimmel and Chris E. Stout (London: Praeger, 2006), p. 49.
147 Ramamurthy, Anandi. *Black Star: Britain's Asian Youth Movements* (London: Pluto Press, 2013), p. 2.
148 Taylor, Stan and Zig Layton-Henry. 'Race at the Polls', *New Society*, 25 August 1977.
149 Benford, Robert D. and David A. Snow. 'Framing Processes and Social Movements: An Overview and Assessment', *Annual Review of Sociology*, 26 (2000), p. 626.

4

FASCISTS AND ANTI-FASCISTS IN THE 1980s AND 1990s

Introduction

Throughout the 1980s and 1990s, another 'protest cycle' developed between fascists and anti-fascists across Britain. This chapter will examine the factors that led to the rise and decline of this cycle, what caused the contest to escalate and de-escalate. Once again, the key questions to be answered are whether and why the interactions between the opposing movement and countermovement altered the levels of support for either side, as well as the extent to which they exerted a radicalising effect that led to increasingly violent protest repertoires.

Although the Socialist Workers' Party (SWP) had created a highly successful mass anti-fascist movement in 1977 with the Anti-Nazi League (ANL), after the National Front's (NF) dismal performance in the 1979 election their focus began to shift away from fascists and towards the new right-wing Conservative government.[1] Furthermore, between 1978 and 1981 there had been a 'growing tension between the political priorities and perspectives of the working class rank and file and a largely upper middle class leadership [of the SWP]',[2] which led to many of the 'Squads' – who had been formed to pursue the strategy of physical force anti-fascism – either being expelled or quitting in solidarity with those expelled.[3]

These expulsions from the SWP were no doubt the result of efforts by the leadership to rein in the use of violence by members of the party, as it was considered to be counter-productive in their current situation. This is another example of Busher et al.'s 'internal brakes on violent escalation' in action. As they argue, while 'some groups use violence to recruit members ... this usually works only for a relatively small number of militants. Most groups require wider bases of support, at least some of whom are unlikely to favour high levels of violence ... Emphasising the importance of achieving or sustaining support among these publics can therefore be deployed as a brake on violent escalation.'[4] No doubt the SWP leadership were cognisant of their party's association with violence after incidents such as the clashes at Red Lion Square and Lewisham in the 1970s and wished to undo these connections in the public's mind's eye. Further, there were those who felt that the violent clashes which the Squads had engaged in had become 'depoliticised ... and cut off from any mass audience' and were thus not actually achieving anything in terms of their political goals.[5] Of course, while this 'internal brake' certainly was effective in preventing further violent escalation within the SWP, as we shall see, the dynamic of escalation was just moved from one group to another within the broader anti-fascist movement.

While the 1979 election had been disastrous for the National Front, this had the result of fracturing the NF into four smaller parties. Some of the party carried on as the NF under the chairmanship of Andrew Brons; the former chairman, John Tyndall, broke away, forming the New National Front (later renamed the British National Party); and two smaller groups called the National Front Constitutional Movement and the British Democratic Party also splintered off.[6] However, as Steve Tilzey observed, while the NF had been shattered, 'its remnants were nastier, more vicious, and less inclined to wait patiently for an electoral break-through to achieve their aims'.[7] So, far from the extreme-right threat vanishing, the 'NF's electoral failure in 1979 was followed by organised and escalating violence.'[8]

1981–1983

Following their respective misfortunes in the 1979 election, a focal point for both former SWP 'Squad' members and some of the remaining, disillusioned, NF members was the Chapel Market in Islington, North London. During the 1970s, both the ANL and the NF had maintained paper-selling pitches in Chapel Market, and there had frequently been clashes between the two groups.[9] However, in the summer of 1981 'the local NF branch, one of the biggest and nastiest in the country... decided, with support from the SWP for the ANL waning, to up the ante.'[10] Upping 'the ante' included publishing hit-lists of the NF's political opponents in *Bulldog*, the paper for the Young NF, setting fire to a community centre, attacking a local left-wing bookshop, and increasingly violent attacks on any left-wing paper sellers.[11]

In particular, one Sunday in July 1981, the usual contingent of NF paper sellers were bolstered by 50 activists from the Brent NF chapter, alongside other members who usually sold NF papers in Brick Lane; this large gang attacked and easily overran the ANL and other anti-fascists in Chapel Market.[12] Far from capitalising on the declining fortunes of the ANL though, the local NF only succeeded in escalating the conflict and invigorating the anti-fascist movement there. At the same time that the SWP were expelling members for 'squaddism', some of these same former members, alongside assorted independent anti-fascists, reacted to the NF aggression in Islington. As one anti-fascist commented at the time: 'All the stuff with the expulsions more or less overlapped with the campaign at Chapel Market, where we were keeping it all together... We were obsessed with it... We were there every week, and there were regular clashes with the Front'.[13]

Following the incident in July 1981, the anti-fascists decided that it had been a decisive attempt to clear them from the area by the NF. 'Offence being the best form of defence',[14] the anti-fascists gathered as big a group as they could and attacked the Brent NF paper sellers at their usual pitch in Kingsbury the following week, hospitalising five of them.[15] The very next day, 100 NF members mobilised at Chapel Market. This pattern of tit-for-tat violence continued for the next two years, with at least two larger-scale clashes. The first, in November 1981, involved a large team of anti-fascists waiting in a pub to ambush some NF members who they correctly assumed would attack an anti-racist rally in nearby Archway. The second involved an NF attack, led by then Chairman Ian Anderson, going awry: they vastly underestimated their enemies and had to flee the area, relying on police presence for help.[16] As Anti-Fascist Action would write some years later:

> [t]he clashes at Kingsbury, Archway and Chapel Market broke the back of the NF paper sale at Islington. The fascists were unable to maintain their presence and by the end of 1982 the sale had collapsed... To make things worse, eight members of Camden and Islington NF were sent down for armed robberies at this time and the branch collapsed. This victory didn't just have a local impact, the collapse of the branch had a domino effect across north London with the NF ceasing to have any organised presence in what was a very strong area for them.[17]

Obviously this is hardly an unbiased account, however the assessment is backed-up by Matthew Collins, who, while an NF member, noted that, as late as 1989, the far right recognised that Islington was effectively 'controlled' by anti-fascists, and was as such a no-go area for them.[18]

It was in this crucible of escalating violence between fascists and anti-fascists around Chapel Market that the militant far-left anti-fascist group Red Action (RA) was formed.[19] In terms of escalation, as already stated, both the groups' paths towards the use of political violence had similar origins, i.e. the 1979 elections and the concomitant fallout on the far left and far right. With regard to those anti-fascists who had been expelled from the SWP for 'squaddism', their former comrades' spurning did little to dampen their militant spirit. Indeed, the waning interest in – or outright hostility towards – the use of physical violence as a tactic held by the majority of the British left seemed only to encourage this as an inherent part of their organisational identity. As RA activists wrote at the time: 'We are proud of the image of being able to back up our words with actions, but we have been accused of being no better than the fascists, a squad of "macho boot-boys".'[20]

Macklin and Busher have rightly highlighted the need to pay close attention to within-movement dynamics and relationships when analysing cases of CE, and that is particularly pertinent here.[21] Mia Bloom has argued that groups competing over the same social base may use radicalisation as a tool to win over converts, a process called 'outbidding'.[22] Similarly, McCauley and Moskalenko have pointed out that as 'competing groups try different tactics, the competition may escalate to gradually more radical acts if sympathisers favor these acts'.[23] It is entirely possible that RA felt that they might be able to gain radical and working class support by emphasising their militant, anti-bourgeois stance; after all, a number of people had quit the SWP in solidarity with those who were expelled over accusations of 'squaddism'. In the first issue of their official bulletin Red Action used the successful use of physical force anti-fascism by the ANL in the 1970s and the historical example of the Nazis as justification for their aggressive strategy.[24]

With regard to the NF, although they had been pursuing a provocative strategy throughout the 1970s, there had still been the pressure to maintain a facade of respectability towards the public so as to win votes; with this pressure gone, many elements decided to more-or-less abandon electioneering and instead pursue a strategy of political violence in order to provoke a race war, and also to gain control of the streets from their political rivals.[25] They joined other groups, such as the British Movement (BM), who, although occasionally contested elections, never attempted to conceal their neo-Nazi ideology and were always a viciously violent street movement.[26]

Other factors notwithstanding, there *is* clear evidence here that the relationship between the opposing groups exerted a radicalising influence on both sides; in short, there is some evidence of the dynamic of CE developing here on a small scale, culminating in the eviction of the far right from the Islington area and the formation of Red Action as a specifically physical force outfit; although it must be noted that there was never an escalation from the use of nonlethal to lethal violence. Another important point brought out by this case study is the importance of the concept of territory as a variable in the occurrence of CE. Social Movement theorists have made similar observations elsewhere; as della Porta notes: 'Socialization to violence happened in action, especially around specific geographical areas, through the radicalization of specific forms of action... Violence often develops in situations of competition over the control of specific spaces.'[27] This suggests that dynamics of CE may be more likely to begin in small (perhaps urban) territories rather than on a national scale.

From 1982 onwards, with both RA and militant far-right elements freed from the pressures of respectability which electioneering encourages, the use of violence gained high probability. However, echoing the relationship between the far right and far left in the 1970s, both groups drew their main support from white working-class communities, and thus their competition over this demographic necessarily had a strong influence over their areas of operation as well as the form their conflict took. As argued in the previous chapter, the nature of the cleavage between movement and countermovement does seem to strongly influence the degree to which CE effects the M/CM contest. Movements and countermovements may be divided along ascriptive (e.g. ethnicity, race, nationality) or non-ascriptive (e.g. ideology) lines,[28] and this distinction is important: if the cleavage is non-ascriptive and both sides of the M/CM are competing over the same social base, they are obviously less likely to use categorical lethal violence for fear of alienating potential supporters. This contrasts with, for example, an M/CM contest fought along ethnic lines, where a movement organisation could hope to win recruits from their ethnic group by bombing an area known to be populated by the other ethnic group; if either RA or the NF bombed a white working class area (from which both sides were mainly drawing their support) then they would obviously be much less likely to benefit from that.

Accordingly, both the far left and far right attempted to dominate 'area[s] of working class culture' such as youth music scenes and football terraces.[29] Indeed, from 1982 onwards, 'one of Red Action's first moves was to renew efforts to curtail the BM presence on the punk circuit.'[30] Fascists had been regularly attacking punk gigs for years, especially ones known to be left-wing or anti-fascist. The punk poet Attila the Stockbroker remembered that 'from my point of view, events reached a climax at a gig at the Brixton Ace in 1983'.[31] A group of fascists turned up and started giving *Seig Heil* salutes and intimidating the crowd. 'Then…there was a big commotion at the door and, again, a load of [Red Action] members charged in. All of a sudden an awful lot of fascists decided to leave the venue very quickly, some of them nursing a number of wounds and injuries. After that I had very little trouble at gigs.'[32]

It was a year later, on 10 June 1984, at the Greater London Council 'Jobs for Change' festival, that the far right would attempt a major counter-attack to the offensive launched by the militant anti-fascists. This was a free open-air event at Jubilee Gardens with lots of left-wing artists playing. As the Redskins played their set on the main stage, roughly 80 NF members stormed the stage, attacked the band, and also attacked many of the attendees.[33] Although there had not been much in the way of security, and the attack came as a complete surprise, some of the attendees, including RA members and a number of striking miners, fought back and drove them off.[34]

However, the incident had a strong impact on RA, who saw it as being a propaganda victory for the far right.[35] This was to be an influential moment for Red Action. The RA members who had been at the event had seen a group of skinheads wearing NF and (White Power band) Skrewdriver t-shirts before the fight; however, at the time, they decided that they may have been wearing the clothes as a fashion statement rather than a political one, and bearing in mind that it was a family event decided not to confront them. The group felt particularly chagrined over this: 'It left Red Action Members cursing ourselves for our reasonableness and moderation.'[36] They stated, rather ominously, that:

> In future, anyone we see at any socialist event wearing any form of fascist, NF, or anti-socialist emblems will be assumed to be there for disruptive reasons, and will be taken out at the first opportunity.[37]

Also, once again the group were unapologetic about how their less militant comrades felt about their approach, referring to criticisms they had received from their 'genteel friends on the left' who disagreed with them:

> If this should mean that we disrupt someone's Sunday afternoon for a while then we apologise in advance, but there it is. There are far more important things at stake here, than sandwiches on the lawn.[38]

Once again, it seems that their strategy, and indeed, organisational self-image, of violent anti-fascism was forged in relation to both their violent political enemies, *and* the disdainful 'comrades' within their own movement.

As della Porta has argued, radicalisation is not only a result of opposition between movements and countermovements,

> but also of competitive escalation within…social movement families. Competitive dynamics tend to intensify during cycles of protest, as social movement organizations multiply and then split over the best strategies to adopt, some of them choosing more radical ones… different groups not only adapt to environmental conditions but exercise agency: they discuss strategies, experiment with them, and divide over them.[39]

1983–1985

The early to mid-1980s was certainly witness to the growth of a 'protest cycle' between the far right and anti-fascists in Britain. It seems likely that fascist organisations had been growing in membership in the early part of the 1980s,[40] with the National Front still the dominant force at this stage. However, the British National Party was gaining support and in the 1983 general election they managed to field 53 candidates, passing the threshold of 50 which entitled them to five minutes of broadcasting time on TV and radio.[41] The NF adopted the same strategy, fielding 50 candidates, presenting them with the same privileges.[42] Also, the British Movement had risen to probably over 2,000 members by 1984, and furthermore 'were known at this time to be even more involved in random violent attacks against black people than NF supporters.'[43]

In response to the far right's growth and their increasingly violent methods, as well as the perceived lack of a suitable response, a conference was held on 28 July

1985 at Conway Hall to address the growing 'fascist threat'.[44] The meeting included around 350 attendees, and groups involved included Red Action, Class War, the Jewish Socialist Group, the Newham Monitoring Project, Workers' Power, *Searchlight*, the Refugee Forum and other local anti-racist groups.[45] At a subsequent 'delegate meeting', consisting of two delegates from each constituent organisation, this group was given the name 'Anti-Fascist Action' (AFA).[46] One of the core parts of the 'statement of aims' for AFA included the commitment to 'oppose racism and fascism physically, on the streets, and ideologically.'[47]

The militancy of the organisation came from the hard-line physical force groups: RA; the anarchist Direct Action Movement (DAM); and Class War. The rest of AFA consisted of groups who, 'in the main, identified with the liberal left-wing of the Labour Party.'[48] Red Action, who were broadly speaking a London-centric organisation, had been pursuing this strategy for years, and were keen for it to be carried out at a national level. Thus, the result of increasing fascist violence was the growth of this militant anti-fascist tendency, from local actions by small groups to a national anti-fascist network.

However, many of the groups involved were wary of violence, and not at all committed to the 'physical opposition' side of the group's mission statement. Further, as the organisation was being founded, the dominant militant group (RA) had consigned themselves to protecting the conference from attacks they felt may come from the far right, and thus muted their voice in the forging of the outfit: 'From the very outset, therefore, the political orientation and agenda of the new group was dictated by others: a basic misreading of the political chemistry at work which would take more than four years to rectify.'[49] It should also be noted that while there is evidence of tit-for-tat exchanges between the far left and far right escalating the conflict, culminating in the formation of AFA, this was really a one-sided affair. Although the far right did provoke the formation of a national anti-fascist network, their motivations for violence came less from their enemies' actions (although these no doubt fuelled many incidents) but largely from the fact that their leaders saw little chance of gaining any political power under the circumstances in which they currently found themselves (in particular, operating under a government that was already taking a hard line on immigration). Consequently, the far right were more interested in using provocative tactics to gain attention and maintain the loyalty and morale of existing members.[50]

The first major mobilisation by AFA was a counter-demo to the NF's annual Remembrance Day march to the Cenotaph in London on 10 November 1985. AFA's plan was to get to the cenotaph first and occupy it, to disrupt or prevent the NF's plans. There were around 300 AFA activists, and between 1,200 and 1,500 NF activists. Despite the disparity in numbers, AFA maintained an occupation of the NF's destination.[51] Around this time anti-fascist and leftist groups had become increasingly concerned about the fascists' links to European terrorist groups, as well as their own paramilitary training and stockpiling of weapons.

These views were not as sensationalist as they might have at first have appeared. The Association of Jewish Ex-Servicemen (AJEX), which kept security files on far-right groups, wrote a report about the BM stating:

> Some para-military training exists for its members, who are also known to have access to arms. … The News of the World… mentions that Leader Guard members participate in 'field training sessions' at which guns are used, and Private Eye (September 15, 1978) quotes an article in the Exeter Weekly News about members training with guns and rifles.[52]

A number of incidents leant credibility to these concerns; on 1 November 1985 the BNP organiser for Redbridge, Tony Lecomber, was arrested after a homemade explosive device prematurely detonated in his car whilst he was in the vicinity of the South London office of the Workers' Revolutionary Party (WRP).[53] On 27 March 1986 seven Chelsea Football Club supporters were 'remanded in custody after Police raids uncovered an array of National Front (NF) literature, an Ulster Loyalist flag as well as various types of weapons.'[54] Finally, on 1 July 1986, 'armed Wiltshire police seized a weapons cache, including nine anti-tank rockets and launchers, as well as guns, ammunition and explosives… Two men were arrested, one of whom… [had] extensive links with the extreme Right… [and] is close to Michael McLaughlin, the former British Movement leader'.[55]

AFA were particularly concerned over the apparent radicalisation of their enemies, arguing in a letter sent out to 'all Labour Movement Organisations' in the mid 1980s that 'the activities of far-Right groups such as the National Front and the British National Party… are becoming more openly violent and *turning to terrorism*'.[56] They further argued in an internal document that:

> Since the days of the Anti-Nazi League, the NF, BM, BNP and like-minded groups have all been busy regrouping, providing a haven for wanted terrorists from all over Europe and openly embracing a new more violent creed… their energies are now concentrated towards paramilitary activities, either in clandestine camps or by infiltrating the territorial army… The fascists hope to wage a campaign of terror against their enemies.[57]

Consequently, AFA were determined to try to weaken their enemies' attachment to their cause by employing radical means themselves. So, when the National Front organised a protest march against American nuclear missiles in England at Bury St. Edmunds, AFA came out in force against them. All in all around 60 members were mobilised, half of whom were RA members.[58] There were several 'skirmishes' before and after the event, and the march itself was disrupted when Red Action members 'ambushed' the march from a side street. Nine anti-fascists were arrested, and charged with public order offences.[59]

The same year AFA once again opposed the NF's Remembrance Day March to the Cenotaph, successfully mobilising a much larger crowd than their enemies.[60] Shortly afterwards, in January 1987, AFA stewarded the Bloody Sunday Remembrance Day march in Sheffield. There were around 2–3,000 marchers. The march was attacked by fascists, leading to skirmishes with AFA stewards. Several AFA members were consequently arrested.[61]

As well as these clashes at political marches and rallies, AFA stuck to their promise to prevent the NF from growing in areas of working class culture. In an internal bulletin they wrote that

> …in the racist heartlands where the potential to harness the frustrations of a white working class left to rot in Thatcher's Britain is at its sharpest. [Fascists] have organised at football grounds – West Ham, Chelsea, Tottenham, Sunderland, Norwich City, Glasgow Rangers, Hearts, Blackburn Rovers, Cardiff City, and Rochdale – where they have been behind some out-rageous acts of violence… The fascists are also trying to build up a base within the white working class…[62]

AFA's observations were correct; indeed, British football had been fertile ground for both racist attitudes and the far right since at least the mid-1970s. Paul Thomas argues that this is in large part due to the relatively high rate at which British-born black players entered the game at a time of economic instability: 'Football was one of the most visible symbols of this developing multicultural society and tension was inevitable. At the same time, the British economy went into structural decline and unemployment grew. These two separate develop-ments led both to racial tension and an historically high level of support for far-right parties.'[63]

In their campaign to exploit these developments, the most important arrow in the NF's quiver was almost certainly their publication *Bulldog*. Arguably 'the first football fanzine', this 'offensive and aggressive publication' was 'was deliberately pitched at the young fans on the terraces.'[64] A significant feature of *Bulldog*, in terms of the NF's attempts to foster a favourable climate at football matches, was their 'League of Louts' table.[65] Later known as the 'Racist League', this regu-lar piece was a league table of football teams according to the levels of racism displayed by their fans.[66] By turning it into a competition, with notoriety as the prize, the NF intended to incentivise further racist behaviour amongst fans. Further, this generated more publicity for the party as national papers wrote articles condemning the competition.[67]

The attempts of the far right to maintain a presence at football terraces did not go unopposed, and unsurprisingly generated concomitant anti-fascist and anti-racist endeavours. Of these, one of the most successful and influential was Leeds Fans United Against Racism and Fascism (LFUARF). This organisation was founded in 1987 by a group of Leeds United fans (including a number of people from the Leeds Anti-Fascist Action branch)[68] who had grown increasingly angry over the displays of racism at the Leed's United football stadium Elland Road.[69] Within a few years of their founding, LFUARF had successfully curbed racist behaviour and all but entirely removed the far-right presence at Elland Road.

Their successes were the result of a considered campaign which was sensitive and responsive to the specific context of Leeds United. In the first instance, the activists were all committed Leeds United fans acting out of a genuine concern for the welfare of their club, and as such were perceived as 'insiders' by other Leeds fans. Earlier anti-fascist mobilisations at Elland Road, such as leafleting campaigns by the Anti-Nazi League, had faltered because the activists involved had not been Leeds United fans (or, indeed, football fans at all). As Thomas observes, the ANL's slogan 'kicking the Nazis out of football' was problematic considering that 'the anti-racists clearly were not part of football themselves.'[70]

Secondly, LFUARF managed to force the club itself to take the issue seriously. Initially Leeds United had been in a state of denial over racism and fascism at the club, with the apparent attitude 'that talking about racism is a much greater problem than racism itself'.[71] After the Labour MP for Leeds Central applied pressure on LFUARF's behalf, Leeds United finally agreed to meet with the activists – but challenged their assessment of the situation and asked them to provide proof. In response LFUARF produced their *Terror on The Terraces* report, which drew data from prior media reports and enquiries to detail the extent of racist abuse and far-right mobilisations that occurred at Elland Road. The report provoked an outcry from the national media who were 'fiercely critical of the racist reality of Elland Road and the lack of action against it'.[72] Suddenly finding themselves under close scrutiny from the media, Leeds United shifted their stance and began producing their own anti-racist leaflets which were given out at the club's turnstiles.

Thirdly, and perhaps most importantly, LFUARF produced their own fanzine *Marching Altogether*. This publication, the first football fanzine in the country to be founded on an anti-racist agenda, was clearly written by committed Leeds United fans. LFUARF made the shrewd decision to give this out for free, reasoning that this was the only way to reach fans who weren't already anti-racists/anti-fascists. Further, unlike the NF *Bulldog* sellers, the vendors of *Marching Altogether* would also be seen in the terraces enjoying the game after selling their paper. 'This, and the evidence in the Terror on our Terraces report, helped us to show fans that the National Front and, implicitly, the ideas they stood for, were 'outsiders' with no interest in or commitment to Leeds United, and who were doing nothing but giving 'us' a bad reputation', recalls Thomas, who was heavily involved in the LFUARF campaign.[73]

The efficacy of the LFUARF campaign inspired similar endeavours at other clubs around the country, 'including "Foxes Against Racism" at Leicester City and "Newcastle United Against Racism"'.[74] As was the case with LFUARF, AFA played a large part in the foundation and operation of many of these campaigns to combat the far right at football grounds.[75] Interestingly, it seems that these victories were achieved, in large part, through non-violent means. By successfully (and sincerely) portraying themselves as part of the Leeds United fan-base, and the NF as opportunistic outsiders, LFUARF managed to starve their enemies of support without *having* to tackle them physically.

Aside from the football scene, RA argued that there was 'another area of working class culture where neo-fascists have a new growing hold. It is the music scene, among young alienated working class youth across Europe'.[76] Describing a network of 'contacts, bands and supporters', RA argue that White Power bands 'build bridges between nihilism and fascism'.[77] AFA had begun to tackle this by disrupting gigs organised by the far right, or having them banned outright.[78] Until this point, the NF had something of a monopoly on the organisation of the neo-Nazi music scene in the UK. However, Ian Stuart Donaldson, lead singer of neo-Nazi band Skrewdriver, became increasingly disillusioned by the NF and felt that they were exploiting the far-right music scene for its money. He thus broke out on his own to launch 'Blood & Honour' (B&H) as an independent network for extreme-right rock bands.[79] This led to a series of clashes on the streets of London as AFA/RA members attacked B&H members and supporters on sight, resulting in the arrests of three AFA members for an attack on the notorious extreme-right street-fighter (and head of security for Skrewdriver) Nicky Crane, and Ian Donaldson allegedly having to move away from London for his safety.[80]

One of the other ways in which AFA responded to this threat was by setting up their own music organisation: Cable Street Beat (CSB). Sponsored by both RA and AFA, CSB was 'set up to provide an alternative. Its function is simple: it is to counter and ultimately negate the propaganda activities and objectives like "Blood and Honour" at home and abroad.'[81] The first CSB concert was on 8 October 1988, at the London Electric Ballroom. A veteran of the actual 'Battle of Cable Street' was invited to the stage, where he gave a speech about fascism and racism. The event made £6,000 in ticket sales.[82]

Despite these successes though, by 1988 the growing tensions within AFA between the militants and moderates were becoming irreconcilable. In December 1988 RA published an article criticising AFA's decision that year to hold another parallel rally to the NF's Annual Remembrance Day rally in London rather than directly disrupting their enemy's rally. They dismissed AFA's theme of 'reclaiming remembrance day', arguing that it was 'a symptom of an appeal to respectability which is little to do with anti-fascism generally and even less to do with the politics of Red Action specifically'. Ignoring AFA's official line, RA and the DAM did attack the fascists, engaging in a series of skirmishes across London.[83] By April 1989 these internal difficulties had become 'insurmountable'.[84]

1989–1994

By the middle of 1989, internal pressure caused by too many competing groups with incompatible aims jostling against each other had effectively left AFA 'on its knees, both in London and nationally'; however, the militant wing fought hard to keep hold of what remained of the organisation.[85] Relaunching themselves in September 1989, AFA (now only consisting of Red Action, DAM, and the Trotskyist 'Workers Power' as well as unaffiliated anti-fascists) became unapologetically hard-line, vowing to emphasise the 'physical' opposition in their aim to combat fascism physically and ideologically.[86] Also, there was renewed emphasis on class over race (the latter formerly being given more prominence by the presence of some of the more moderate and liberal anti-racist groups within AFA). They argued that it was vital that their propaganda should carry a class message, not only to provide rebuttals to 'common prejudices' but also to prevent AFA from being presented as middle class 'outsiders'[87]; that is, part of the establishment and thus part of the problem: 'We moved away from protest actions and calls for the government and police to lead the fight against fascism… AFA's objective was to clear the fascists out of working class areas and create the space for a progressive alternative to be built.'[88] This was a shrewd move, as the far right had often made political capital from the perceived middle-class make-up of far-left groups.[89]

AFA saw their conflict with the fascists as being, at core, a battle for the hearts and minds of the working class. The more disenfranchised members of society, they argued, had nowhere to turn to, as the Labour Party was now more interested in courting the bourgeoisie than protecting the interests of workers. In their absence, far-right parties were often seen as the only 'radical alternative':[90]

> Any advances by the right in this territory represents a dangerous retreat by the left. The working class is the natural constituency of socialism, not fascism. Racism and socialism are incompatible… The 'success' of the far right is due to the fact that the far left are not seen as a credible option.[91]

The fascists' successes, argued RA, were a product of the left's failure, not a cause of it. Interestingly, there was at least tacit agreement from the highest level of the BNP that, at that point in time at least, they were chiefly aiming to mobilise the working class, this being considered the most fertile demographic for them. While always keen to stress the primacy of race and nation over that of class, BNP leader John Tyndall did nevertheless state in a lengthy article that

> … we ought straight away to recognise the moral cowardice that has been described as predominant among our middle classes in the present climate will, for some time to come, preclude their massed participation in our struggle in any circumstances and under any conditions… [However] The young skinhead who, with his friends, drove hundreds of miles overnight to attend a party activity a long way from home, and all at personal expense… typify the spirit of our movement… For the moment, and much to my regret, the professional classes do not…[92]

Similarly, the BNP's paper the *British Nationalist* ran an article titled 'What About the Workers?' the following year. There, they argued that the BNP was the real defender of workers' rights, not the SWP; although, naturally, this concern only stretched as far as white British workers.[93] AFA's argument that the far right had been more concerned with targeting the working class than other constituencies was further reinforced by a report by the Board of Deputies of British Jews who found evidence that the 'National Front (NF) has attempted to recruit [far-left] Militant Tendency supporters in Liverpool. Militant, which has rebuffed the move, is considered by the NF to be the only genuine working class Left-wing group, and therefore a likely source of political converts.'[94]

AFA's rebirth marked a point of intensification in the conflict between fascists and anti-fascists, although this escalation was as much to do with the exodus from AFA of those opposed to violence as it was the provocation from the far right. At the turn of the decade, the BNP had now replaced the NF as AFA's chief antagonists, having managed to build the biggest profile on the extreme right in Britain.[95] This was a transitional period for the BNP, who, in the early 1990s, decided that the political climate was becoming favourable enough to sufficiently attempt to start taking electoral politics seriously.[96] Yet they were also, for the time being, pursuing the strategy of 'march and grow' which Tyndall believed had served the NF well in its early days.[97] These tactics involved confronting and attacking their opponents.

Such was the case when a large group of BNP members attacked a meeting at Welling Library which had been called to discuss the problem of the BNP's local HQ. The BNP stated that around 45 of their members had gone there peacefully, but on arrival had been set upon by a group of 50 Labour members.[98] Their claim was contradicted by Matthew Collins however, who joined the BNP at this event, and claims it was a planned BNP 'hit' that he describes as a 'massacre'.[99] Similarly, in February 1990 a group of around 15 to 20 BNP members attacked an SWP meeting in Glasgow, seriously injuring several members.[100]

The first big clash between militant anti-fascists and fascists after the re-launch of AFA was at a BNP election meeting at Weavers Field School, Bethnal Green, on 21 April 1990.[101] Between 50 and 60 AFA members approached the meeting, where police were keeping a picket organised by the SWP and Labour Party activists away from the BNP. On nearing the school, the militants were told to enter by the police, who mistook them for far-right activists. Once they got close to the BNP they launched a fierce attack. After a few minutes of intense fighting, around a dozen AFA members had been caught by the police, and the remainder decided to escape before being rounded up by any incoming police reinforcements. The BNP blamed the incident on poor policing, claiming that there had been insufficient protection on the way to the meeting and that BNP members had been picked off in small numbers.[102]

Sean Birchall argues that, as 'well as defining its relationship with the BNP, events on this day also defined AFA's relationship to the far left.'[103] AFA had attempted to engage with other left-wing groups, such as the SWP, but had been ignored by them. Therefore, while AFA considered Weavers Field an important victory, they also felt that much more could have been achieved if the left had united under the militants' strategy.[104] Once again, the militants' bitter experience of the attitudes of the more moderate anti-fascists cemented their identity as a physical force outfit. Their violent confrontation with the BNP, which was witnessed by around 150–200 SWP and Labour members, juxtaposed the two approaches and reinforced the efficacy of their strategy over that of the rest of the left's in their own eyes.

On 21 February 1991, the black teenager Rolan Adams was stabbed to death by a group of white youths in East London. Along with much of the British left, AFA helped to mobilise a string of protests in Adams' name. The reaction to Adams' murder was mainly focused on the area around Welling, in South East London, where the BNP had established a new headquarters the same year that AFA had relaunched.[105] AFA's campaign involved mobilising people around not just Adams' murder, but the rising incidence of racially motivated attacks in London more generally, which they attributed to the presence of the BNP's HQ and their activities there:

> In line with A.F.A. policy of 'setting the agenda' and so wresting the initiative from the neo-nazis and race attackers... Anti-Fascist-Action [sic] returned to Brick Lane market on Sunday 17 March. This time we announced the event by distributing over 15,000 leaflets on the neighbouring estates... Since [the BNP] arrived [in Welling] in 1989, race attacks... have doubled.[106]

AFA orchestrated a number of anti-fascist activities around the same time, mainly throughout London, where they caused trouble for pubs that allowed BNP members to drink in and marched on the BNP's HQ (which had been vacated on the police's advice), but also in Glasgow and Hertfordshire.[107]

The BNP responded to these actions by organising a march from where Rolan Adams was attacked on 25 May 1991, and a counter-demo was arranged by a broad group of leftist and community organisations.[108] Once again, AFA argued for a confrontational stance, and in the meetings running up to the demo and counter-demo secured some agreement that their response to the fascists would only make an impact if they disrupted, or even stopped outright, the latter's march. On the day, however, only AFA and some militant individuals attempted to disrupt the BNP demonstration, while the bulk of the anti-fascists marched away from them. This caused some friction between the militants and non-militants within the Rolan Adams campaign, and further distanced AFA from their more moderate comrades.[109]

In fact, the rivalry between different groups in the anti-fascist movement only continued to grow from this point, as the field became increasingly crowded by an influx of new groups. Throughout 1992 three major national anti-fascist bodies were launched (or re-launched): the SWP's Anti-Nazi League (ANL), Militant's Youth Against Racism in Europe (YRE), and the Anti-Racist Alliance (ARA).[110]

AFA argued that the formation of these groups was 'demonstrative proof' of the successful impact of their 'setting the agenda' strategy.[111] This was not a baseless claim: only a year earlier leading SWP member John Molyneux had argued in the *Socialist Worker* that 'the overall fascist threat is not of the size and strength to justify or even make viable a general national response on the lines of the Anti-Nazi League'.[112] Given that in the interim the fascist threat had not hugely increased, but thousands of people had been mobilised in anti-fascist events, including 3,500 being mobilised by AFA for a single march through Bethnal Green on 11 November 1991,[113] it seems reasonable to assume that at least part of the motivation behind the formation of these new anti-fascist groups was opportunism inspired by the militants' successes.[114]

The effect this development had on the M/CM dynamic may have been a radicalising one. As Nigel Copsey has noted: 'AFA's response was to differentiate itself from this competition by further emphasising its physical mettle.'[115] Indeed, it is entirely possible that the overcrowding of the anti-fascist scene by moderate groups led to AFA further eschewing moderate tactics, such as marches, in favour of more clandestine and radical ones. Having organised mass marches to oppose the BNP up to 1991, they became much less willing to carry on this approach after other national anti-fascist rivals began to operate similarly. Rather, across 1992, AFA redoubled its commitment to physical opposition of the fascists (although they did still occasionally commit stewards to protect anti-racist marches organised by other groups).

Instead of marches, AFA members attacked BNP and B&H members in Hertfordshire (including then-leading B&H members Neil and Paul Parish), who were involved in an assault case at Hertfordshire Magistrates Court.[116] AFA also attacked BNP members and pubs popular with the BNP in Glasgow and Edinburgh throughout 1992, culminating in several large fights 'before, during and after' an annual march against racism and fascism in Glasgow, which resulted in seven BNP members being hospitalised.[117] As a former AFA member recalled:

> The end result of [the formation of the ANL, YRE, and ARA] was that… anti-fascist unity had suddenly become a competitive market place, with organisations that were better funded, and better connected in terms of media publicity than AFA. AFA did continue to help organise and provide stewards for specific broader anti-racist marches… but there were no more AFA marches.[118]

Another march was organised against the BNP's HQ in Welling in the first half of 1993 but, whereas two years before AFA had participated, this time the militants stayed clear of the march and instead attacked a contingent of Combat 18 (C18) members who were drinking nearby in Abbey Wood.[119]

Mirroring the anti-fascist mobilisation around racist attacks and the murder of Rolan Adams, the BNP began their 'Rights for Whites' campaign. Launched initially by Eddie Butler in Tower Hamlets, the 'Rights for Whites' campaign represented the BNP's first real, concerted, attempt to succeed at electoral politics, by pursuing a strategy of community campaigning on issues of local salience.[120] Just as anti-fascists marched in protest of racist violence, the BNP argued that whites were the real victims of racist violence and mobilised people against alleged racist attacks on white people.[121] Although they maintained their commitment to provocative street-politics for a few years to come, this can be seen as the beginning of the BNP's 'quest for legitimacy' and their drift away from political violence.[122] Nevertheless, AFA's campaign of violence had led many on the far right to the conclusion that it was necessary to have a stewards group that could protect them from the far-left street-fighters. To this end, BNP Chief Steward Derek Beackon and Party Election Officer Eddy Butler organised a meeting at the City of Paris Pub in London, inviting the most hardened brawlers of the far right. With the express aim of being able to take on the militant-left physically, Combat 18 was born.[123]

Straight from their inception C18 were, on the whole, more willing to use extreme tactics than other groups operating in the far right at the time. Throughout 1992 and 1993 they engaged in a series of violent attacks which was to give them a reputation as a terror group.[124] They firebombed a number of buildings belonging to perceived political opponents: the Communist Party building in March 1992; the headquarters of the *Morning Star* in April; and the offices of the Democratic Left and the Sandwell Unemployment and Community Resource centre in Birmingham that August. In early 1993 five Combat 18 members, wearing balaclavas, forced their way into the Freedom Bookshop and Press in London, vandalising the computer equipment and Printing Presses while terrifying the people inside. C18 also printed magazines and fanzines with hit-lists containing the names and addresses of left-wing activists, gay clubs, people they saw as 'race traitors', and later published bomb making blueprints with instructions to go out and 'Bomb the Bastards'.[125]

Given the group's genesis as a hard-line response to the activities of AFA and RA, C18 are an *a priori* example (and product) of CE. Yet there is also more to their radicalisation and mobilisation than just interactions with opposing groups. One reason for their embrace of extra-legal means was a perception that the white working class had been *de facto* disenfranchised by 'The System', and therefore to pursue legal avenues was pointless.[126] As they stated in one of their publications, they felt that they were 'AT WAR WITH THE BRITISH STATE!'[127] Another reason was the inspiration drawn from both Loyalist and Nationalist paramilitary groups in Northern Ireland who, C18 felt, were also faced with the task of changing the system from the outside. As C18 leader Charlie Sargent stated: 'Loyalist paramilitaries or Sinn Fein, when they stand for elections, they're humiliated basically, but as a paramilitary group they get respect. That's how we've got to go.'[128]

Still, for all the talk of being a 'terror' or 'paramilitary group', it is easy to exaggerate the real threat posed by Combat 18, who were in reality little more than a small and poorly organised, if very violent, football hooligan 'firm' with delusions of grandeur,[129] who tended to focus on 'soft' targets rather than tackle the more aggressive Red Action or AFA. One particular episode provides an illuminating vignette of C18's character: in 1996 a group of them travelled to *Searchlight* editor Gerry Gable's house in the middle of the night with the express intention of throwing a petrol bomb at his house, only to realise on arrival that they had left their masks at home. Not to be discouraged, they used plastic bags with eye-holes cut out instead, only when it came time to do the deed a gust of wind blew the bag around the main perpetrator's face, causing him to send the bomb flying in the wrong direction (the bomb, being incompetently made, would have caused little damage anyway).[130] This combination of extreme malice and incompetence is a good summary of C18's character. As Nick Ryan has described: 'Despite its propaganda, the group was rarely a national danger, other than to individuals or small groups. It was never really a committed terrorist organisation, with a few notable exceptions.'[131]

The rise of C18 occurred around the same time that the BNP began to seriously embrace electoral politics and drift away from political violence. As the 1990s had drawn on, modernisers within the party such as Tony Lecomber and Eddy Butler had recognised that certain factors – including the Gulf crisis, the creation of the European Union and the construction of the Eurotunnel – all made for conditions much more conducive to the goals of an ethno-nationalist party then they were during the 1980s.[132] Furthermore, the mid-1990s growth of European parties such as the Austrian Freedom Party and the French Front National demonstrated the efficacy of the more respectable 'Euro-Nationalist' approach over the more belligerent 'street politics' style which had dominated the British far right for decades.[133] In 1993, the BNP won their first council seat in Millwall, Tower Hamlets. Although the party only managed to hold the seat until the following year, the modernisers felt vindicated. On 15 March 1994 Tony Lecomber, one of the architects of the Millwall victory, announced in a BNP meeting, to which the press had been invited: 'The days of street warfare were over... [there would be] no more meetings, marches, punch-ups'.[134] Importantly, another major factor in the BNP's deradicalisation had been the ongoing street-war with AFA. As Nigel Copsey has argued, 'far from destroying the BNP in a war of attrition, militant anti-fascism actually *encouraged* its modernization'.[135]

Mark Hayes has taken exception to this analysis, arguing that it relies on a degree of 'counter-factual guessing', since 'who is to say whether, if left unopposed to control the streets, the BNP would not have earned the space to elect parliamentary representatives? How many more people would have suffered brutality at the hands of racist bullies?'[136] However, it seems that Hayes may have missed the point somewhat; while he is correct in stating that, had things been different, the BNP could have been more successful (of course, by the same token, it is at least possible that clashes with the militant-left *attracted* supporters, and so they may have been less well-off under these different circumstances), the point is that AFA and RA *did* engage physically with the BNP. Accordingly, drawing a causal link from this to the BNP's success via their modernisation is a reasonable conclusion. Importantly, the BNP themselves, or at least the modernising element within it, recognised this as being the case, and boasted in the pages of *Spearhead* that they recognised the 'historical theme' of violence hindering their political progress years before the left did.[137] This suggests that without the circumstances being in place to propel an M/CM conflict beyond the threshold of non-lethal street violence into the realm of paramilitary and/or terror tactics – circumstances which, judging by this case, may well need to include the absence of any group desiring electoral success, as well as the absence of a relatively free and fair democratic state – it is likely that the conflict will naturally lead to a downwards trajectory towards moderation.

The BNP's gradual modernisation and C18's growth led to a distancing between the two groups. Indeed, despite their intended *raison d'être* as guardians of the BNP, 'many on the right, including BNP members, grew to fear C18 more than the Left did, as it viciously attacked members of what it saw as rival organisations.'[138] Relations between the London-based BNP leadership and C18 had begun to deteriorate as early as 1993 – only a year after the 'stewards group' had been formed – as the BNP first began to distance itself from political violence. In early 1994, in two separate incidents, leading BNP members Tony Lecomber and Eddy Butler were attacked by C18 second-in-command Will 'Wilf the Beast' Browning.[139] BNP leader John Tyndall responded to C18 hostilities by proscribing them from the BNP, and later suggested that the group may be state assets; pointing out that, despite several of their members being arrested for producing highly offensive propaganda (such as their *C18* magazine) that was illegal under the Public Order Act, charges did not quickly follow.[140] Tyndall later described the two groups as being at war with each other.[141]

Despite Tyndall's claims, however, there remained a significant overlap in rank-and-file membership between C18 and the BNP throughout much of the country. Certain BNP members believed 'that a C18-type group was necessary as a parallel organisation', and there is even evidence that in some areas BNP members would use their dual C18 membership as a kind of alter-ego for when they felt they needed to act in a less than respectable (or legal) manner.[142] As one former AFA member recalls:

> in lots of places, particularly outside of London, the demarcation between who was Combat 18 and who was BNP was incredibly hazy. It was essentially the same people but you know, they wear one hat one day and one hat the next day. And I think in London it was a little bit more demarcated because C18 operated as a kind of distinct gang, you know, who obviously fell out very badly with the BNP, and people properly broke away, whereas my experience in the North was that you had people who were essentially wearing both hats.[143]

Tyndall and other modernising BNP leaders knew that to actually discipline their members for supporting C18 could be devastating to their party's unity. Indeed, several entire BNP branches had switched allegiance to the C18-linked National Socialist Alliance, 'among them Dundee, Liverpool, Oldham, Halifax, Derby and Northampton. In London, home to much of the BNP leadership and of its only electoral success, members switched to the NSA in droves.'[144]

With the BNP beginning to avoid physical confrontations, C18 started to become the focus for militant anti-fascist street fighters. As AFA stated at the time: 'While the BNP adopt a low-key electoral strategy… the threat of fascist violence has been taken up by C18'.[145] Indeed, one member of AFA remembers that the 'injection of that kind of Combat 18 style model' did lead to an escalation in the protest repertoire of the far right operating in the North:

> There were attacks on universities, there were attacks on pubs near the universities, which a lot of anti-fascist and left-wing students drank in. So there was a real escalation in the level of harassment really … it became much more targeted at soft targets, like, a pub with left-wing students in, or much more focused on individual anti-fascist activists.[146]

Further, the far right also began 'intelligence gathering, like university notice boards, if they had contact numbers for a local anarchist group or an anti-fascist group, then, they were coming into universities and taking down those details and then phoning people up and harassing them.'[147]

It seems likely that this development on the far right was largely in response to developments on the left, where there had been a spurt in activity since the formation of YRE, the ARA and the reformation of the ANL:

> I think that means that there's much more of a kind of visibility on the streets of you know left wing anti-racism or left-wing anti-fascism. So that then I think, gave more targets, if you like, to the far right. So, I know that in Leeds, for example, there were a number of attacks on either the SWP or the Anti-Nazi League, kind of in the centre of town, and that happened elsewhere. I know of attacks that happened in Newcastle as well.[148]

Interestingly, though, the far right's renewed campaign did not have a significant radicalising effect on the anti-fascist movement. In terms of the more moderate anti-fascist groups, rather than employing more violent strategies, they instead quickly became much more security conscious and implemented measures to better protect themselves:

> I remember the SWP kind of got different organisers in, people who were a bit more street smart and maybe could handle themselves a bit better, they kind of improved their security a bit, they took some steps to protect their members a bit more. You know, they'd just do sensible things like

they'd group up in one place so that when they went down to sell their papers you're going down on mass, not two people going down with Anti-Nazi League badges on who are easy to pick off. The kind of basic security stuff that AFA did all the time. So I think the more liberal anti-fascists in the Anti-Nazi League improved some of their security measures.[149]

For their part, AFA did orchestrate a few noteworthy attacks on the far right after the emergence of C18. In 1993 an 80-strong contingent of AFA members infiltrated and then successfully disrupted BNP pre-election rally in Colne, leading to the arrests of three anti-fascists. This 'had quite a demoralising effect on the BNP in the North West. Because it was kind of around this time Combat 18 were having, or perceived to be having, physical successes against the left, and this was the BNP getting badly turned over on their own doorstep.'[150] Further, A C18 'recruitment drive' in the Clarence Pub, Manchester, was shut down by a large 'red dominated anti-fascist group'.[151] However, on the whole, the introduction of C18 did not lead to a radicalisation in terms of an increase in violent tactics by the militants either. Combat 18 continued to avoid attacking militant anti-fascists, whereas AFA began to concentrate on its own intelligence gathering operations against the far right. In Manchester 'they used to bug BNP meetings and things like that, and they used to infiltrate people into the BNP.'[152] Elsewhere, particularly throughout the Northern Network, AFA 'spent quite a bit of time photographing people, following people, trying to find out you know where they live, where they work, what their names were' before then publicising this information.[153]

As was the case when AFA/RA were combating the NF and the BNP, with both belligerents perceiving their main demographic as being the (white) working class, once again there was a hegemonic struggle as the opposing sides attempted to gain both recruits and resources in areas of working class and youth culture. The first significant development in this area for Combat 18 was the move to tap into what they perceived as being latent groups of recruits from amongst football fans, while simultaneously using football matches as sites to sell their publications and spread their propaganda. They quickly started distributing their magazines, such as *Putsch*, *The Order* and *Stormer*, at football grounds.[154] AFA noted that, although most of their propaganda was often fantasy, C18's explicit claim had been made very clear: 'Getting all the football fans, or firms, mobs, whatever and getting them all behind a Nationalist cause as one, that's when we start to progress.'[155] While this had been a strong area of activity for the National Front, the BNP had failed to capitalise on it in the same way, which left room for C18 to build up a profile in various clubs.[156]

For their part, AFA continued to set up and support left-wing fanzines and fan associations, much like they had with Leeds in 1987. Indeed, just as LFUARF had set up *Marching Altogether*, AFA helped to set up a number of other anti-fascist fanzines at football clubs. One of the most prominent of these was the publication *Red Attitude* which was published by AFA members and Manchester United fans 'who were concerned that fascists in the North-West were beginning to get active around football grounds in the area.'[157] Similarly to *Marching Altogether*, *Red Attitude* was written by and for committed Manchester United fans. Much of each issue was devoted just to news and reports on the club itself, though there was also regular updates on AFA's national campaign against the far right. Another significant move, in a joint effort with Celtic Football Club fans, was to set up the pro-Republican and anti-fascist fanzine *Tiocfaidh ár lá* in 1991, which was later complemented by the group Celtic Fans Against Fascism.[158]

As C18 appeared on the scene and developed strong connections to various football hooligan groups, most noticeably the Chelsea Headhunters and Glasgow Rangers, AFA helped form more anti-fascist football fanzines and groups in other football clubs, which culminated in the formation of the Football Fans Against Fascism Network.[159] The football scene was strategically useful for both sides, as it provided experienced street fighters who were already very aware of police tactics due to previous encounters with them. Indeed, both sides claimed that the football terraces were where they got their best recruits. As one AFA steward stated: 'The thing is you get people ready-made … If they come from football, they know how to deal with the police, they understand the gang mentality, they know how to fight and understand the psychology of the other mob.'[160] In some regions, this led to a strong intensification of the conflict; for example, on-going fights between anti-fascist Celtic fans and far-right Rangers fans in Glasgow were linked to the murder of three young Celtic fans in 1996, which in turn led to AFA orchestrating several revenge attacks on Combat 18/Rangers fans there.[161]

However, despite thinking that uniting football hooligans was one of the most effective way to grow their ranks, C18 faltered in their efforts. Nick Lowles argues that this is largely due to three key reasons: firstly, the hooligans that C18 could mobilise for street fights tended to only to be interested in that one activity – once the excitement of fighting was over, they had little interest in serious political work like leafleting or organising meetings.[162] Secondly, many hooligan firms were multiracial in composition, and unsurprisingly non-white members of these groups were less than enamoured by C18's overtly racist position. Thirdly, by their very nature hooligan firms held long-standing rivalries with firms from other clubs – and these animosities were a serious barrier to unity. 'While committed fascists would put aside club hostilities for a political cause, the bulk of hooligans would not.'[163] Thus, although C18 'became widely known on the hooligan scene in the mid'90s', 'few recruits were made directly through football.'[164]

Likewise, the other main area in which the two sides attempted to gain traction was youth music scenes. For C18 this meant the neo-Nazi skinhead music scene, which was still largely centred around Ian Stuart Donaldson and the Blood & Honour network. B&H had been earning around £1,000 a week through its merchandising, making it a very inviting prospect to other groups on the far right; accordingly, C18 'hovered like vultures around the skinhead scene'.[165] The attempts by B&H to openly organise musical events provoked some of the most large-scale political violence seen on English streets in decades.

The biggest example of this was the 'Battle of Waterloo' which occurred on 12 September 1992. AFA mobilised around 1,000 militant anti-fascists who managed to occupy the redirection point for another B&H concert, Waterloo station in central London, and successfully disrupted B&H's plans. Due to the scale of the violence, five tube stations and two British Rail stations were closed; moreover, with hundreds of far-right skinheads retreating from AFA over Waterloo bridge, traffic in that area of London was effectively brought to a standstill. There were some 44 arrests, mainly anti-fascists, and a similar number of people hospitalised.[166]

AFA considered this to be quite a victory, and it is indeed the case that B&H were cowed into trying to hide their gigs wherever possible from AFA thereafter. Yet it is worth noting that, four days later, the BNP gained 20% of the vote in a by-election on the Isle of Dogs.[167] Furthermore, the debacle surrounding B&H's event paved the way for C18, who had been vying for full control of the network, to finally achieve their aim, placing at their disposal an organisation that would provide them hundreds of thousands of pounds in capital through merchandising and their newly formed ISD Records CD wing (named after Ian Stuart Donaldson, who had died in a car crash on 24 September 1993).[168] With C18 at the helm, B&H would once more try to openly organise a concert in the capital; this time a memorial concert for Donaldson on 15 January 1994. Predictably, this attempt fared no better than the previous initiatives as militant anti-fascists once more came out in force to violently disrupt the planned proceedings – leading to the event's cancellation.[169]

As well as preventing their enemies' attempts at organising events, AFA continued its commitment to providing a left-wing alternative to the encroachments of the far right in working class and youth areas. Concerts and events were organised through the Cable Street Beat label, while an anti-fascist electronic dance music collective called Freedom of Music was formed, which later put out a double CD titled 'This is Fascism' and organised a 'number of very well attended raves around the country'.[170] Another important aspect of AFA's work was their highly successful Unity Carnivals. The first was held on 8 September 1991 on Hackney Downs, in East London, and attracted around 10,000 people.[171] The second one was held the next year at the same site and was similar in size.[172] They had one more, again attracting around 10,000 people, at Newcastle in 1993.[173]

The attempts to exploit these music scenes had a pronounced effect on the M/CM contest. Apart from directly leading to a number of the biggest and most violent clashes between the warring groups, these various musical enterprises provided both capital and recruits for both sides. AFA claimed that their second Unity carnival in Hackney Downs generated most of the activists who would then join in the fight at the 'Battle of Waterloo' a few days later.[174] From Combat 18's perspective, when they took control of Blood and Honour they obtained a highly successful operation, estimated to be worth around £100,000 a year.[175] While in the short term this benefited them immensely, it also led to their downfall, and so ultimately de-escalated the conflict. Their demise was strongly linked to the huge amounts of money they were making. Firstly, this led to them concentrating on B&H at the expense of activism at football grounds, which seriously diminished their number of new recruits. In the pages of *The Order* it was argued that when C18 swapped the 'terraces' for the 'gig-halls' the 'recruiting died'.[176] Secondly, the leaders became increasingly distrustful of each other with such large amounts of money, which contributed to a leadership split that culminated in the murder of neo-Nazi Chris Castle in 1997 by former Skrewdriver guitarist Martin Cross and C18 founder Charlie Sargent.[177]

Thirdly, and perhaps most relevantly here, the schism occasioned by C18's takeover of B&H had other long-reaching consequences. Sargent's rival in the split was Will Browning, who was intent on leading C18 down the road to becoming a committed paramilitary terror group.[178] In a bid to cement the organisation's reputation as such, as well as to truly establish himself at the helm of the group, the same year that Castle was murdered Browning had a Danish neo-Nazi send several letter-bombs to targets around England, including the London branch of AFA. Fortunately, acting on information provided by Scotland Yard (strongly suggesting that at least one police informant was working within the organisation), Swedish police intercepted the bombs before they could cause any damage.[179] By 1998, due to the murder of Chris Castle, the organisation of the letterbombs, and the distribution of racially inflammatory materials, most of the C18 leadership were in jail and the 'organisation, always greatly exaggerated, [was] essentially finished'.[180]

The aforementioned street battles and bomb plot notwithstanding, C18 had little impact on their political opponents in terms of cumulative extremism; their violence towards the moderate wing of the British Left and anti-fascist groups had no noticeable radicalising effect, and their attempts to attack the militant wing were far and few between. This was likely due to at least three factors; the first being the lack of commitment to the cause the average C18 activist held, and the extra-political activities many of them engaged in at the expense of organisational goals. Although Combat 18 did have a poorly articulated 'white power' agenda, and an ideology of sorts based loosely on the writings of the American neo-Nazi Harold Covington, members were often preoccupied by illicit or suspect money making projects such as drug dealing, illegal debt collection or the merchandising and CD wings of the Blood & Honour music network.[181] Furthermore, it seems likely that many people involved in C18 street actions were chiefly motivated by a lust for violence and were not 'particularly right-wing, not in the C18 sense anyway'.[182] This contrasts starkly with the militants in RA and AFA who approached their activities with an almost obsessive, ideologically driven, zeal.[183]

Secondly, although they were more willing to use extreme means, they were also significantly smaller than other groups on the far right, meaning that their potential impact was necessarily less widespread and coordinated. Gathering accurate figures of C18 activists is very difficult, not least of all because they eschewed traditional models of membership and instead argued for a system of independent cells organising themselves according to Louis Beam's strategy of 'leaderless resistance'.[184] However it has been estimated by academics that the group only ever had around 200 core members.[185]

A third reason for C18's decline was the volatile temperament and behaviour of their leaders, particularly Charlie Sargent and Will Browning, which led to many bitter disagreements with other groups on the far right. This acted as a barrier to co-operation, thereby further limiting the potential impact of the group. Browning's right-hand man once remarked that he 'confronts things head on. He couldn't be sneaky if he tried… His first action is that violence is the only option.'[186] In one particular instance of self-limiting misjudgement, C18 printed a personal attack on the renowned American neo-Nazi David Lane, an imprisoned member of the American neo-Nazi organisation The Order. Lane wrote a pointed retaliation, which was published online, and his near-legendary status amongst the global National Socialist community meant that this incident damaged the credibility Combat 18.[187] Undoubtedly, this violently unstable outlook was also a huge contributing factor to the internal struggles which ultimately led to the organisation tearing itself apart.

1995–2001

It is, again, necessary to examine why dynamics of CE did not develop from nonlethal forms of political violence to lethal forms, or in Alimi *et al.*'s terms, from the 'emergence of violence… [to] the escalation of violence' (with the notable exceptions of the murder of Chris Castle and the attempted letter-bomb strikes).[188] By the second half of the 1990s, the far right was not offering much of a target for militant anti-fascists. C18 was more occupied with clashes with rival fascist groups and internal strife than it was with the far left, and the BNP was doing its best to avoid giving its political opponents the opportunity to attack them. In fact, far from 'reciprocal radicalisation',[189] the dominant dynamic that existed between the fascists and anti-fascists in this period was one of reciprocal deradicalisation; that is, the BNP's shift away from extreme tactics was probably the biggest single contributing factor in the downward trajectory of the M/CM conflict.[190] As the BNP increasingly favoured the 'hearts and minds' approach over their earlier 'march and grow' tactics, AFA were deprived of a focus for their direct action strategy. An AFA member later reflected that 'unless AFA adapted to the new BNP strategy, AFA would 'atrophy' and wither. AFA was geared for confrontation. Without confrontation AFA – as it then was – would have no reason to exist'.[191]

With this thought in mind, many members of AFA decided it was necessary to follow the BNP down the electoral road by setting up their own party, the Independent Working Class Association (IWCA). However, this project, conceived as 'filling the vacuum' in working class areas which had been created by AFA having cleared fascists from the streets, was rife with problems right from the start. In the first instance, although the Marxists of RA, the chief architects of the IWCA, may have been the dominant faction in London and Manchester, throughout much of the rest of the country – particularly in AFA's Northern Network – anarchists held sway over the organisation, and they naturally rejected any electoral strategy.[192] This dispute between the different ideological camps within AFA ultimately hastened its demise, which had been instigated by the BNP's moderation and C18's volatility.

In truth, however, the changing nature of AFA was not only influenced by developments on the far right; AFA was 'coupled' to more than one social movement or political actor, and co-evolved with these third parties.[193] First of all, the 'vacuum' which members of AFA felt needed filling was not just the political space created by the absence of the far right on the streets, but also by the absence of the left. As RA argued:

> Their total ineptitude; and the tangible contempt that exists between Labour and its erstwhile constituency has locally and nationally begat the BNP... Labour has openly abandoned the politics of milk and water socialism for the politics of milk and water monetarism... Labour's demise should be the Left's opportunity.[194]

The radicalisation towards aggressive violent tactics occurred in part due to RA and AFA's relationship with the rest of the left, and clearly their deradicalisation was also influenced in a similar fashion. Particularly, it was the drift to the right by the Labour Party, the perceived abandonment of the working class and the subsequent absence of a political party to representing their interests (at the same time that the far right were seriously trying to enter this space) that animated their electoral plans.

Another group that AFA, or more particularly RA, were coupled with, and who likely had an influence on the militants' drift toward electioneering, was the Irish Republican Movement. This movement was so significant to Red Action that two members even became activists for the IRA, detonating bombs in London and on a train in 1993 for the republican group, leading to thirty-year prison sentences.[195] Indeed, RA's Commitment to their support for armed struggle against British occupation in Northern Ireland was probably second only to their commitment to physical force anti-fascism in the pages of *Red Action*: 'You would not have to be particularly familiar with Red Action to realise that support for the armed struggle of the IRA and INLA is something which we push very much to the forefront of our political activities and identity.'[196] By 1994 AFA argued that the IRA had 'Britain bombed to the negotiation table', and that 'the architects of the peace process' were 'the leadership of the Provisional IRA.'[197] Between 1994 and 1998, with Sinn Fein and the IRA's Gerry Adams growing from 'Mr 10%' to the leader of the fourth biggest party in the Northern

Irish Assembly, it is at least possible that the substitution of political violence for electioneering by the Irish republicans influenced the militant anti-fascists.[198] Certainly one former anarchist member of AFA felt this to be the case:

> Red Action had always been a strong supporter of the Irish Republican movement – and the move of Republicans from the armed struggle to community organising, and the electoral success of Sinn Fein, may well have also played a role in the rethinking of Red Action's strategy.[199]

The third and final factor influencing the trajectory of de-escalation of the M/CM conflict between militant anti-fascists and fascists in Britain was the growing powers and capabilities of the state to interfere in their battles. On 3 November 1994, the Criminal Justice and Public Order Act was introduced, which gave the police increased powers and limited some civil liberties in removing a suspect's right to silence.[200] Furthermore, the Act placed limitations on citizens' rights of peaceful assembly:

> The police may now declare any gathering of five or more people to be illegal. They may apply this to a political gathering, a trade union strike or a music festival. They may break up any musical event on private land without a warrant, a bit of venality that is a declaration of war by ageing politicians against young people.[201]

Every antagonist in the M/CM contest recognised the threat that this Act presented to their ambitions. Red Action argued that the Act 'allows the police to do much as they please in questioning people and cordoning off areas.'[202] Their fears over the legislation were justified when, in 1997, several AFA members leaving a peaceful and legal meeting were stopped by the police under the Act, and had their names and addresses, as well as identifying features such as clothes and tattoos, noted down.[203] Combat 18 argued that the Act was yet another weapon in the increasing arsenal of the state in their war with the far right,[204] and the BNP complained about the infringement on their right to free speech after Nick Griffin and Paul Ballard were arrested under the Public Order Act for publishing and distributing 'racially inflammatory material' in *The Rune*.[205]

Aside from the Criminal Justice and Public Order Act, *Red Action* noted the enormous growth in CCTV cameras, 'the ending of telephone privacy', the introduction of CS spray for police officers, and the development of a centralised computer system which could hold data on people's DNA representing some of the growing disincentives for people to join the militants' cause.[206] Further, these were all points generally agreed upon by Combat 18.[207] From the mid-1990s onwards, although AFA made a valiant attempt to keep their mission alive, the evolution or disintegration of their enemies and the shifting circumstances around them proved too big an obstacle. In May 1997, AFA made a couple of successful attacks on the BNP during election counts in Glasgow and Bristol,[208] but at a Bloody Sunday Memorial event in London on 24 January 1998, at which the NF had organised a counter-demo, a vast police presence prevented AFA from effectively tackling the fascists, leading to their observation that the 'lesson for AFA was the amount of resources the police were prepared to use on the day to prevent the anti-fascists being effective.'[209] Not only were anti-fascists again faced with a situation of the police photographing, videotaping and writing down details of them, but now officers were also carrying 'mugsheets' of AFA 'ringleaders'.[210] AFA were faced with similar problems on 28 February 1998 at an NF-organised anti-immigrant demonstration at Dover, where 'the police outnumbered the anti-fascists themselves by a least 3 to 1. Again the police had camera teams busy all day, including at least one from Bloody Sunday.'[211] All of this, combined with an ageing pool of activists and a diminishing supply of new recruits due to the shrinking profile that AFA was projecting after the BNP's retreat from the streets, meant that 'by 2001 – though probably a long time before – AFA as a national organisation hardly existed.'[212]

Conclusion

The first main point to be made about the foregoing discussion is the effect that elections, and the organisational need for votes, has on the development of CE. Throughout this case study, both the escalation of the M/CM contest at the beginning of the 1980s, and the gradual de-escalation away from violence from 1993, were linked to the failure of the NF at the 1979 elections and the evolution towards electoral politics by the BNP and parts of AFA during the 1990s respectively. This suggests that if one or more of the organisations involved in the M/CM conflict are political parties, elections can have either a radicalising or moderating effect on them – depending on whether the results signal that this is a potentially successful pathway or not.

When the moderating pressures that electioneering can confer on an M/CM contest are absent, escalation does not seem to happen evenly across a country. Indeed, the concept of territory, or the locality in which groups develop tit-for-tat dynamics of violence, is important. In a smaller geographical area such as Leeds or East London, dynamics of CE can develop much faster and evenly than on a national scale. The clashes between fascists and anti-fascists in North London at the beginning of the 1980s escalated quickly and were resolved relatively quickly with the formation of Red Action and the perception of the anti-fascists 'winning' the 'turf war' there.

The formation of Red Action, and then the subsequent formation of AFA and C18, highlights the need to be sensitive to how within-movement dynamics can cause radicalisation. This happens both as organisations try to 'outbid' their moderate rivals to gain support from the radical flank, and also as, in dialogue with the more mainstream groups within their movement, their own organisational self-image is solidified in relation to more moderate counterparts. As with the presence of elections, within-movement dynamics and interactions do not necessarily lead to further radicalisation. Labour's shift to the right – in conjunction with the BNP's eschewing of violence – also helped to create the 'political vacuum' which AFA/RA felt it necessary to fill, demonstrating that within movement dynamics can also produce a moderating effect on militant groups.

Within-movement dynamics and other external factors aside, the formation of RA, AFA and C18 does also demonstrate the existence of patterns of CE, as they were all formed, to a large extent, in response to provocation from, or the growth of, their political enemies. RA, and to a lesser extent AFA, always operated in what Copsey refers to as the 'radical' rather than the 'legal' tradition of anti-fascism. Later the M/CM contest provoked the formation of C18 who were in some ways the fascist equivalent (i.e. eschewing electoral politics and legal forms of protest in favour of violent radical tactics).[213] Although these groups were all fairly hard-line, none of them managed to escalate the contest further by provoking, or themselves using, a sustained shift in tactics from non-lethal street-brawling to lethal violence. C18 made some notable attempts, but their lack of competence and commitment were an effective barrier to this goal. A far-right solo-actor terrorist and ex-BNP member, David Copeland, did attempt to start a race war by detonating several bombs in London; but this had no noticeable effect on the M/CM conflict and only served to shock the public. Rather, both the far right and the far left exerted significant amounts of energy in trying to achieve hegemonic dominance in areas of working class and youth culture, such as music and football scenes, so as to eventually be a dominant ideological force within that demographic.

Notes

1 Hann, Dave. *Physical Resistance: A Hundred Years of Anti-Fascism* (Alresford: Zero Books, 2013), pp. 314–315.
2 Birchall, Sean. *Beating the Fascists: The Untold Story of Anti-Fascist Action* (London: Freedom Press, 2010), p. 55.
3 *Red Action*, Issue 1, February 1982, p. 1; Birchall. *Beating the Fascists*, Chapter 1.5.
4 Busher, Joel, Donald Holbrook and Graham Macklin. 'The Internal Brakes on Violent Escalation: A Typology', *Behavioral Sciences of Terrorism and Political Aggression*, 11, no. 1 (2019), p. 10.
5 Renton, David. *Never Again: Rock Against Racism and the Anti-Nazi League 1976–1982* (Oxon: Routledge, 2019), p. 164.
6 *Spearhead*, No. 135, January 1980, p. 18; Hill, Ray and Andrew Bell. *The Other Face of Terror: Inside Europe's Neo-Nazi Network* (London: Grafton Books, 1988), pp. 90–91.
7 Hann, Dave and Steve Tilzey. *No Retreat: The Secret War Between Britain's Anti-Fascists and the Far Right* (Lytham: Milo Books, 2003), p. 71.
8 Miles, Robert and Phizacklea, Annie. *White Man's Country: Racism in British Politics* (London: Pluto Press, 1984), p. 124.
9 *The Guardian*, 4 July 1981, p. 17; *Fighting Talk*, Issue 19, April 1998, p. 20.
10 *Red Action Bulletin*, Vol. 3. Issue 4, January 1999, p. 5.
11 *The Guardian*, 30 June 1981, p. 2; *Fighting Talk*, Issue 19, April 1998, p. 20;
12 *Red Action Bulletin*, Vol. 3. Issue 4, January 1999, p. 5; *Fighting Talk*, Issue 19, April 1998, p. 20.

13 Hann, *Physical Resistance*, pp. 318–319.
14 *Fighting Talk*, Issue 19, April 1998, p. 20.
15 Ibid., p. 20.
16 *Fighting Talk*, Issue 19, April 1998, pp. 20–21.
17 Ibid., p. 21.
18 Collins, Matthew. *Hate: My Life in the Far Right* (London: Biteback Publishing, 2011), p. 35.
19 *Fighting Talk*, Issue 19, April 1998, p. 20; Hann, *Physical Resistance*, pp. 318–319.
20 *Red Action Bulletin*, Issue 1, February 1982, p. 1.
21 Busher, Joel and Graham Macklin. 'The Missing Spirals of Violence: Four Waves of Movement–Countermovement Contest in Post-war Britain', *Behavioral Sciences of Terrorism and Political Aggression*, 7, no. 1 (2015), p. 11.
22 Bloom, Mia. *Dying to Kill: The Allure of Suicide Terror* (New York: Columbia University Press, 2005).
23 McCauley, Clark and Moskalenko, Sophia. *Friction: How Radicalisation Happens to Them and Us* (Oxford: Oxford University Press, 2011), p. 125.
24 *Red Action Bulletin*, Issue 1, February 1982, p. 1.
25 Miles, Robert and Phizacklea, Annie. *White Man's Country: Racism in British Politics* (London: Pluto Press, 1984), pp. 124–128; Hill, Ray and Andrew Bell. *The Other Face of Terror: Inside Europe's Neo-Nazi Network* (London: Grafton Books, 1988), pp. 155–158; Collins, Matthew. *Hate: My Life in the Far Right* (London: Biteback Publishing, 2011).
26 Hill, Ray and Andrew Bell. *The Other Face of Terror: Inside Europe's Neo-Nazi Network* (London: Grafton Books, 1988), pp. 155–158.
27 Della Porta, Donatella. *Clandestine Political Violence* (Cambridge: Cambridge University Press, 2013), pp. 71–72.
28 Alimi Y. Eitan, Charles Demetriou and Lorenzo Bosi. *The Dynamics of Radicalization: A Relational and Comparative Perspective* (Oxford: Oxford University Press, 2015), p. 48.
29 Birchall, *Beating the Fascists*, p. 40.
30 Hann, *Physical Resistance*, p. 319.
31 Ibid., p. 321.
32 Ibid., p. 321.
33 Copsey, Nigel. *Anti-Fascism in Britain* (London: Macmillan Press Ltd, 2000), p. 160.
34 Birchall, *Beating the Fascists*, p. 93.
35 *Red Action Bulletin*, Issue 13, N/D, p. 3.
36 Ibid., p. 3.
37 Ibid., p. 3.
38 Ibid., p. 3.
39 Della Porta, *Clandestine Political Violence*, pp. 75–76.
40 Hill and Bell. *The Other Face of Terror*, p. 122.
41 Copsey, Nigel. *Contemporary British Fascism: The British National Party and the Quest for Legitimacy* (Basingstoke: Palgrave, 2008), p. 32.
42 Ibid., p. 32.
43 Hill and Bell. *The Other Face of Terror*, p. 122.
44 *Red Action Bulletin*, Issue 19, August 1985, p. 3.
45 Hann, *Physical Resistance*, p. 327.
46 *Red Action Bulletin*, Issue 19, August 1985; *Red Action Bulletin*, Issue 20, December 1985.
47 Birchall, *Beating the Fascists*, p. 107.
48 Ibid., p. 107.
49 Ibid., p. 107.
50 Goodwin, Matthew J. *New British Fascism: Rise of the British National Party* (Routledge: Oxon, 2011), pp. 41–44.

51 *Red Action Bulletin*, Issue 20, December 1985.
52 Searchlight Archive (SCH): SCH/01/Res/AF/04/003: Box 3: Board of Deputies Reports Box 1, 1970s + 1980s: *Action Briefing*, Association of Jewish Ex–Servicemen & Women Issue No. 26, August 1985, pp. 5–6.
53 Board of Deputies of British Jews, Confidential Weekly Summary of Events, 3rd–10th March 1986, p. 1.
54 Board of Deputies of British Jews, Confidential Weekly Summary of Events, 24th–31st March 1986, p. 2.
55 Board of Deputies of British Jews, Confidential Weekly Summary of Events, 30th June–6th July 1986, p. 1.
56 SCH/01/Res/AF Series 4: Anti–Fascist Material: Letter to Labour Movement groups and organisations from Anti–Fascist Action, emphasis added.
57 SCH/01/Res/AF Series 4: Anti–Fascist Material: AFA Internal Bulletin January 1986, p. 3.
58 Bullstreet, K. *Bash the Fash: Anti-Fascist Recollections 1984–3* (London: Kate Sharpley Library, 2001), pp. 7–9; *Red Action Bulletin*, Issue 26, February 1986.
59 Bullstreet, *Bash the Fash*, pp. 7–9; *Red Action Bulletin*, Issue 26, February 1986.
60 *The Guardian*, 10 November 1986, p. 2.
61 *The Sunday Times*, 1 February 1987; *Red Action Bulletin*, Issue 31, March 1987.
62 SCH/01/Res/AF Series 4: Anti–Fascist Material: AFA Internal Bulletin January 1986, pp. 1–2.
63 Thomas, Paul. 'Kicking Racism Out of Football: A Supporter's View', *Race and Class*, 36, no. 4 (1995), pp. 95–101.
64 Ibid., p. 96.
65 Lowles, Nick. 'Far Out With the Far Right', in *Hooligan Wars: Causes and Effects of Football Violence*, Edited by Mark Perryman (Edinburgh: Mainstream Publishing Company, 2002), pp. 109–110.
66 Bebber, Brett. *Violence and Racism in Football: Politics and Cultural Conflict in British Society, 1968–1998* (London: Routledge, 2011), p. 163.
67 Ibid., p. 163.
68 Garland, Jon and Michael Rowe. *Racism and Anti-Racism in Football* (Basingstoke: Palgrave, 2001), p. 73.
69 Thomas, Paul. 'Marching Altogether? Football Fans Taking a Stand Against Racism', in *Sports and Challenges to Racism*, Edited by Jonathan Long and Karl Spracklen (Houndmills: Palgrave Macmillan, 2011), p. 187.
70 Ibid., pp. 190–191.
71 Ibid., pp. 188–189.
72 Ibid., pp. 188–189.
73 Ibid., p. 192.
74 Garland, Jon and Michael Rowe. *Racism and Anti-Racism in Football* (Basingstoke: Palgrave, 2001), p. 73.
75 Bebber, Brett. *Violence and Racism in Football: Politics and Cultural Conflict in British Society, 1968–1998* (London: Routledge, 2011), p. 195.
76 *Red Action Bulletin*, Issue 45, August 1988, p. 3.
77 Ibid., p. 3.
78 *Red Action Bulletin*, Issue 33, June 1987, p. 4.
79 Lowles, Nick. *White Riot: The Violent Story of Combat 18* (Guernsey: Milo Books, 2001), p. 101.
80 Birchall, *Beating the Fascists*, pp. 161–166.
81 *Red Action Bulletin*, Issue 45, August 1988, p. 3.
82 *Red Action Bulletin*, Issue 47, November 1988, p. 2.
83 *The Guardian*, 10 November 1988, p. 2; *Red Action Bulletin*, Issue 48, December 1988, p. 2.
84 *Red Action Bulletin*, Issue 51, April 1989, p. 2.

85 Birchall, *Beating the Fascists*, p. 169.
86 *Fighting Talk*, Issue 12, 1995, pp. 8–9.
87 Birchall, *Beating the Fascists*, p. 170.
88 *Fighting Talk*, Issue 12, 1995, pp. 8–9.
89 *Nationalism Today*, Issue No. 25, November 1984, p. 19.
90 *Red Action Bulletin*, Issue 58, Spring 1991, p. 2.
91 Ibid., p. 2.
92 *Spearhead*, No. 272, October 1991, pp. 5–9.
93 *British Nationalist*, No. 124, October 1992, p. 4.
94 Board of Deputies of British Jews, Confidential Weekly Summary of Events, 12th–19th May 1986, p. 2.
95 Trilling, Daniel. *Bloody Nasty People: The Rise of Britain's Far Right* (London: Verso, 2013), p. 62.
96 Goodwin, *New British Fascism*, p. 43.
97 Ibid., p. 43.
98 *Spearhead*, No. 246, August 1989.
99 Collins, *Hate*, pp. 53–56.
100 *Red Action Bulletin*, Issue 58, Spring 1991, p. 2.
101 *The Guardian*, 18 April 1990, p. 3; Birchall, *Beating the Fascists*, p. 183.
102 *British Nationalist*, May/June, 1990.
103 Birchall, *Beating the Fascists*, p. 186.
104 Ibid., p. 186.
105 Copsey, *Contemporary British Fascism*, p. 47.
106 *Red Action Bulletin*, Issue 59, June/July 1991, p. 1 & p. 8.
107 Ibid., p. 1 & p. 8.
108 *The Guardian*, 25 May 1991, p. 3; *Red Action Bulletin*, Issue 60, September/October 1991.
109 Ibid.
110 *Red Action Bulletin*, Issue 63, July/August 1992.
111 Ibid., p. 1.
112 *Red Action Bulletin*, Issue 60, September/October 1991, p. 6.
113 *Red Action Bulletin*, Issue 61, January 1992, p. 1.
114 Birchall, *Beating the Fascists*, Chapter 3.8.
115 Copsey, Nigel. 'From Direct Action to Community Action: The Changing Dynamics of Anti-fascist Opposition', in *British National Party: Contemporary Perspectives*, Edited by Nigel Copsey and Graham Macklin (Oxon: Routledge, 2011), pp. 127–128.
116 *Red Action Bulletin*, Issue 63, July/August 1992, pp. 1&8.
117 *Red Action Bulletin*, Issue 65, Spring 1993, p. 12.
118 Anon. *Anti-Fascist Action – An Anarchist Perspective* (London: Kate Sharpley Library, 2007), p. 9.
119 *The Independent*, 23 October 1993, p. 21; *Red Action Bulletin*, Issue 67, Spring 1994.
120 Copsey, *Contemporary British Fascism*, pp. 56–57; Goodwin, *New British Fascism*, p. 46.
121 *British Nationalist*, No. 122 July 1992, p. 8.
122 Copsey, *Contemporary British Fascism*.
123 Lowles, *White Riot*, pp. 14–17.
124 *Searchlight*, January 1995, No. 235, p. 4.
125 *Combat 18*, Issue No. 3, c. 1993; *Searchlight*, January 1995, No. 235; Lowles, *White Riot*; Goodrick-Clarke, Nicholas. *Black Sun: Aryan Cults, Esoteric Nazism and the Politics of Identity* (New York: New York University Press, 2002).
126 Ryan, *Homeland*, pp. 21–22.
127 *SCH/01/Res/BRI Series 13: British Far Right: The Order*, Issue 12, 1995, p. 4.
128 Ryan, *Homeland*, p. 21.

129 Ibid., p. 29.
130 Lowles, *White Riot*, p. 136.
131 Ryan, *Homeland*, p. 30.
132 Goodwin, *New British Fascism*, pp. 47–49.
133 *Spearhead*, No. 325, March 1996, p. 11; *Fighting Talk*, Issue 19, April 1998, p. 11; Copsey, *Contemporary British Fascism*, p. 70; Goodwin, *New British Fascism*, pp. 47–49.
134 Birchall, *Beating the Fascists*, p. 355.
135 Copsey, 'From Direct Action to Community Action', p. 130.
136 Hayes, Mark. 'Red Action – Left-Wing Pariah: Some Observations Regarding Ideological Apostasy and the Discourse of Proletarian Resistance', in *Against the Grain: The British Far Left from 1956'*, Edited by Matthew Worley and Evan Smith (Manchester: Manchester University Press, 2014), p. 241.
137 *Spearhead*, No. 346, December 1997.
138 Ryan, *Homeland*, p. 19.
139 Lowles, *White Riot*, p. 58.
140 *Spearhead*, No. 299, January 1994; *Spearhead*, No. 319, September 1995.
141 *Spearhead*, No. 320, October 1995.
142 Lowles, Nick. *White Riot: The Violent Story of Combat 18* (Guernsey: Milo Books, 2001), p. 88.
143 Interview with former Anti-Fascist Action activist, 13 June 2019.
144 Lowles, Nick. *White Riot: The Violent Story of Combat 18* (Guernsey: Milo Books, 2001), p. 142.
145 *Fighting Talk*, Issue 12, 1995, p. 9.
146 Interview with former Anti-Fascist Action activist, 13 June 2019.
147 Ibid.
148 Ibid.
149 Ibid.
150 Ibid.
151 *Man. Utd Anti Fascists*, Newsletter no. 1, Winter 1995, p. 2.
152 Interview with former Anti-Fascist Action activist, 13 June 2019.
153 Ibid.
154 SCH/01/Res/BRI Series 13: British Far Right: *The Order*, Issue 12, 1995; SCH/01/Res/BRI Series 13: British Far Right: *The Order*, Issue 19, April/June 1997; SCH/01/Res/BRI Series 13: British Far Right: *The Stormer*, Issue 5, N/D.
155 *Fighting Talk*, Issue 9, 1995, pp. 3–11, a quote of a C18 member.
156 Ibid.
157 *Man. Utd Anti Fascists*, Newsletter no. 1, Winter 1995, p. 1.
158 *Tiocfaidh ár lá*, Issue 40, N/D; *Fighting Talk*, Issue 9, 1995, p. 8.
159 *Tiocfaidh ár lá*, Issue 18, N/D, p. 11.
160 *The Guardian*, 25 November 1994, p. 4.
161 *Red Action*, Issue 73; *Fighting Talk*, Issue 14.
162 Lowles, Nick. 'Far Out with the Far Right', in *Hooligan Wars: Causes and Effects of Football Violence*, Edited by Mark Perryman (Edinburgh: Mainstream Publishing Company, 2002), pp. 112–113.
163 Ibid., p. 115.
164 Ibid., p. 119.
165 Lowles, Nick. *White Riot: The Violent Story of Combat 18* (Guernsey: Milo Books, 2001).
166 *Red Action Bulletin*, Issue 64, January 1993; Bullstreet, *Bash the Fash*, pp. 14–15; Birchall, *Beating the Fascists*, Chapter 3.17;
167 *Red Action Bulletin*, Issue 64, January 1993.
168 *The Independent*, 1 February 1998; Lowles, Nick. *White Riot: The Violent Story of Combat 18* (Guernsey: Milo Books, 2001).
169 *Fighting Talk*, Issue 7, 1994.

170 *Fighting Talk*, Issue 20, August 1998, p. 14.
171 Birchall, *Beating the Fascists: The Untold Story of Anti-Fascist Action* (London: Freedom Press, 2010).
172 Fighting Talk, Issue 20 page 15.
173 *SCH/01/Res/AF Series 4: Anti–Fascist Material:* TWAFA Unity Carnival Programme, 12 June 1993, p. 9.
174 *Fighting Talk*, Issue 20, August 1998, p. 15.
175 Lowles, Nick. *White Riot: The Violent Story of Combat 18* (Guernsey: Milo Books, 2001), p. 119.
176 SCH/01/Res/BRI Series 13: British Far Right: *The Order*, Issue 19, April/June 1997, p. 3.
177 Ryan, *Homeland*, p. 29.
178 Ibid., p. 29.
179 *The Herald*, 26 August 1997.
180 *Fighting Talk*, Issue 19, April 1998, p. 4.
181 For the basis of C18's ideology, see Lowles, *White Riot*, Chapter 2; C18 leader Charlie Sargent had two convictions for drug-related offences by 1997, and many other members were involved in drug dealing, see: *The Independent*, 1 February 1998; and Ryan, *Homeland*, p. 17.
182 Lowles, *White Riot*, p. 80; Also see Testa, M. *Militant Anti-Fascism: A Hundred Years of Resistance* (Edinburgh: AK Press, 2015), pp. 236–237.
183 For example see London AFA's 'Operation Zero Tolerance': Birchall, *Beating the Fascists*, p. 391.
184 SCH/01/Res/BRI Series 13: British Far Right: *Combat 18*, Issue 3, c. 1993.
185 Ryan, *Homeland*, p. 17; Goodrick-Clarke, Nicholas. *Black Sun*, p. 46;
186 Ryan, *Homeland*, p. 45.
187 Lowles, *White Riot*, pp. 195–195.
188 Alimi *et al. The Dynamics of Radicalization*, p. 12; Also, see Busher, Joel and Macklin, Graham. 'Interpreting "Cumulative Extremism": Six Proposals for Enhancing Conceptual Clarity', *Terrorism and Political Violence* (2014), Vol. 27. Issue 5, p. 2.
189 Bailey, Gavin and Phil Edwards. 'Rethinking 'Radicalisation': Microradicalisations and Reciprocal Radicalisation as an Intertwined Process', *Journal for Deradicalization*, 10 (2017), p. 266.
190 Copsey, Nigel. 'From Direct Action to Community Action: The Changing Dynamics of Anti-fascist Opposition', in *British National Party: Contemporary Perspectives*, Edited by Nigel Copsey and Graham Macklin (Oxon: Routledge, 2011).
191 Anon. *Anti-Fascist Action – An Anarchist Perspective* (London: Kate Sharpley Library, 2007), p. 13.
192 Ibid., p. 11.
193 Busher, Joel and Graham Macklin. 'Interpreting "Cumulative Extremism": Six Proposals for Enhancing Conceptual Clarity', *Terrorism and Political Violence* (2014).
194 *Red Action Bulletin*, Issue 68, Summer 1994, p. 2.
195 *The Independent*, 14 May 1994, p. 5.
196 *Red Action Bulletin*, Issue 35, October 1987, p. 2.
197 *Red Action Bulletin*, Issue 69, Autumn 1994, p. 1.
198 *Red Action Bulletin*, Vol. 3. Issue 3, October 1998, p. 5.
199 Anon. *Anti-Fascist Action – An Anarchist Perspective* (London: Kate Sharpley Library, 2007), p. 11.
200 *The Independent*, 9 November 1994, p. 18.
201 Ibid., p. 18.
202 *Red Action Bulletin*, Issue 74, Spring 1997, p. 14.
203 Ibid., p. 14.
204 *The Order*, Issue 12, 1995.
205 *Spearhead*, No. 342, August 1997, p. 18.

206 *Red Action Bulletin*, Issue 74, Spring 1997, p. 14.
207 *The Order*, Issue 12, 1995.
208 *Fighting Talk*, Issue 17, September 1997, p. 3.
209 *Fighting Talk*, Issue 19, April 1998, p. 3.
210 Ibid., p. 3.
211 Ibid., pp. 3–4.
212 Anon. *Anti-Fascist Action – An Anarchist Perspective* (London: Kate Sharpley Library, 2007), p. 13.
213 Copsey, Nigel. *Anti-Fascism in Britain* (London: Macmillan Press Ltd, 2000), p. 3.

5

NORTHERN IRELAND FROM 1960–1976[1]

Introduction

The population of Northern Ireland (NI) has, since the creation of the state in 1921, been divided into two communities: the Catholics and the Protestants. While other important divisions, such as class, do, of course, exist, it is this boundary which is most salient; and certainly the one most pertinent to this study.[2]

In the 1960s, the nature of the relationship between the two communities was one of political alienation of the Catholics in a region where the Parliament of Northern Ireland was exclusively controlled by Protestants through the Ulster Unionist Party; a socially conservative ethnoreligious party which held power from 1921 to 1972. But during the 1960s, 'the post-war free education system and the increase in university scholarships was creating a much larger, better-educated Catholic middle class, ambitious, anxious to participate in politics and to end their second-class status',[3] ultimately sparking off a civil rights movement, just as similar movements spread throughout other parts of the world. Yet as Finn points out, in contrast to other countries of the same era, such as France and Italy, where leftist revolutionary groups aimed to provoke the population into confrontation against the 'repressive character of capitalist rule', the same results could not be expected in NI:

> French and Italian politics had been divided along class lines since 1945, with a Communist-led working-class movement facing the ruling conservative bloc in both countries… In Northern Ireland, on the other hand, political life had been chiefly organized around two sectarian camps since 1920, with alignments based on class relegated to second place. If social polarization was to occur, it would most likely be communal in nature.[4]

Accordingly, the (almost exclusively Catholic) civil rights movement soon provoked a backlash from Protestant loyalists, and as violence escalated between the two sides the British Army (BA) was also forced to enter the fray. By the 1970s, paramilitary groups from both communities were using lethal force against both their 'rival' communities and the BA. This period of violent conflict, known as 'the Troubles', lasted until 1998.

This chapter will examine the escalation from the emergence of a peaceful civil rights movement (CRM) in the early 1960s to the outbreak of civil war in Ulster and its violent peak between 1972 and 1976.[5] The escalation of hostilities between the opposing movements shall be assessed and the factors which are conducive to cumulative extremism (CE) emerging identified. Further, the state's different strategies for managing these developments – and the reasons for their successes and failures – shall also be analysed.

1963–1966

Sectarianism was a 'social fact' of life in Northern Ireland from the state's formation in 1921.[6] This is arguably the most important difference between the case studies of this book: the social structure of NI was characterised by two distinct communities whereas the fascists and anti-fascists faced each other in a more pluralistic context. In the previous chapters, social movement organisations (SMOs) were eager to present themselves as the representatives of a broader social group, and the defenders of that group's interests against its enemies (as defined by the SMO). This process was much easier when it reflected both the genuine concerns of that social group and broader social divisions. This explains why the NF were keen to exacerbate communal antagonisms along 'racial' lines, and why they benefited when anxieties about immigration were inflamed by the arrival of refugees in 1972 and 1976.

However, on the whole British society was never structured according to these divisions in the same way that Northern Irish society was. The deep social divide that existed between Catholics and Protestants was a useful foundation for an SMO wanting to present itself as the representative or defender of one of those groups. Further, as has already been stated in an earlier chapter, when the cleavage of an M/CM contest is non-ascriptive and the groups are both competing over the same social base there is much less of an incentive to use categorical or indiscriminate lethal violence, as this could alienate potential supporters. This is obviously not the case when the M/CM conflict is being fought across ascriptive lines and between two communities, whereby violence towards the 'enemy' group could potentially win support for a social movement organisation.

Communal consciousness was maintained by the political architecture of NI. As Bourke has argued, the Ulster Unionist Party's dominance of the Parliament of Northern Ireland meant that the will of the Protestant community was 'permanently enfranchised at the expense of the inclusive will of the people as a whole'.[7] Further, the existence of the Special Powers Act, an Act which gave Stormont a vast array of coercive powers, ultimately meant that communal 'antagonism in the form of emergency legislation was therefore embodied in the permanent political machinery of the State.'[8] It is, perhaps, unsurprising then that although the two communities did live in relative peace for decades, and in areas co-existed with enough congeniality to allow their children to grow up playing together,[9] the social and political inequality experienced by the Catholic community led to a rising feeling of discontent at their situation and hostility towards the Unionists.[10] Of particular frustration were the issues of representation in local government, as the franchise 'only extended to ratepayers' and thus was skewed in favour of the generally more wealthy Protestant population, and the fair allocation of public housing; all of which was felt more sharply by those living in the mainly Catholic areas of West Ulster, such as the city of Derry.[11] Catholic discontent over these issues eventually manifested itself in a civil rights movement which aimed to bring about reform of the province. The key observation here is that this sense of grievance ensured a strong connection between the growing CRM and the Catholic population.[12]

The nascent civil rights movement grew out of earlier organisations such as the Homeless Citizens' League (HCL), founded in Dungannon in May 1963, and the Campaign for Social Justice (CSJ), founded in January 1964.[13] These groups undertook and published thorough research on the housing situation to highlight the discrimination faced by the Catholic community, and made a real effort to not be drawn into sectarian arguments.[14] While the seeds of the CRM were taking sprout during the mid-1960s elements of the Protestant community were also being mobilised although not, at first, in direct response to the burgeoning CRM.

Within the Protestant community there were long-standing fears over both the Catholic population in Northern Ireland and the neighbouring Republic of Ireland.[15] These fears had been given a new urgency by Terence O'Neill's ascension to the position of Prime Minister for Northern Ireland in 1963, and, more specifically, his apparent efforts to build bridges between the Catholic and Protestant communities. Concerns over O'Neill's premiership grew significantly after he attempted to improve relations with the Republic of Ireland by inviting the Taoiseach Seán Lemass to Stormont in January 1965.[16] The fact that O'Neill's efforts were really just symbolic, as these 'sympathetic gestures far outran O'Neill's ability or capacity to deliver real improvements in the circumstances' of the Catholics,[17] was either irrelevant to, or not grasped by, a growing number of Protestants. As Lemass travelled through NI, the firebrand Reverend Ian Paisley rallied Protestants against the meeting, throwing snowballs at his car as he passed, before leading a protest outside of Stormont parliament.[18]

The disproportionate response to such seemingly anodyne developments, as well as the ease with which Paisley was able to inflame loyalist sensibilities, speaks to the insecurities felt by Protestants in NI over the continued existence of their state and by extension their community. Indeed, the relationship between the Protestants and the NI state explains a great deal about why events unfolded as they did and was in large part shaped by events that occurred at the time that the state was born. Buckland has argued that when Ireland was partitioned, the British government was juggling three priorities: extricating itself from the crisis in Northern Ireland that had been fuelled by 'a strident Irish republicanism', but in so doing upholding promises to Ulster Unionists that they would not fall under 'Dublin rule' while also appearing 'relatively acceptable to Irish nationalists'.[19] The result of pursuing these disparate goals was 'that the governmental structure established in Northern Ireland was ill-thought-out and the new regional government and parliament were given responsibility without real power.'[20]

This precarious situation was exacerbated by developments south of the border. From 1921 to 1925 republicans orchestrated border raids and operations in Belfast, 'activities connived at by certain leading Free State politicians.'[21] Further, after the February 1932 general election Fianna Fáil formed a minority government in the South. The new President of the Executive Council, Éamon de Valera, was a devout Catholic and staunch republican who 'indulged in anti-partition rhetoric and tried to wring concessions from the imperial government.'[22] The anxieties of the Unionists were added to when, on 29 December 1937, the new constitution of Éire came into effect which 'formally claimed Northern Ireland as an integral part of Éire, asserting that the national territory consisted of the whole island of Ireland, its islands and its territorial seas'.[23] Moreover, De Valera's irredentist rhetoric was 'accompanied by, and may have encouraged, a revival of I.R.A. hopes and activities.'[24]

The Unionists found themselves in a position where they faced both internal and external threats to their new state's survival. Internally they faced the hostility of the NI Catholic community and the possibility of the labour movement turning even the Protestant working class against them to some degree. Further, they were inexperienced statesmen with limited political powers. Externally they were faced with the irredentist desires of the South and the ambivalent attitudes of the British towards the fate of Ulster. To deal with the former problem and stabilise their position, the Unionists attempted to forge a class alliance with the Protestant working class of NI against the threat of republicanism. To this end, 'the Unionist leadership increasingly 'exposed' the connection between socialism and republicanism, a process in which it was assisted by the British labour movement's (verbal) support for the national struggle.'[25] The Unionists and Protestant middle-class were successful in their endeavour, and they managed to sow antagonism between Catholic and Protestant workers to the extent that attacks on Catholic and Protestant socialists began and around 8,000 Catholic workers, and 1,500 protestant trade unionists, the so-called 'rotten prods', were expelled from their positions in the engineering and linen industries of Belfast.[26] Yet in forging the alliance, the Unionists had to cede some measure of their power to the 'Orange section of the working class'.[27] As Farrell observed, the 'Unionist bosses had ensured the loyalty of the Protestant masses. But it was at a price, the price of permanently maintaining discrimination and Protestant supremacy.'[28] These developments combined to produce a 'siege mentality'[29] amongst the

Protestant population of the North, and an NI state that was 'sectarian-populist' in character.[30] These were to be enduring features of Northern Ireland, and it is within this framework that Protestants interpreted the developments of the 1960s and onwards.

1966

1966 was a critical year for the increasing friction between Catholics and Protestants in Northern Ireland. It marked the fiftieth anniversary of both the Easter Rising and the Battle of the Somme, both of which 'brought hostile political traditions onto the streets of Northern Ireland', and was the year that O'Neill himself felt that things began to 'go wrong'.[31] The Republican tricolour was proudly displayed on houses throughout Catholic areas of Belfast for weeks either side of the Easter Rising commemorations, and Ian Paisley 'thundered against ecumenism and appeasement in response' throughout the spring and summer.[32] Genuinely concerned that the Easter Commemoration would see the IRA mobilised again, Paisley helped to found the Ulster Constitution Defence Committee (UCDC) to take whatever measures were necessary 'to maintain Northern Ireland's constitutional position within the United Kingdom', and which acted 'as an umbrella for the… Ulster Protestant Volunteers (UPV), whose numbers ran into many thousands'.[33]

The Ulster Protestant Volunteers, despite Paisley's protestations to the contrary, had more overtly paramilitary pretensions, and, more worryingly, had links with the newly formed Ulster Volunteer Force (UVF).[34] This latter group, who named themselves after the Protestant militia of 1912 and considered themselves to be 'the true inheritor of [their] predecessor's mantle', was by far the most alarming development of 1966.[35] The UVF was formed between April and May 1966 by a group of Protestants from the Shankill Road area of Belfast, who would meet every Thursday evening at the local Standard Bar,[36] and would be the first organisation to bring lethal sectarian violence back to the streets of Northern Ireland since the end of the IRA's Border Campaign in 1962. However, after murdering three people across May and June the organisation was proscribed and three of its members (including leader Augustus 'Gusty' Spence) were imprisoned for life.

Gusty has always claimed that he did not commit the murders, and, perhaps more interestingly, that the UVF was not formed by him in response to the rising threat from the IRA but by rogue elements within the Unionist Party who intended for it to be used as 'a bargaining counter against some of the things which O'Neill had brought out into debate.'[37] Novosel agrees with Gusty's case, although his only real evidence, beyond interviews with biased parties, is a Progressive Unionist Party policy document from 2002 which states that 'The UVF was reformed again in 1965 by concerned members of the Ulster Unionist Party (UUP) who opposed the liberalism of Terrence O'Neill, then Prime Minister of Northern Ireland.'[38]

Novosel's argument is not unconvincing but suffers from a lack of firm evidence. The relevance to this study, however, is the contention that the UVF was formed because of a conspiracy within 'Big House Loyalism' rather than in response to communal tensions, and was thus not a part of the dynamic of CE. But this argument suffers the same as most 'elite manipulation' arguments; that is, even if Novosel (and Gusty) are right that elite members of the UUP orchestrated the beginning of the UVF, they certainly did not create the very real and sincere feeling of sectarian antagonism that was driving people's behaviour on the streets. As Purdie noted, in '1966 communalist incidents took on a more serious character than usual. There was a clustering of cases of arson, desecration, violence and intimidation.'[39] Whoever created the UVF, they did not create this environment.

Both the emergence of the UVF and the heightening communal tensions point to the part that the symbolism of historic interactions between the two communities, and in particular the role that marches, parades and commemorations, helped to play in creating the conditions in which sectarian violence could occur. Kenney posits that in 'Northern Ireland, through ritual and folklore, the present and future are cast in the mold of the past… [and riots] sometimes accompany traditional marches and rallies, especially if the message is being delivered in a manner more challenging or aggressive than usual.'[40] Kenney's point is supported by the Northern Ireland Civil Rights Association (NICRA) who, in their official history, state that marches 'were therefore a physical manifestation of Northern Ireland politics and the recognised territorial divisions of the two sectarian groups meant that marching had become a form of sectarian one-up-man-ship.'[41] These marches and commemorations served to be a regular source of communal mobilisation, to exacerbate and entrench communal difference, and to bring the groups into direct contact with the 'communal other'.[42] Gusty Spence even claimed that the decision to turn to violence was influenced by the climate created by the lead up to the republican Easter Rising celebrations.[43]

This was fruitful territory for political entrepreneurs wishing to make capital out of the growing sectarian strife. Whereas John Tyndall and Martin Webster struggled to have their ideas of racial incompatibility find purchase amongst the white British population, and the SWP similarly struggled to have their class war find acceptance amongst the working class, Ian Paisley found it much easier to spread his divisive ideology. This demonstrates that the greater the extent to which social movements and SMOs are perceived to represent the interests of broader communities, and the greater the extent to which they can exploit extant societal divisions and animosities, the more likely that processes of CE will develop.

As militant Protestant groups were being mobilised, other forces were also propelling Catholics and civil rights activists into expressing their political aims on the streets. In particular the Northern Ireland Labour Party (NILP), which, throughout the 1960s had been 'moving towards more and more explicit endorsement of what were to become the civil rights demands',[44] had made a genuine and concerted effort to forge a 'radical, non-sectarian alternative' to the Unionist Party's hegemony.[45] However, due to an array of reasons including a deliberate effort by O'Neill to torpedo the project, the NILP failed by 1966, 'and its failure was one more factor in the inexorable process that was forcing opposition onto the streets.'[46] At a conference of the republican Wolfe Tone Society (WTS) in Maghera over the weekend of 13–14 August 1966 the decision was made to form what would arguably be the most important manifestation of this process, the Northern Ireland Civil Rights Association (NICRA).

1967

Formed on 29 January 1967, and then officially launched a few months later on 9 April, NICRA's initial thirteen-person steering committee consisted of people drawn from 'the Amalgamated Union of Engineering Workers, the CSJ, the Communist Party of Northern Ireland, the Belfast Wolfe Tone Society, the Belfast Trades Council, the Republican Clubs, the Ulster Liberal Party, the National Democratic Party, the Republican Labour Party, the Ardoyne Tenants Association and the NILP'.[47] As shall become apparent, the prominent presence of republicans in the creation of, and control over, NICRA made it difficult for the organisation, and the wider CRM, to portray itself as genuinely non-sectarian and accordingly it provoked fears amongst the Protestant community that it was really just a front for the republican movement aiming to unite Ireland. This would become a major influence on the development of CE over the coming years.

For the first eighteen months of its existence NICRA did very little in the way of direct action. One notable exception to this was their reaction to William Craig's decision, in March 1967, to ban the commemorations of the 1867 Fenian Rising and to proscribe the Republican clubs. Realising that 'a ban on street demonstrations was an effective Government weapon against political protest', NICRA took part in protest rallies against these measures.[48] A noteworthy aspect of NICRA's demonstrations was Ian Paisley's counter-rallies: on 8 March, when a march had been organised to Belfast City Hall in protest over Craig's bans, Ian Paisley

> announced that he was going to hold a public meeting of the Ulster Protestant Volunteers in Shaftesbury Square on the proposed route of the protest march. [However, at] the last moment it was decided to re-route the march to the home of the Minister of Home Affairs and thus avoid the possibility of a sectarian faction fight which Paisley hoped for.[49]

Whether or not a confrontation had been his aim is nothing but conjecture. But his confrontational tactics gave succour to both their causes, deepening and widening their support. This tactic of Paisleyites holding counter-demonstrations at the same time and place as civil rights marches to prevent them from proceeding became an increasingly prevalent pattern in Northern Ireland as NICRA, and the broader CRM, gathered momentum.[50]

Social movement scholars have noted that, by demonstrating the efficacy of mobilisation and threatening other groups' interests, social movements 'create the conditions for the mobilization of counter-movements.'[51] Moreover, particularly in their early stages, the degree to which a movement is successful influences the likelihood of them generating opposition: 'Movements that show signs of succeeding, either by putting their issues on the public agenda or by influencing public policy, are the most likely to provoke counter-movements.'[52] Further, through their constant confrontations, these groups also created the conditions for each other's increasing radicalisation. When groups regularly organise their actions in ways that are likely to bring them into close contact with opposing groups – for example, by organising mass demonstrations or public marches – then physical confrontation becomes much more likely. If these types of 'performances' become routinised and regularly involve physical confrontations then there is a risk that the actors will develop entrenched views of their opponents as 'essentially' bad, which can lead to them dehumanising them and further adding to their willingness to commit violence towards them.[53]

1968

In the summer of 1968, the civil rights organisation Derry Housing Action Committee (DHAC) was preparing for a protest action which would seriously escalate the situation in Northern Ireland. The plans were for a civil rights march in Derry on 5 October 1968, and the 'route was to lead across the centre of the city, from the Waterside, over the River Foyle, through the city walls to the Diamond. This would take the marchers, mostly Catholic, through traditionally Protestant areas.'[54] The DHAC was successful in convincing NICRA to sponsor the event, and it is likely that it would have only been these two groups, the local Labour party and Republican Clubs, as well as the radical Catholics and civil rights activists involved, as the more moderate elements were wary of these organisations; however, after William Craig banned the march, 'many prominent Nationalists and Catholic moderates turned up to take part',[55] suggesting that repressive measures towards perceived reasonable action will escalate situations such as this.

The loyalist Apprentice Boys of Derry announced that they would hold a march at the same time and place as the civil rights march. In defiance of both the government and the loyalists, on the planned day the CRM activists assembled at the Waterside railway station and began their march. They only managed to proceed for around 200 yards before they came into conflict with the RUC, who trapped the protest between two lines of police before using a water cannon and their batons indiscriminately against the civil rights marchers; among those batoned was prominent Westminster MP Gerry Fitt.[56] The chaotic scenes of state violence were captured on film and broadcast across the world, and this coverage 'changed the course of Irish history. The media gave widespread coverage to the unrestrained batoning by the RUC of civil-rights demonstrators, including MPs.'[57]

The immediate results of the events that occurred on 5 October 1968 was 'three days of rioting as flimsy barricades were erected and crowds of up to 1,000 people armed with bricks and the occasional petrol-bomb fought running street-battles with the RUC'.[58] But of more far-reaching consequence was the damage to community relations, the loss of faith in the state and RUC on the part of the Catholics, and the huge boon the television coverage provided to the civil rights movement; within weeks NICRA had branches in the majority of towns in Northern Ireland that had a large Catholic population, and several more civil rights organisations were formed.[59] Indeed, various commentators have argued that the 5 October march transformed the civil rights movement into an actual, country-wide, mass movement.[60] William Craig and other prominent Unionists defended the actions of the police as necessary in keeping order, and proportionate to the threat of sectarian violence presented by the civil rights marchers; furthermore, they claimed that the CRM was a 'Republican front.'[61]

The causal link between repressive police tactics and movement radicalisation has been well explored by social movement theorists,[62] and reinforces the observation that the most important actor in M/CM conflicts is almost always the state, rather than any social movement or organisation involved. Situations such as this are highly emotionally charged, and people previously sympathetic to the CRM may well have become much more inclined to become active. This dynamic would have likely been amplified by the fact that the RUC had, since its earliest days, been widely perceived as a Protestant organisation that operated in a partisan manner.[63] Likewise strong supporters of the government could have believed the state line that the problem was unruly Catholic troublemakers and thus have been more likely to become active in loyalist groups. Repressive policing can influence the emergence of CE in other ways too. De Fazio argues that 'when protesters, counterprotesters and state agents clash with relative regularity during protest events, a process of socialization to violence is likely to occur among activists. Being socialized to violence is part of the process of radicalization, as protesters are initiated into political violence and learn how to use it for self-defence, as well as for proactive purposes.'[64] Once socialised to violence, people may be more likely to use violence in general, rather than just in the circumstances in which the socialisation has occurred.

Immediately after the Derry march, which had occurred just before the start of the academic year, a sizeable group of radical Queen's University Belfast (QUB) students, motivated by the civil rights movement and the police violence at Derry, began to start organising protests. On 9 October 1968 three thousand students attempted to march from the university to the City Hall, but were ultimately frustrated in reaching their target because of a loyalist counter-demonstration; it 'was a classic case of the police restricting a legal civil rights demonstration because they had not been quick enough to prevent an illegal counter-demonstration.'[65] Later that day the students had a large meeting, out of which emerged the radical civil rights organisation that would be known as People's Democracy (PD). Their first action was to organise another march to the City Hall, on 16 October.[66] This time the 1,500 strong crowd of students actually reached their destination, despite opposition from a Paisleyite counter-demo of around 150 people, and the students were praised for their restraint and responsibility.[67]

A month later, on 16 November, in Derry, 1,500 civil rights activists led by the Derry Citizens' Action Committee (DCAC) defied a ban from Craig, who had proscribed all marches there for a month, and attempted to march through the city. Although they were prevented from proceeding by a large RUC force, the action inspired factory workers there to march in and around the city walls over the next few days in open defiance of Craig's ban.[68] The continued mobilisation of the Catholic population by the civil rights campaign provoked a similar reaction amongst some of the Protestant community who 'were being mobilised and politicised in opposition to the campaign.'[69] The relationship between the opposing social movements was now clearly very strongly coupled, as the actions of one group all but forced an oppositional response from the other. As their tactics were becoming more mirrored, it seemed probable that once one group started using violence regularly then so would the other. Indeed, by mid-November there were 'street battles every weekend [which] were beginning to have serious political repercussions.'[70]

In an attempt to calm down the situation, on 9 December O'Neill gave his famous 'Ulster at the Crossroads' speech on television, in which he warned that the Province was 'on the brink of chaos, where neighbour could be set against neighbour', and appealed to the civil rights movement to suspend their activities so as to 'allow an atmosphere favourable to change to develop'.[71] The speech seemed to be fairly successful, receiving both widespread public support and a cessation of activities from NICRA and the DCAC.[72] However, declaring that the CRM was 'in danger of great betrayal…from those who appeal for moderation' and that 'this is the moment when the movement must maintain its impetus; when the advantages gained must be pressed home with greater urgency', PD announced on 20 December that they would be holding another march from Belfast to Derry in the new year.[73]

1969

The PD's 'Long March', as it would become known, from Belfast to Derry was to be a transformative event. Setting off on the morning of Wednesday 1 January 1969, the march lasted four days and took the activists through many areas where they were met with highly aggressive resistance from Paisleyites, often led by Major Bunting (Paisley's right hand man), causing the RUC to reroute the activists.[74] By far the most shockingly violent attack against the protestors occurred on the last day of the march, 4 January, when they reached the

Burntollet Bridge on the road to Derry. Here around 200 loyalists waited in the field running adjacent to the road, where they had amassed piles of missiles the previous night to use in an ambush of the PD members. As the march approached they hurled rocks, bottles, and pieces of masonry at the young radicals. When the marchers tried to escape from the loyalist onslaught they were met with another group of loyalists, led by Major Bunting, who viciously attacked them with heavy blunt instruments. Through all of this the RUC, who were present, not only did nothing to help, but some of them were openly mingling with the loyalists; and, perhaps more worryingly, around half of the loyalists were in the Ulster Special Constabulary.[75]

The march had initially faced criticism from both NICRA, the main nationalist newspaper *The Irish News*, and the broader Catholic community for being an irresponsible action in the present climate, but the general consensus shifted towards full support for the march following the violent reaction of the loyalists and the failure to protect them on the part of the state.[76] The DCAC held a rally for the PD activists after their arrival into the city, which faced some trouble from loyalists, and after its conclusion there was severe rioting throughout Derry as communal tensions were brought to the fore by the events of the past four days, reinforcing della Porta's hypothesis that repressive police action can radicalise populations and lead to support for clandestine political violence.[77]

However, the 'most ominous feature of this was a breakdown in discipline by some policemen, who attacked shoppers in a city-centre supermarket and broke windows, kicked doors and sang sectarian songs in Catholic areas into the early hours of the morning.'[78] In response to this, the next day thousands of people gathered in the Bogside area where it was decided to organise vigilante patrols and raise barricades to prevent any more incursions by the RUC.[79] The barricades of 'Free Derry' were eventually brought down peacefully after the DCAC called for moderation, however the event radicalised many people and led to the emergence of a new community leadership 'which was not averse to violence'; this in turn created the conditions in which the few republicans in the area, who were even less averse to violence and illegal direct action, could take on more prominent roles and 'advance the Republican cause'.[80]

In this instance the civil rights radicals had been attempting to force the hand of the state by provoking a violent reaction from the loyalists. Farrell, the march organiser, has himself admitted he had wanted to expose the 'sectarian thuggery' of the NI state so that 'Westminster would be forced to intervene' (although the result was no doubt far in excess of what he had expected, or indeed, wanted).[81] The reaction of the loyalists, and parts of the NI security services, then radicalised sections of the Catholic community by reinforcing their view that the state was a Protestant one in which they were a disenfranchised minority. This allowed those more in favour of violent and illegal means to gain some purchase on the civil rights movement/Catholic community. This in turn reinforced loyalist fears over the claims that the civil rights movement was really a republican insurgency, thereby exerting a radicalising influence on them. As Ó Dochartaigh argues, the events of January 1969, and particularly the creation of Free Derry, both allowed republicans to begin 'to exert their influence', and also reinforced the Unionist/loyalist claim that 'at the very least...the civil rights campaign was being exploited by the IRA.'[82]

This dynamic is an example of a form of McCauley's 'Jujitsu Politics': causing provocation in the hopes that the 'state response, to the extent that it hurts or outrages those less committed than [the activists] themselves, does for [those activist] what they cannot do for themselves. This is Jujitsu politics: using the enemy's strength to mobilize against itself'.[83] McCauley refers explicitly to terrorists, but the same principle can apply to social movement activists and their rivals (which is exactly what happened at Burntollet), and this can then lead to 'vicarious retribution':

> when a member of a group commits an act of aggression toward members of an outgroup for an assault or provocation that had no personal consequences for him or her, but did harm a fellow ingroup member. In these situations, the retaliatory aggression is often directed at outgroup members who themselves were not the direct causal agents in the original attack against the person's ingroup. Thus, retribution is vicarious in the sense that neither the agent of retaliation nor the target of retribution were directly involved in the original event that precipitated the intergroup conflict.[84]

These are perhaps the two key mechanisms at the centre of CE. In this case, the PD provoked loyalists to highlight ineffectual state protection and thereby delegitimize Stormont and the suggested package of reforms. In actuality, it seems that the ferocity of the response that the PD marchers elicited from the loyalists took them wholly by surprise.[85] Regardless, the attacks 'on the march by Protestant workers automatically ensured Catholic support for it',[86] where before Catholics had been highly critical of the venture, and ultimately it ended in violence, barricaded communal enclaves, and clashes between the Catholics and the police.

In an interview in early 1969, the PD leaders discussed the movements' progress, with Michael Farrell stating that they had managed to mobilise the Catholic working class and got across 'to them the necessity of non-sectarianism and even the fact that their Protestant fellow worker is almost as much exploited as they are', however, Eamonn McCann disagreed, and argued, far more accurately, that

> I believe that we have failed to get our position across in the last six months. It is perfectly obvious that people do still see themselves as Catholics and Protestants, and the cry 'get the Protestants' is still very much on the lips of the Catholic working class. Everyone applauds loudly when one says in a speech that we are not sectarian, we are fighting for the rights of all Irish workers, but really that's because they see this as the new way of getting at the Protestants.[87]

That is not to say that the CRM *itself*, as opposed to elements of the Catholic community in general, had become sectarian in nature. Not only were leaders such as Farrell and Bernadette Devlin genuinely motivated by non-sectarian socialist ideals, but so also were most of the rank-and-file genuinely campaigning for civil rights rather than viewing the CRM movement as a 'new way of getting at the Protestants.' However, much of the Protestant population were affronted by the CRM regardless of how sincere their claims were. The truth was that many Protestants were just as impoverished as working-class Catholics, and they resented the way in which they felt that the CRM marginalised their hardships.[88]

A corollary of the claims and actions of the CRM, then, was to hold a mirror up to working-class Protestants' lives and social conditions, which gradually politicised them and led to a break between working-class loyalists and the middle and upper-class Unionists.[89] The class alliance which Unionists had fostered since the 1920s to maintain Protestant supremacy was not as robust as they would have liked, and the deepening crisis was opening old fault lines.[90] Hugh Smyth, who would go on to be a Progressive Unionist Party representative, described how

> There was a snap and all of a sudden your eyes had been opened… You see, for all too long, nobody ever questioned their political masters – that was the unseemly thing to do… When the troubles started we looked around us and there was no one to help… where was our politicians? They run [sic] away and left us…[91]

Working-class Protestants, increasingly concerned about the growing crisis, began to organise themselves into vigilante groups, paralleling the activities of Catholics in Free Derry. Growing tensions between the two communities came to breaking point a few weeks later. In Belfast a loyalist march passed the predominantly Catholic Unity flats on 2 August, provoking clashes between the two groups. Later that evening a crowd of several thousand Protestants then attacked the unity flats, resulting in 'the worst rioting in Belfast since 1935.'[92] Unusually, this rioting pitched Protestants against the RUC, leading to barricades being thrown up along the Shankill as the RUC attempted to restore order over the Protestant area; the 'loyal Shankill was now a community in rebellion'.[93]

As news of the Unity Flats riots spread to Derry, the newly formed Derry Citizens' Defense Association (DCDA) began collecting materials for barricades and weapons in preparation 'for expected attacks by the RUC and loyalists during the annual loyalist parade on 12 August'.[94] The Apprentice Boys of Derry, an offshoot of the Protestant Orange Order, declared that they would go ahead with their provocative annual march despite the tinderbox situation. At one o'clock, around 15,000 marchers, displaying Protestant and Orange symbols, began their traditional route around the city's walls, and 'tossed penny coins into the Bogside as a 'gesture of contempt' towards the Catholics below.'[95] Around an hour and a half later missiles began to be thrown from Catholic areas over the police lines at the marchers from the Bogside. The situation soon escalated as Catholics clashed with the RUC, the B Specials and loyalist groups.[96]

The rioting in Derry lasted for three days, but elsewhere in Northern Ireland Catholics held demonstrations in an attempt to divert the RUC's resources and thereby provide some respite to their coreligionists in Derry.[97] After several days of violent disorder throughout Ulster, eight people lay dead, around seven hundred 'people had been wounded or injured and nearly three hundred buildings [had been] destroyed or badly damaged.'[98] Furthermore, on 14 August the Stormont government had been forced to request assistance from Westminster, and later that day the 'first contingents of British soldiers took to the streets of Derry.'[99]

A key observation about the relatively spontaneous riots at the Unity Flats and at Derry is that these events further polarised the ethnic communities and strengthened and emboldened the extremist ethnic groups. Horowitz argues that 'states experiencing extensive riots are also likely to experience other kinds of political violence. It is easy to see why this is so. Ethnic violence can serve as the proving ground of extremist organisations, which sometimes provide its leadership. The riot may test their mettle, cement their *esprit de corps*, and aid their recruitment efforts.'[100] In Northern Ireland, there is little doubt that these riots contributed to the conditions under which the paramilitaries could eventually flourish.

Indeed, fitting with Horowitz's observation, the riots of August 1969 marked the unambiguous shift away from civil-rights oriented protests and demonstrations and loyalist led counter-protests to fully-fledged interethnic conflict. Although a key player in the developing conflict had been the state, and continued to be even more so with the arrival of the British Army (BA), the dynamic between the two ethnic communities had escalated through their violent interactions, particularly their marches and counter-marches which increasingly descended into riots. Reflecting on a widely read editorial in *The Times,* published after the August riots, which stated that politics in Northern Ireland was now driven by something 'primitive and volcanic, tribal fears and hatreds', Bourke argues that this common perspective on the situation misses the point, as 'the trouble had not risen from obscure historic depths [but was rather] the product of a set of recent circumstances where the burgeoning of modern democratic expectations had collided with the absence of democracy in Northern Ireland.'[101]

Bourke is correct that this is a hugely reductive argument which should not have gained the traction that it has; indeed, the most obvious flaw with an 'ancient hatreds' argument is its failure to explain why the violence should erupt at that point rather than at any other point during the nearly fifty years of the state's existence. However, Bourke's account is deficient in that he does not acknowledge the role that historical intercommunal relations *did* play in fuelling the escalating tactics. Just as Tarrow has pointed out that you 'are more likely to call an episode a revolution if your country experienced one in the past than if it never had one',[102] people are more like to perceive the collective action of an outgroup as hostile if there's recently been, or there is a recurring pattern of, violent conflict with that group. In NI, there had been a reoccurring pattern of violence perpetrated by (Catholic) republican and (Protestant) loyalist groups since the formation of the Province.

The rioting in the street and the clashes taking place between Catholics, loyalists and the RUC meant that the situation was now conducive for the IRA to begin to exert more influence over the Catholic population. There was a boost in recruitment, particularly in Belfast, but this very quickly led to internal strife as older IRA veterans who had previously left the movement argued that the IRA 'leadership had failed to defend nationalists', and existing members felt contempt over the perceived opportunism of the returning men: 'they thought the republic was going to be got without them… and they were afraid to be left out of it'.[103] This division only got worse, with the older Belfast IRA men feeling increasingly dissatisfied with the Dublin leadership, whose Marxist leanings had alienated much of the more conservative republicans in the north. However, the split was not along neat left–right ideological lines and had as much to do with laying blame for the unsatisfactory condition of Northern IRA units.

On 28 December these tensions came to a head, and a group of secessionists formally announced their existence as the Provisional IRA while claiming the support of the majority of volunteers (although outside of Belfast this was certainly not the case). 'There was now a frantic scramble to secure dumps and the controls of arms locally, and to bulk up support.'[104] As the IRA was splitting, and both wings were desperately trying to find weapons and train recruits,[105] the Protestants and loyalists were also mobilising. On 11 October, after a riot on the Shankill Road, RUC constable Victor Arbuckle was shot by loyalist gunmen; he was the first RUC man to be killed in the conflict.[106] Towards the end of 1969 'reports of widespread recruitment to the UVF were sufficient to raise alarm in Westminster.'[107]

1970

Commenting on the development of the Official IRA (OIRA, as the remaining group came to be known) and Provisional IRA, the PD criticised the latter for displaying 'the most backwards and hillbilly attitudes to the problems in the North, they are rabidly sectarian and nationalist in their outlook', and the former for being 'retarded by their tradition of being a militant clandestine army [which has led them to] consider political agitation to be of secondary importance'.[108] They argued that the violent approach displayed by both was counterproductive in that it both reinforced sectarian antagonisms and was pursued at the expense of serious political work.

PD were correct that sectarian antagonism was on the rise. The General Officer Commanding (GoC) of the British forces in Northern Ireland, General Freeland, had petitioned the British Prime Minister Heath and Home Secretary

Maudling to override Prime Minister of Northern Ireland Chichester-Clarke's decision to allow the annual communal marches to proceed, but the appeal was rejected.[109] An Orange march on 27 June 1970 through North Belfast precipitated rioting, and as this spread to the East of the city a UVF unit attacked St Matthew's Church on Newtownards Road, (part of a small Catholic enclave in a majority Protestant area) with guns and firebombs.[110] However, the Provisional IRA were more prepared than the republicans had been in 1969, and, armed with guns, fought a battle against the loyalists in defence of the Catholic church and the Catholic Short Strand area of East Belfast where it was situated.[111] The firefight, along with clashes in the north of the city, resulted in the deaths of five Protestants and one Catholic.

The Provisional IRA generated a great deal of goodwill from the Catholics of Belfast through their actions on Newtownards Road, and further legitimised their claims that they were the protectors of the nationalists in Northern Ireland.[112] Their reputation became an effective 'recruitment sergeant', and inevitably also served to widen the gulf between the two communities. As Catholics faced increasing discrimination and retribution for the Protestant deaths – around 500 Catholic workers were forced out of the Protestant dominated Harland and Wolff shipyard in the East of the city – the Officials criticised their rivals, arguing that 'the hatred and bitterness engendered by the killing of six Protestant civilians can only increase the likelihood of further pogroms'.[113]

There is some evidence that the Officials' criticisms were valid, as it seems that this incident indirectly contributed to the eventual formation of the Ulster Defence Association (UDA), the organisation that would go on to be the largest paramilitary group in Northern Ireland. Following the shootings on 27 June a meeting was held in the Protestant Woodvale area of Belfast, at which a group of Protestant men decided there was a need for loyalists to have military training. This was the beginning of the Woodvale Defence Association (WDA), and its example was soon followed by other groups of men elsewhere in Belfast; many of these groups would go on to unite as the UDA in September 1971.[114] While there had already been Protestant defence associations prior to this, the leap from vigilantism to paramilitarism seems to have been made here, in response to Catholics arming themselves.[115] This seems to be an example of della Porta's 'gradual reciprocal adaptation to increasingly dangerous weapons' mechanism.[116]

As the summer drew on, it was the British Army who became an increasingly prominent focus for, and cause of, the Catholic's ire. Only a few days after the 'Siege of St. Matthews' the Army conducted rigorous house searches throughout the Lower Falls Road area, looking for weapons dumps. This angered the locals who threw stones at the army as they left, cornering some, leading to reinforcements being called into the area. Soon three thousand troops occupied the Lower Falls Road and a curfew was imposed which lasted three days, during which time several houses, shops and businesses were searched and damaged.[117] This provoked a backlash from the Officials and the Provisionals, both of whom engaged in gun battles with the Army. Four Catholics were killed by the Army during the battle. This was a tremendous boon to the Provisionals, as it seemed to demonstrate the necessity of the physical force struggle and so pushed people towards the more militant republican group[118]; although for the time being the Lower Falls area would remain a stronghold of the Officials. This would by no means be the last time that the actions of the Army caused more support for the Provisionals than anything the republican or loyalist paramilitaries could do. Indeed, by 'the end of 1970 support for the Provisionals in Belfast was increasing in direct proportion to the weight of the British military presence in nationalist areas.'[119]

1971

In February 1971, elements of the civil rights movement noted that many of their aims – such as '[p]lural voting...for businessmen' and the disbandment of the B Specials – had actually been achieved.[120] But this had no moderating effect on the crisis, demonstrating that the issue of civil rights had been all but totally eclipsed by the dynamic of CE. Indeed, the violence was increasing sharply. In April the Provisional IRA detonated 37 serious explosions, 47 in May and 50 in June[121]; yet of far more significance in terms of intercommunal radicalisation/mobilisation was the murdering of three young off-duty Scottish soldiers.

On 10 March Dougald McCaughey, Joseph McCaig, and John McCaig, all members of the Royal Highland Fusiliers, were lured from the Belfast pub they were drinking in and murdered. The killings were widely condemned, and the IRA even denied involvement, but it was widely accepted that they were the perpetrators.[122] The killings mobilised huge numbers of Protestants onto the streets, many of whom felt a strong cultural connection to Scotland, demanding that further action be taken against the IRA. This generated enormous pressure on Prime Minister of NI James Chichester-Clark, who met with the British Home Secretary on 16 March in Westminster to discuss the worsening situation.[123] The British response to the situation was insufficient in Chichester-Clark's eyes, leading to his resignation and replacement by Brian Faulkner on 23 March.[124]

Faulkner's appointment did not stem the rising tide of violence. The following month participants of an Orange Lodge procession towards the Catholic enclave of Newtownards Road attacked some youths who had been shouting abuse at them and were consequently fired upon by Catholic adults in the area. Later that night a mob of around 2,000 loyalists once more attacked the area around St. Matthews church. This continued for the next week, 'with further attacks being launched against the chapel and the trouble even spreading to the Shankill Road.'[125] This intercommunal conflict was now becoming a self-sustaining cycle of violence, growing more lethal by the day. In De Fazio's words, the 'antagonist movement' for both sides 'and the spiral of violence and radicalization' had become a reason in and of itself to mobilise, over and above 'the original aim of mobilization'.[126] Sectarianism and revenge, as much as any republican or loyalist goals, became one of the main factors propelling the conflict and motivating the parties involved.

Indeed, becoming swept up in the currents of CE was becoming an increasingly prominent reason for people to join the different paramilitary organisations. Michael Stone, who would go on to join the UDA, stated that the eviction of some of his family members from their home by a mob of Catholics was the direct inspiration for both his membership of the paramilitary group and the burning hatred which fuelled his violent behaviour:

> This sectarian attack on my family sowed the seeds of hatred and resentment that would stay with me for most of my adult life… [and set him] on a path of no return, that would eventually take me to prison, or to my death.[127]

One of the Provisional leaders admitted that many of his recruits 'joined because they hated Protestants… [and the] actions of the Protestant murder gangs in the following years ensured that sectarian assassinations became part of the Provisionals' routine activities'.[128] English has observed that by 1971 it was no longer just the Army that was the target of paramilitary violence:

> Cycles of revenge and hatred involved defending your own community and avenging it upon its more local enemies too – in the chilling words of one north Belfast Provisional, looking over a Protestant area of the city: 'that's my dream for Ireland. I would like to see those Orange [Protestant or Loyalist] bastards just wiped out.' Sectarian influences played a vital part in moulding the thinking of the Provisionals.[129]

Nevertheless, the BA remained the most important player in the M/CM dynamic, capable of (unintentionally) exerting a huge radicalising effect over the population. The most significant example of the Army/State contributing to the wider dynamic of mobilisation and radicalisation up to this point was to occur in August when they introduced internment. Faulkner had been minister for home affairs during the IRA's 1956–62 border campaign, which had been tackled with the introduction of internment both sides of the border, and he was keen to attempt the same thing again. On 9 August 1971 the British Army began Operation Demetrius, with the aim of interning IRA members, and predictably provoked an enormous reaction from the Catholic population. The Officials commented that:

> The raids by the British Army and the RUC Special Branch in the North were accompanied by the now usual assaults of men, terrorising of women and children, stealing of personal possessions from the working class homes, and wrecking of the houses. The only apparent result of this viciousness

has been to increase the determination of the people to resist, and to show who represents the major threat to the security of British imperial exploitation of Ireland.[130]

And the Provisionals similarly stated that:

> In a last desperate gamble, Mr Faulkner and Mr Heath decided to introduce the Special Powers Act of Internment without trial or charge ... Since August 1969 the British government and the Stormont government were warned by the minority that if internment was brought in they would resist violently. As can be seen, the minority reacted as threatened and a massive resistance campaign began with the return of the barricades and full scale rioting.[131]

Both groups were fairly accurate in their appraisal of the boost to the support of the republican movement the Army's actions had given. Indeed, it had been a disastrous move on the part of the state, 'the arrests were ineffectual from the point of view of security while the measures wildly exacerbated existing Catholic estrangement.'[132] Interestingly, Michael Farrell argues that this marked the point at which the majority of the Catholic population shifted from supporting the civil rights movement and calling for reform within the existing state to wanting to 'destroy it.'[133]

The aftermath of Operation Demetrius certainly saw deep and lasting damage to the relationship between the two communities.[134] It was not just the republicans who experienced a boost in support, as the explosion of Catholic violence reinforced Protestant fears that 'the very structures of security and government that had protected them would be pulled down.'[135] The actions of the state in interning suspected IRA members added a huge stimulus to the dynamic of CE. Accordingly, there was a significant increase in both republican and loyalist violence.[136] On 12 August the Officials and the UVF fought gun battles on the Grosvenor Road, and the following day both the Officials and Provisionals cooperated with each other as they engaged in firefights with both the UVF and the British Army.[137]

With regard to the loyalists, up until Operation Demetrius there had been no more 'than a score of active UVF men', but the 'explosion of Catholic violence that followed internment in August was to change that.'[138] Not only did new recruits flock to the UVF, but 'protestant vigilante groups sprang up everywhere',[139] and the following month many of these groups coalesced into the UDA.[140]

Across the summer of 1971 a series of sectarian attacks were perpetrated by the PIRA and loyalist groups. Processes CE continued to displace organisations' explicitly stated goals, e.g. a united Ireland and the expulsion of British troops from the country, as they became embroiled in cycles of violent revenge.[141] A series of lethal tit-for-tat bombings were carried out by the PIRA and UVF across November and December, culminating in the Provisionals detonating a car bomb in a busy shopping area on the Shankill Road, killing two adults and two young children. 'Many Shankill men who subsequently joined the paramilitary ranks say they were in the vicinity and most of them recount the same story: of a dead child still in its buggy and a headless infant corpse.'[142]

As well as the M/CM conflict escalating, the relationship between the British Army and the IRA(s) was also strongly affected. Before internment was introduced, the British Army killed seven people in 1971: five Catholic civilians and two members of the PIRA.[143] From 9 August onwards the British Army killed 37: six PIRA members and 31 Catholic civilians. The PIRA killed nine British soldiers before internment in 1971, and 27 after.[144] The Officials killed one soldier before, and four after.[145] The introduction of internment clearly caused the dynamic between all parties involved in the contest to develop in an increasingly lethal direction.

1972

1972 witnessed the peak in violence of the troubles in terms of sectarian killings, but it was also without 'doubt the year of the Provos. Never again would the IRA be as strong as it was that year and never again would it come as near to achieving its military goal, forcing the British out of Northern Ireland.'[146] Despite these dangerous circumstances, once again the actions of the British Army escalated the situation and mobilised more people under the banners of paramilitary groups than any single incident of sectarian violence. On 30 January 1972 NICRA organised a march through Derry, which attracted thousands of participants. Anticipating that the IRA would be drawn on to the streets for the march, the British commanding officer sent the elite First Parachute Regiment to police the event. As the marchers approached the British soldiers, some of them began throwing missiles at the soldiers who retaliated with excessive force. Within an hour 'thirteen men lay dead and seventeen wounded, one of whom died a few weeks later. None were in the IRA, and eyewitness testimony said they had been killed in cold blood.'[147] The day famously became known as Bloody Sunday.

Once again there was a violent and widespread reaction to what was perceived as British oppression, with even more Catholics swarming to join the ranks of republican paramilitary groups.[148] South of the border in Dublin, the British Embassy was besieged and firebombed in response.[149] However, perhaps the most dramatic result of Bloody Sunday was that Faulkner and his ministers resigned, and at the 'end of March the parliament and government of Northern Ireland were prorogued, and their powers transferred to Westminster and to a secretary of state.'[150] In retaliation for Bloody Sunday, the following month the Officials detonated a bomb at the Parachute Regiment's HQ in Aldershot, England. However, the operation was a public relations disaster, as they only succeeded in killing seven civilians including a Catholic priest.[151] Later, on 25 May, OIRA members abducted and killed a 19-year-old Catholic from Derry called Ranger Best who was home on leave from the British Army. This was yet another blunder; the young man, who 'had been known to join his friends in the Provisionals in throwing stones at the British Army'[152] in his youth, had been a local to the Creggan area of Derry, and his murder 'provoked several hundred "enraged women" from Catholic nationalist and republican areas to march on Derry's Official IRA Headquarters'.[153]

Shortly after the Aldershot and Ranger Best incidents, and the backlash both incidents had incurred, a meeting of the OIRA commanding officers was held over the weekend of 27–28 May to discuss the merits of a ceasefire. The response to Best's murder was seen as indicative of a growing distaste for violence amongst the Catholic community.[154] However, beyond this, the OIRA were much more concerned over the rising tide of sectarian violence than their rivals in the Provisionals. The UDA, which was still a legal organisation, 'had held its first mass rallies during May, at which thousands of masked men paraded in military fashion' and the number of Catholic civilians being murdered was rising steeply.[155] The OIRA announced a ceasefire on 30 May 1972, stating that they would limit their military operations to defensive actions.[156]

The prorogation of Stormont and the introduction of home rule had been a major aim of the PIRA (and, indeed, the entire nationalist community), and this apparent victory, along with the massive fillip in support they experienced following Bloody Sunday, further emboldened them in their war against the British. They detonated thirty bombs in Northern Ireland on 14 April alone, and conducted over a thousand operations in May,[157] killing at least forty people.[158] In response, loyalists set up 'no-go' areas similar to those that had been set up in Catholic areas, with over 160 barricades patrolled by UDA members being set up between 9 and 11 June. Furthermore, the UDA began to terrorise the Catholic community in an attempt to scare them away from supporting the IRA, by kidnapping, torturing and killing randomly selected Catholics, almost all of whom had no connection to the IRA.[159]

Part of the impetus for this strategy was the fact that the UDA, despite its now impressive size which now numbered in the thousands,[160] did not have 'the firepower to take on either the army or the IRA' and so the Inner Council argued 'the case for 'producing an equal or greater amount of terror among [the IRA's] followers than they can among us,' an ominous justification of the serial killing of Catholics already taking place.'[161] Further, the UVF was developing its fighting cadres and they were just as enthusiastic in their approach to sectarian murders.[162] The Provisionals had, since their inception, presented themselves as the protectors of the Catholic population (and for the most part had acted in what they considered to be a genuinely non-sectarian manner), but after the loyalist sectarian killings began, the Army Council 'sanctioned the use of retaliation' which ultimately 'amounted to authorising revenge killings.'[163] The reality of the situation was that the Provisionals were not capable of protecting Catholics from the random loyalist kidnappings and murders, and so their 'only effective tactic was to convince the loyalists that their campaign was futile by engaging in random killings in return… With each killing and reprisal the horror seemed to deepen.'[164]

This demonstrates that the relationship between the opposing SMOs and their social base is a fundamentally important aspect of the development of CE. As stated earlier, the chances of an M/CM contest escalating to include lethal force increase to the extent that the opposing SMOs are perceived as both representing the interests of a wider community and also threatening the interests of another community. But once the threshold of lethal violence has been passed, and groups are committed to using deadly tactics, if an SMO is strongly associated with or supported by a community then that group becomes a target for the SMO's enemies. Not only are they easier to attack, being on the whole unarmed and not trained in the military arts, but also attacking them is perceived as a way of cutting off support for the paramilitary organisations they have links to. However, when attacking their enemy's social base, an SMO (e.g. the UDA) then provides members of that community (e.g. the Catholics of NI) with motivation (e.g. revenge and/or protection) for joining the SMO associated with their community (e.g. the PIRA). As CE develops, then, and civilian populations become the focus of violence, the grounds are laid for the dynamic's perpetuation.

On Friday 21 July one of the most disastrous events in the Provisionals' history occurred. The PIRA detonated between nineteen and twenty-six car bombs throughout Belfast within the space of an hour. 'Nine people were killed and a hundred and thirty injured' on the day which would notoriously come to be known as 'Bloody Friday'.[165] At the time, the PIRA attempted to shift the blame onto the security forces, arguing, unconvincingly, that:

> IN EVERY CASE AT LEAST 30 MINUTES WARNING WAS GIVEN…
> The only conclusion one can come to is that the authorities, seeing that they were failing to beat the people and the IRA, callously allowed civilians to remain in the danger areas intending to use the resulting injuries and deaths as propaganda in their war against the struggle for liberation.[166]

However, this account has since been disputed by Brendan Hughes, the commander of the Bloody Friday operation.[167]

The aftermath of Bloody Friday was disastrous for the republican movement. In the first place, nationalist opinion towards the PIRA armed campaign became increasingly negative,[168] as it had already started to following the prorogation of Stormont and the car bombs detonated in Derry and Claudy.[169] Secondly, the mechanism of 'vicarious retribution' went into full effect, and there was a huge influx of recruits into loyalist paramilitaries eager to enact violent revenge on the republicans, not to mention the Catholic population in general.[170] The pages of *Loyalist News* raged that:

> We the Loyalist people of Ulster have known all along, and to our cost, what the IRA and the people who support them, namely the Roman Catholic minority of this Province, are capable of doing… the only way

to beat the terrorists is to hit them hard again and again. We know where they operate from and who they are, so let's go and get them, before another outrage happens…ATTACK NOW…CLEAR THEM OUT… DEATH PENALTY TO THOSE CAUGHT WITH GELIGNITE.[171]

However, the worst consequence of Bloody Friday to the operational ability of the PIRA was the justification it gave to the state to decisively act against them. 'The British quickly realized that events had moved to their advantage [after the damage Bloody Friday did to the IRA's popularity and legitimacy, and ten] days later, on July 31,'[172] they executed 'Operation Motorman', which involved large numbers of troops invading the previously republican 'no-go' areas of Derry and Belfast,[173] an operation which would have been potentially disastrous prior to Bloody Friday.[174] In a very short time military forts were constructed in the middle of former IRA strongholds, severely curtailing their operational capability.

Although the Army was now moving swiftly and decisively against the PIRA, they were far more conservative in their response to the emergence of the UDA[175] This was possibly because the two wings of the IRA had killed seventy-nine soldiers that year and so had stretched the Army's resources thin; further, the UDA did not claim responsibility for the deaths of the Catholics they murdered,[176] making them a more difficult group to combat. Also, throughout at least some of 1972, Westminster viewed the actions of the UDA as 'comparatively harmless vigilante activity'.[177] This view was arguably highly inaccurate when one considers that the month following Operation Motorman a Catholic woman named Sally McClenaghan's house was invaded by UDA members who raped and shot her before murdering her 14-year-old son.[178]

Another reason for the government's softer view of the loyalist organisation could well be the existence of a certain degree of collusion between loyalist groups and the security services. Cadwallader has pointed out that some of the weapons used to assassinate Catholics, such as the '1958 Model 36 Mills hand grenade' which was thrown through the window of the Catholic Connolly's family home in Portadown, killing Patrick Connolly, was 'used exclusively by British and commonwealth forces'.[179] 'Intelligence reached the RUC Criminal Investigation Department (CID) that an ex-serviceman in Portadown was the most likely source [of the weapons]. He was neither arrested nor interviewed.'[180] It was soon established that 'loyalists were routinely taking guns from British armouries', and a British Army internal investigation report concluded that the 'possibility of collusion is therefore highly probable'.[181]

Later that year, In August 1972, the Provisionals claimed that:

The inner council of the UDA have recently made their public debut. Although they have aped the IRA in manner and dress – note combat jackets, sunglasses, facial disguises – there the resemblance ends. The UDA specialise in assassinating Catholics, and as is suspected, Protestants who are 'too' friendly with Catholics.[182]

While this is a fair description of the levels of indiscriminate violence being employed by the UDA, who by this stage were 'outkilling the UVF',[183] this was nonetheless somewhat hypocritical of the republicans. The truth is that both movements had become extremely tightly coupled *and* did not just ape each other in 'manner and dress' but in lethal tactics as well. By this stage both republican and loyalist groups had embraced the widespread use of categorical sectarian murders, and across 1972 loyalists killed around 83 Catholic civilians while republican groups were responsible for the assassination of around 49 Protestant civilians.[184]

In October 1972 the UVF planned an operation to detonate bombs in the Republic so as to dampen the support that the PIRA was receiving south of the border. So far the PIRA's tactic of instilling terror through the use of car bombs had been restricted to the North, but the 'UVF determined that this should change, bringing the IRA's tactic of city centre car bombings south.'[185] As violence from the Troubles began bleeding over into the South, the Dublin Government was debating over whether to introduce new emergency legislation which 'allow detention for questioning without charge for seven days and imprisonment for membership of an illegal organisation on the word of a senior Garda officer'.[186] The bombs were extremely well timed, and the legislation passed through with huge public approval due to the misconception that the PIRA had perpetrated the acts. The UVF's plan had worked, and the Republic's new legislation became a major thorn in the side of the IRA.[187]

By the end of 1972, 480 people had been killed, and between the beginning of the troubles in 1969 and the end of 1972 693 people had been killed. At the end of 1972, the year which bore witness to more deaths than any in the Troubles, the civil rights movement was effectively dead and buried. NICRA carried on trying to achieve its goals, but the more important groups to the two communities were now the paramilitary organisations doing the killings.

1973

Across January and February 1973 around eighteen civilians were murdered by loyalists.[188] This wave of assassinations resulted in the first loyalists being interned on 5 February, which in turn provoked a violent backlash from the Protestant community in much the same way that the introduction of internment for republicans had amongst Catholics years earlier; though, it should be noted that only two loyalists were interned compared with the 342 Catholics that were interned in 1971.[189] There was rioting in Belfast and firefights in which several people were killed.[190] On 7 February, a two day general strike was called by William Craig under pressure from several loyalist groups such as the UDA and the Loyalist Association of Workers (LAW).[191] While the strike was successful in disrupting public transport and causing some power outages, it was also accompanied by violence, with four people dying as a result.[192] The strike was 'widely condemned by the Protestant population.'[193]

Extending the policy of internment without trial to loyalists and Protestants was not the only intervention that the British had up their sleeves. A referendum was held on 8 March to establish whether the people of NI wanted to remain a part of the UK. The poll was boycotted by the Nationalist community, meaning that it essentially became a referendum of the Protestant community's feelings on remaining a part of the UK, with entirely predictable results. Of the 59% of the population who did take part, 99% voted in favour of remaining within the UK.[194] Even with virtually the entire Nationalist community boycotting the referendum, the Secretary of State for Northern Ireland William Whitelaw still felt that this 'result cleared the way for a new experiment in devolved government'.[195]

On 20 March Westminster published a White Paper in which it was proposed that there should be a 'Northern Ireland Assembly of about 80 members elected' which should include 'committees…whose members will reflect the balance of parties, associated with each Northern Ireland Department.'[196] This 'shared assembly' would, then, include both Unionists and nationalists; although Britain would retain control over certain sensitive matters and 'exceptional measures in the law and order field'.[197] An important suggestion included in the White Paper was the 'establishment of institutional arrangements for consultation and co-operation between Northern Ireland and the Republic of Ireland'.[198] Two of the objectives of this 'Council of Ireland' were to be 'the acceptance of the present status of Northern Ireland, and of the possibility – which would have to be compatible with the principle of consent – of subsequent change in that status.'[199] Although this was clearly meant to reassure all parties, Catholic and Protestant, 'the psychological impact of the Dublin link was to prove fatal to the entire White Paper vision.'[200]

On 3 May the 'Northern Ireland Assembly Act' became law, and on 28 June the Assembly elections were held. Those in favour of power-sharing gained a majority, and Faulkner was able to secure an agreement 'from the SDLP and the Alliance to the formation of a devolved executive which he would lead as Prime Minister with Gerry Fitt of the SDLP as his deputy'.[201]

Likely in response to progress being made on the power-sharing project, the paramilitaries increased the intensity of their violent campaigns. This was particularly true of the UVF, who significantly increased their attacks on Catholics and their businesses.[202] The increase in UVF attacks was partly facilitated by their ties to the Ulster Defence Regiment (UDR) – a regiment of the British Army that recruited specifically from Ulster and had been founded to replace the hated B Special militia – and the RUC. Indeed, the British government was becoming increasingly concerned over the level of loyalist involvement in the security services, and in August commissioned a report titled 'Subversion in the UDR'. As Cadwallader notes, the 'findings were hair-raising – or they should have been, given that the UDR was increasingly being deployed in Catholic areas.'[203]

Among the more concerning conclusions in the report were that since 'the beginning of the current campaign the best single source of weapons…for

Protestant extremist groups has been the UDR', with 190 UDR weapons 'lost' or stolen during 1972 compared to 16 regular Army weapons:

> We believe that the vast majority of weapons stolen from the UDR during this period are in the hands of Protestant extremists ... In no case is there proof positive of collusion: but in every case there is considerable suspicion, which in some instances is strong enough to lead to a judgment that an element of collusion was present ... It is likely that there remain within the UDR significant numbers of men (perhaps 5–15%) who are, or have been, members of Protestant extremist organisations.[204]

The issue of collusion once again raises the question of the state's role in both M/CM conflicts in general and the dynamic of CE in particular. The direct interactions between state forces and clandestine SMOs often occurred in the realm of what the journalist Martin Dillon terms 'the Dirty War': 'the war which takes place in the shadowy world of agents, double agents and informers; the world in which intelligence agencies and terrorists seek to outwit and kill each other.'[205] This is not an area in which the state acted with parity towards the opposing social movements.[206] Bruce points out that in a lethal M/CM conflict one can often label the various actors as 'anti-state' and 'pro-state' terror groups, and if a state engages in acts of terror then that can be labelled as 'state terror'.[207] This observation has two implications on the development of CE.

Firstly, this may mitigate the even development of CE because it places the pro-state group in competition for recruits with the state security services. If Protestants wanted to defend their communities and homes from the threat of the republicans then they could join the RUC or UDR rather than the UVF or UDA; a decision which would bring them a well-paid job and some level of prestige in their community without the risk of being imprisoned. The republican paramilitaries, on the other hand, had 'access to all sections' of the Catholic working class.[208] This gives the anti-state group an advantage over its counter-movement. Furthermore, the fact that loyalists and the security forces shared a social base made it easier for the latter to infiltrate the former (although, as we have seen, it also made the reverse true).

Secondly, and conversely, what Campbell terms the 'public-private mix' of acts of terror – that is, the spectrum of pro-state and state terror acts – became an important aspect of CE in Northern Ireland.[209] In terms of those acts positioned in the middle of the spectrum – combined state and pro-state acts of terror – it has become increasingly clear that state collusion happened at fairly senior levels (on which more later), something which the Catholic community became increasingly sure of over this period.[210] Purely 'private' acts of terror – those perpetrated by loyalists and republicans without input from the state – have been discussed earlier, and will be dealt with again later. But purely 'public' state acts of terror possibly contributed to the radicalisation of moderates and the mobilisation of radicals in much the same way as 'public-private' ones. One such agency who, it has been alleged, carried out such acts was the Military Reconnaissance Force (MRF) of the British Army. The MRF was led by elite special forces soldiers, operated in civilian clothes and vehicles,[211] and was linked to various shootings in nationalist areas which were initially thought to be perpetrated by loyalists.[212] Indeed, Rolston argues that one of the main tasks of MRF units was 'the policy of drive-by shootings in republican areas.'[213] In November 2013 the BBC's *Panorama* documentary series aired an episode in which a number of (alleged) former MRF soldiers anonymously admitted to, amongst other things, killing unarmed civilians.[214]

These acts obviously had a direct influence on the nationalist community. On 3 February 1973 six Catholics, three civilians and three PIRA volunteers, were murdered in what has been alleged to have been an MRF operation.[215] The PIRA claimed that this was the work of 'British Army snipers' and 'loyalist gunmen', and stated that 'all this evil and suffering is caused because of British occupation and oppression in Ireland, and until we are rid of that we can never have peace'.[216] Other nationalists from the New Lodge area declared that the event

> only steels us in our resolve to struggle endlessly until finally we achieve our country united and free from the shackles of British Imperialism… Long live the memory of the men who died in the New Lodge massacre. Your deaths further confirm the justice of our cause.[217]

Many Catholics were in no doubt that this was an intentional and indiscriminate attack on their community by the Army or a loyalist/Army team.

State-terror and 'public-private' terror, or collusion, alienated the Catholics and eroded trust in law and order. This situation was exacerbated by the knowledge amongst the Catholics that Brigadier Frank Kitson's books *Low Intensity Operations: Subversion, Insurgency and Peacekeeping* and *Gangs and Counter-Gangs* had become the British Army's manuals for managing counterinsurgency operations.[218] Kitson described in his books his successes in dealing with insurgencies in British colonies by forming 'Counter-gangs' and 'pseudo gangs' from members of the local population to help gather information and sow disinformation, as well as for use 'as an offensive weapon' by 'killing terrorists'.[219] That this was interpreted by many Catholics in NI as tacit acknowledgement of British involvement with loyalist paramilitaries should come as no surprise. Indeed, the Social Democratic and Labour Party (SDLP) politician Paddy Devlin argued that Kitson 'probably did more than any other individual to sour relations between the Catholic community and the security forces'.[220] This connection between loyalist paramilitaries and British security services both legitimised the Provisionals as the 'defenders' of the Catholic community and quite possibly encouraged some to actively join them. Further it is at least likely that covert co-operation between loyalists and state forces emboldened and encouraged the former in their sectarian campaign. This demonstrates one of the more direct ways in which the state's interventions into M/CM conflicts can produce processes of CE.

Progress towards the finalisation of the power-sharing Executive for NI continued apace. On 9 December 1973 the Sunningdale Agreement was signed by the Prime Minister, the Taoiseach, and the Northern Ireland Executive. Brian Faulkner was there representing the pro-assembly Unionists (a minority faction within the Unionist Party), and he was joined by members of the SDLP and the Alliance party.[221] The agreement had something for each party: the Unionists could legitimately claim that they achieved the acceptance of the Northern Irish state from the Irish Government. On top of this, the 'British Government solemnly declared that it was, and would remain, their policy to support the wishes of the majority of the people of Northern Ireland.'[222] For the SDLP there was the promise of the 'Council of Ireland' which would consist of 'representatives of the two parts of Ireland'.[223]

1974

The Sunningdale Agreement had an interesting effect on the M/CM dynamic. While it had initially created an impetus for the paramilitaries to increase their use of violence in the hopes of derailing it, it also briefly mitigated CE by fostering an atmosphere in which the loyalists and republicans attempted to find common ground as the basis of their own political solution. This was first demonstrated on 18 November 1973, as arrangements were still being made for the Agreement, when the UVF 'and its subordinate groupings commenced a cessation of aggressive military activity so that it could devote more time and energy to seek a political solution to the present crisis in Ulster.'[224]

Although none of the other paramilitaries, republican or loyalist, reciprocated the UVF's gesture, there was agreement on both sides of the divide that Sunningdale needed to be opposed (even if they did have different reasons for believing this). In January 1974 the Official IRA stated that the

> ruling classes of Britain and Ireland agreed to impose a federal 'solution' on the Irish people at Sunningdale. Their meeting was planned in secret, held in camera and surrounded by mystifying clouds of stage-managed publicity. The agreement is being pushed on the people with a combination of lies and blackmail. It will not succeed…[225]

The UDA, unsurprisingly, was more concerned over the inclusion of the Council of Ireland in the agreement, claiming that the

> Republic of Ireland will shortly have legal jurisdiction over the citizens of Northern Ireland. Before the Sunningdale Agreement the Republic could only claim jurisdiction in THEORY. The new Commission on LAW for the 32 counties now makes this a reality… Some of you after careful thought may be prepared to accept a United Ireland. That's fair enough. We intend to FIGHT whatever the cost to ourselves or our families. We would like to know just how many are prepared to stand and fight with us.[226]

The consensus that Sunningdale must be opposed seemed to present an opportunity for the republican and loyalist paramilitaries to find some common ground and attempt to pursue a political rather than military solution. The basis for this apparent potential for political dialogue between the opposing movements was the idea, touted by renowned Unionist politician and barrister Desmond Boal, of a 'federal' or 'amalgamated' Ireland which would be united but would also allow Ulster a degree of sovereignty.[227] This solution was somewhat similar to the Provisionals' own idea of *Éire Nua* which had been officially adopted by the PIRA in 1971.[228] *Éire Nua* had called for Ireland to be divided into a federation of four provinces with each area possessing devolved powers under a national parliament; crucially, to ease Unionist concerns, Ulster was one of these provinces. After Boal first suggested his idea there was a brief outpouring of effusive praise for the idea from elements within both the republican and loyalist camps.

The PIRA went so far as to declare on the front page of *An Phoblacht*:

> LOYALISTS AND REPUBLICANS ON WAY TO PEACE
> … The Republican Movement is confident that there exists firm grounds for reconciliation and peace now between its aspirations and the propositions announced by Boal and endorsed by several of the 'loyalist' groups.
> If these favourable overtures can be fostered, peace and a real settlement is at hand.[229]

Adding that

> A much clearer vision of a new Ireland was offered before and is now being offered again. Desmond Boal's plan provides grounds for negotiations between the I.R.A. and militant Loyalists.
> It has much common ground with other Loyalist leaders, notably John Taylor, who thinks on the lines of a Nine County Independent Assembly for Ulster and with Sinn Féin's idea of a federal structure of government.[230]

In later issues of *An Phoblacht* the Provisionals attempted to further demonstrate the potential for loyalist/republican cooperation. For example, they claimed that it had 'been welcomed by the "men of violence" in the IRA, the UVF and the UDA as a "talking point", and should be rejected only for very good reasons.'[231]

In the pages of *Combat* the UVF stated that they had

> …committed [themselves] to working for the establishment of a federal system…
> The Federal solution as looked at reasonably by both loyalists and republicans is the only sane solution to the Irish question.[232]

They also argued that 'Sectarian violence is the most powerful and vicious weapon in the hands of the pre-Sunningdale politicians… the greatest danger to the implementation of the Sunningdale Agreement is the growing movement amongst the paramilitary organisations towards seeking a political solution.'[233]

These statements were not simply bluster. There were some influential voices within the UVF calling for dialogue with the republicans, including UVF founding member Gusty Spence and the editor of *Combat* Billy Mitchell.[234] To this end, secret meetings were arranged between the UVF and both the Officials and the PIRA in February 1974, and some small progress seemed to have been made in these talks.[235] For instance, in one memo from these talks the UVF seemed to concede that the British were indeed legitimate targets for the republicans, stating to the PIRA that: 'If the Provisional IRA wish to combat British imperialism, we believe that they should direct their bombs and bullets against the armed British forces…and not against the Ulster businessman and worker.'[236] Another memo from the meetings with the PIRA suggests that there was some working-class solidarity between the groups, with the UVF delegates stating that they had had enough 'of the fur-coat brigade and were resolved to seek some form of government and leadership that excluded the landed gentry and upper/middle class. The UVF men stated that they saw no difference between green Tories and orange Tories, between the fur-coat brigade and the castle Catholics; they wanted no more to be cannon-fodder for the politicians. The Provisionals agreed on this part too.'[237]

However, ultimately Boal's ideas could not bridge the opposing aims each side had. Even during their attempt to promote Boal's ideas, the PIRA published Michael Farrell's observation that:

> Republicans of all shades have fallen over themselves to welcome the Boal plan…Most of this has been based on wishful thinking, praising him for the things he didn't say…He did not advocate the withdrawal, immediate or otherwise, of British troops…
>
> What Boal did say was that, if Britain was intent in getting out of the North, he would support an amalgamated Ireland with a provincial parliament in the North, 'possessing the powers recently held by Stormont'. And he made clear that he was 'concerned fundamentally with the Protestant community and the preservation of its way of life.'[238]

For their part, the UVF was only interested in Boal's idea to the extent to which it facilitated their continued status as a part of the UK. Further, having been excluded from these talks, the UDA began to sense that 'the UVF was taking some kind of leap forward', and so they intensified their attacks on Catholics including 'a number of bombings for the first time' in a bid to disrupt any progress possibly being made.[239] Moreover, the UVF men involved in these talks were not speaking for the whole organisation, and many of their comrades (and other loyalists and Unionists) would have been very hostile to these talks. Gusty Spence himself felt that the main reason they folded was the uncompromising attitude of some of his fellow Protestants: 'There need not have been any loss of principle, but the super-Prods would not wear it so all further talks with the IRA were hit on the head.'[240]

In the literature on peace processes, parties involved in a conflict who have a vested interest in derailing a negotiated political solution are called 'spoilers'.[241] 'Outside spoilers' are parties who have been excluded from negotiations. This exclusion creates an incentive for them to use 'overt violence as a strategy toward undermining peace', as any settlement would exclude their interests and threaten their existence.[242] This theory usefully explains the behaviour of both republican and loyalist groups as news of a peace process emerged: if their interests were going to be ignored than they would use the most effective tool at their disposal – violence – to 'spoil' it; indeed, as shall be seen, the exclusion of the paramilitaries by the government was the downfall of the Sunningdale Agreement. An interesting observation here though, and an addition to the literature on 'Spoilers' and peace processes, is that the closed structure of political opportunity did not just provoke a violent response from the 'outside spoilers', but also channelled *some* of their efforts towards at least *attempting* to develop their own alternative political solution.

In February 1974 a General Election was held, returning a minority Labour government to office. In Northern Ireland the election was widely seen as a referendum on the Sunningdale Agreement, and while the pro-power-sharing parties had not thought to band together with an electoral coalition, the anti-power-sharing parties managed to build a very successful pact under the United Ulster Unionist Council. Consequently, the anti-power sharing bloc garnered 51% of the vote and eleven of the twelve Westminster seats in NI.[243] The next month a group calling themselves the Ulster Workers' Council (UWC) 'issued a statement demanding fresh assembly elections and warning that there would be widespread disruption if its demands were not met.'[244] The UWC was a successor to the Loyalist Association of Workers, and comprised of loyalist workers, trade unionists, the UDA, and to a lesser extent the UVF and other loyalist paramilitaries.[245] On 14 May a debate was held in Stormont over a motion rejecting the Sunningdale Agreement, on the basis of the February election results, and was defeated by 28 votes to 44. Shortly afterwards Harry Murray, one of the UWC leaders, announced to the BBC that a general strike was to begin the following day.[246]

On 15 May, the UWC released a press statement saying that they were 'determined that the Government shall not ignore the will of the majority of the people as to the form of Government or the Sunningdale Agreement. The attitude of Government has made a nonsense of political action. The Workers have resolved to make an all out effort to bring about a change.'[247] Initially very few people paid any attention to the UWC's strike, and most workers carried on as usual.[248] However, by the middle of that day UDA members 'were, as [UDA leader] Tyrie put it, "persuading" workers that they should not be working.'[249] As well as maintaining a strong presence on the streets, the loyalists had control over the Six Counties' electricity supply. Shortly after the beginning of the strike the UWC managed to reduce power output to 60%, thereby forcing businesses to close and workers home.[250] On 28 May, after Merlyn Rees refused to enter into talks with the UWC, Brian Faulkner resigned and the executive collapsed. This was an impressive victory for Ulster loyalism; by successfully standing up to the British they gained a lot of credibility in the eyes of the Protestants.[251]

During the period around the UWC strike, the state made some inroads in their war on the Provisionals. Their counter-terrorism strategy had improved to the extent that not only were key leading PIRA members from Belfast – such as Brendan Hughes, Gerry Adams, Ivor Bell – locked up, but their weapons caches and safe houses were being raided.[252] Beyond this, the sustained use of solid counterinsurgency tactics and routine police work such as random car searches was making the PIRA's operations increasingly difficult to carry out.[253] By July 1974 hundreds of PIRA volunteers had been interned, with the Belfast brigade taking the brunt of the damage. Consequently, the number of operations being run there had dropped significantly: in the first six months of 1974 only three British soldiers had been killed in Belfast, 'compared to sixteen in the same period the year before.'[254]

Once again, the successes of the state caused the Provisionals to shift the focus of their campaign. Consequently, while in 1974 they did kill less British soldiers, and there was actually a steep decline in the total number of shooting incidents and explosions in Northern Ireland in general, they actually killed nearly twice as many civilians, and slightly more people in total than in 1973.[255] They also shifted their focus from NI and intensified the bombing campaign in Britain, killing dozens of people. It seems likely that an unintended result of the security services' improved counter-terrorism measures was to exacerbate CE by channelling paramilitary violence back towards civilians. As they made it harder for the PIRA to attack military targets, so civilians became the focus.

As 1974 progressed, there developed a growing feeling amongst the IRA and Sinn Fein leadership 'that in light of a high level of attrition, a readjustment had to be made.'[256] 'Backdoor' channels of communication had existed between the PIRA and the British government since the first years of the Troubles, and to this end on 10 December 1974 the PIRA leaders Ruairí Ó Brádaigh and Dáithí Ó Conaill took a delegation of high ranking Provisionals to meet with a group of Protestant clergymen near the village of Feakle. There the clergymen raised the possibility of a ceasefire, to which the Provisional Army Council replied that they would be open to discussing this with the British government as 'long as they led to a British declaration of intent to withdraw, the details of which were negotiable'.[257] The clergymen took the PIRA reply to the Secretary of State on 18 December, and two days later the PIRA Army Council announced that there was going to be a 'suspension of offensive military action in Britain and Ireland' from 22 December to 2 January 1975.[258]

1975

At the start of the new year the Provisionals announced that they would be extending the ceasefire by fourteen days to the 17 January. Although they resumed hostilities after the extended deadline passed, carrying out terror attacks in both

Northern Ireland and Britain, they did also pass a document containing conditions for a more permanent truce to Westminster.[259] On 11 February, following more talks and promises of concessions from each side, the IRA announced an indefinite ceasefire.[260] They stated in *An Phoblacht* that the 'whole purpose of the Truce was to secure from Britain the announcement of her intention to withdraw her troops and an end to interference in Irish affairs at all levels.'[261]

However, it seems that the 'old guard' of the Provisionals, Ruairí Ó Brádaigh and Dáithí Ó Conaill, may have been the victim of British subterfuge. As they had first began to reach out to the British, they had been careful to do so without some of the younger and more militant PIRA members, such as Gerry Adams and Ivor Bell, from finding out. Across 1974 these two groups diverged over their assessment of the appropriate future strategy of the PIRA. The 'old guard' had decided that they did not have the capabilities to win the war, and as such their best option was to achieve what they could through a negotiated political settlement. The 'young Turks' of Adams' camp, however, felt that British promises of concessions were 'a ruse, that a long war was inevitable, and that the emphasis on physical force would have to be broadened to include political activity.'[262] This latter group were becoming convinced that the British were using their improved intelligence to shape the IRA into an organisation more receptive to a ceasefire. To this end they were removing 'people such as themselves who would be obstacles in the way of this plan' and replacing them, 'via internee releases, with more pliable leadership candidates.'[263] Certainly several 'old guard' IRA leaders were released in the run-up to the ceasefire, such as Billy McKee, Jimmy Drumm and Seamus Loughran.[264] Further, in an interview with Bishop and Mallie, Merlyn Rees admitted that when the peace talks were threatened by a renewed IRA bombing campaign in response to the loyalist murder of a Catholic boy, he fired 'a warning shot over the heads of the hawks' on the Army Council by signing some interim custody orders.'[265] This admission is not significantly far removed from the accusation levelled at the British by the 'young Turks'.

Thus, it seems that the state's machinations did indeed help to bring about the ceasefire, and in turn it played an enormous part in redirecting the flow of M/CM interactions. By engaging in a truce with the deadliest of the paramilitary organisations, the British actually intensified the dynamic of cumulative extremism in three ways: by giving an incentive to loyalists to increase their sectarian campaign; by shifting the focus of the Provisionals away from military and towards civilian and loyalist targets; and, less directly, by contributing to a climate in which within-movement feuding was more likely to occur.

Firstly, even if the British government attempted to describe it as a unilateral ceasefire rather than a truce at the time, it soon became quite apparent to anyone interested that they had indeed made concessions to the PIRA. Across 'six months, a high-ranking British civil servant, James Allen, liaised with the Belfast [PIRA] O/C Billy McKee as Long Kesh was emptied of its inmates.'[266] Further, a series of seven 'Incident Centres' were set up across Northern Ireland, staffed by Sinn Féin and the government, to monitor the activities of the IRA and the British Army to ensure that the truce was upheld.[267] These developments became a source of serious anxiety and anger for loyalist paramilitaries. The UDA claimed that the 'Incident Centres set up by the IRA are being used as undercover recruiting offices by this organisation. Crimes are also organised on a massive scale by this so-called Community Policing Scheme.'[268] But beyond these particular instances of British acquiescence, it was the fact that there was any cooperation between the IRA and the British at all that exacerbated the usual loyalist insecurities: mistrust of the British, fear of a united Ireland, and their own political impotence. The UVF stated during its 1975 conference that the 'Conference expressed concern at speculation concerning the granting of concessions to the Provisional Alliance in return for the PIRA's cessation of hostilities against the people of Ulster',[269] and threatened an increase of violence should any of their members be served with a temporary custody order during the ceasefire. Similarly, the UDA stated in *The Ulster Loyalist* that

> what is certain is that [the truce] has been achieved by naked violence. The gunmen have come a long way. Shots in the night and bombs in the market have paid a dividend. And patient law-abiding Loyalists are bound to ask whether militancy is not always the right tactic against the British …[270]

The basis of the IRA ceasefire had been a promise of withdrawal of British troops from Northern Ireland, and on 26 May the Reverend William Arlow, who had participated in the Feakle talks, publicly stated that the British government had agreed to this. Westminster was quick to deny the statement, but the loyalists had little trust left for the architects of the Sunningdale agreement.[271] Convinced that negotiations between the IRA and the British would lead to the Catholics' interests being prioritised over their own, the loyalists became determined to derail the truce. Moreover, as the UDA's statement attests, the ceasefire only served to prove the efficacy of violence in bringing about a paramilitary group's goals in their eyes. Indeed, leading UVF figure Gusty Spence himself stated that:

> Violence had worked for the IRA who were engaged in talks with the political process. The UVF took a conscious decision to give the British government a message that if republican violence could get them to the conference table, the use of indiscriminate violence with a terrible rationale, a 'terrible beauty', the UVF could commit more violence than the IRA.[272]

Just as during the embryonic rumblings of the Sunningdale Agreement the republicans and loyalists increased their use of violence – as their only tool to avoid political irrelevance – now the UDA and UVF were to do the same thing. But whereas in late 1973 and early 1974 both sides of the M/CM contest had been excluded from the process, which seeded ground for the possibility of mutual co-operation, this time it was very much one sided. This only increased the urgency to stop a political solution from developing. Seen in this light, by engaging in a truce with the IRA but not including the loyalists in any kind of formal talks, the British were once again indirectly encouraging an increase in sectarian violence by the loyalists. This seems a reckless oversight on the part of the British, especially when one considers that on 15 May 1974 a paper written for the government stated that waves 'of sectarian assassinations seem to start from the Protestant side. When the Protestants feel threatened … they turn to a campaign of murder'.[273]

Secondly, the ceasefire fundamentally changed the M/CM dynamic. The Provisionals had always claimed to be primarily targeting British military or economic targets, but with these temporarily out of bounds, the PIRA's role as 'defenders' of the Catholic community was suddenly front and centre. Moreover, some of the IRA cadres, used to waging their war, were loathe to take a passive approach:

> Itchy trigger fingers proved especially difficult to restrain during ceasefires. The frustration at being unable to attack the security forces meant that the aggression of the volunteers was often re-channelled onto the Protestant community.[274]

These were deadly circumstances for the civilian population of Northern Ireland. Paramilitary groups from both sides of the divide now had a stronger incentive to wage war on each other, and both sides had an established strategy of targeting the support base of their enemies rather than the actual opposing paramilitaries themselves. Indeed, given the clandestine nature of the groups this was the only reliable way of finding a target. Accordingly, less than two months after the start of the ceasefire on 5 April, the UVF, acting under the cover name the Protestant Action Force, detonated a bomb at McLoughlin's Bar in the Catholic New Lodge area of Belfast, killing two Catholic civilians. In retaliation, on the same day the PIRA detonated a bomb at the Mountainview Tavern on the Shankill Road killing four Protestant civilians and one UDA volunteer. 'A week later the UVF retaliated again, with a bomb at the Strand Bar in the Short Strand which killed six customers.'[275]

On 31 July 1975 three members of the Miami Showband, a popular band from the Republic, were killed by the UVF as they attempted to return home to Dublin after playing a concert in the North.[276] The massacre shocked the North, including the loyalist community, leading the UVF to claim that their patrol had merely been investigating a suspicious looking van when a bomb detonated and they were fired upon.[277] This version of events was not widely accepted,[278] and the PIRA were quick to retaliate; sparking off another round of 'tit-for-tat' inter-communal killings.[279] There are different sources for data on the numbers of deaths during the Troubles; the Police Service of Northern Ireland's (PSNI) data shows 1975 as having more deaths in total than the previous year (247 compared to 220),[280] whereas Malcolm Sutton's *Index of Deaths* shows there as being less (260 compared to 294),[281] however both sources agree that overall deaths in Northern Ireland (as opposed to deaths in the Republic or Britain) went up across 1975 compared to the year before.

The third way in which the 'truce' intensified CE was by fostering conditions whereby within-movement violence – or, 'feuding' – could take place. As with the increase in sectarianism, the removal of the state as a direct target for the Provisionals redirected the flow of the violence. On 29 October a deadly republican feud erupted between the Officials and the Provisionals. As darkness fell the Provisionals put into action an impressive operation involving one hundred of their gunmen. They orchestrated attacks on Officials across Belfast, and in just an hour's time thirty-one had been attacked, nineteen were wounded and one lay dead. This in turn led to yet another series of 'tit-for-tat' killings between the two wings of the republican movement. In the following two weeks eleven people were killed because of the feud.[282] The PIRA justified the attack on their fellow republicans on the grounds that they had allegedly been colluding with the British 'in areas controlled by the Provisionals' so as to 'undermin[e] Provo influence'.[283]

It seems likely that at least twenty-five people were killed as a direct result of feuding across 1975; this compares with eight loyalists killed by republicans and two republicans killed by loyalists.[284] The reasons that within-movement violence is more costly for social movement organisations than M/CM violence are strongly linked to the reasons that M/CM violence tends to be directed at civilians rather than opposing paramilitaries as the conflict grows increasingly lethal. Whereas movement organisations go 'underground' so as to avoid infiltration and arrest from state forces, which makes them similarly difficult to target by opposing movements, rival organisations within the same movement share similar social networks, territorial areas and communities with each other. This makes it much easier for lethal violence to occur between them. Moreover, they are often in direct competition with each other over resources, recruits and support.

By November 1975 the PIRA-Government truce was *de facto* over, even if for the time being both parties publicly acted otherwise. The Provisional Army Council had come to realise that 'nothing of any substance would be forthcoming from the British, despite all the assurances they had received in the secret meetings', and, furthermore, over the seven months of the ceasefire 'nothing had been achieved beyond the release of a few prisoners.'[285] For their part, 'there is considerable reason to doubt whether or not the British were ever sincere about delivering' on the terms of the ceasefire.[286] Certainly by the end of the year, after it had become clear that no political solution would be found, the British were overlooking even the most flagrant breaches of the terms of the ceasefire in an effort to buy time for them to implement their policy of Normalisation.[287] This included the phasing out of internment, the building of the new Maze prison in preparation for the new policy of criminalisation of paramilitaries, and the restructuring of the RUC.[288] However, the government had another reason for dragging the ceasefire out for as long as possible. The PIRA let their guard down during the truce,[289] and this allowed the British to significantly increase their infiltration and intelligence-gathering operations.[290]

1976

1976 was the second bloodiest year of the Troubles after 1972, and the first few days foreshadowed this fact. On 4 January five Catholic civilians were killed by loyalists in South Armagh. The next day a group of twelve republican gunmen calling themselves the Republican Action Force stopped a bus near Kingsmill, ordered the ten Protestant workmen on the bus to line up on the side of the road, and then murdered them. The Republican Action Force is all but universally believed to have been a *nom de guerre* for a group of rogue PIRA gunmen.[291] In response to these killings it was announced that the Special Air Service (SAS) would be sent to Armagh – this was the first public official acknowledgement that the SAS was operating in Northern Ireland – but this had little short-term effect on the dynamic of CE[292]: by the end of January alone 36 civilians had been killed by paramilitaries as well as three policemen and three soldiers.[293]

On 10 February the last formal meeting between the PIRA and the British government was held, and as it ended so did any remaining hope for a political solution to the conflict.[294] The following month the PIRA, and loyalist para-militaries, were dealt another blow when Merlyn Rees began phasing out special category status for people convicted of crimes connected with the Troubles. Henceforth arrested paramilitaries would have to wear penal uniforms and be treated like ordinary criminals.[295]

One of the crucial elements of the new British counter-terrorism strategy was what became known as 'Ulsterisation'. This was the policy of the RUC and the UDR, across 1976, taking over from the regular Army the responsibility for tackling the paramilitaries.[296] As the regular British Army passed the baton to the Ulster security services, deaths of RUC and UDR men increased. O'Malley has argued that the increased murder rate of RUC and UDR personnel was due to a need for the PIRA to keep the conflict alive and provoking a loyalist backlash by attacking these Protestants was the perfect way to achieve this.

> Thus the need for 'help' of the Loyalists, and this the Provisionals have set out to secure. Hence the increasing emphasis on the murder of UDR and RUC men… In short, the most successful IRA operations are those that create conditions of optimal instability, maximising the likelihood of a Protestant backlash against the Catholic community and provoking Protestants to challenge the British government in a way that is inimical to their own best interests.[297]

Of course, it should be noted that any regiment taking over front-line duties should expect to experience a sharp increase in fatalities, precisely because they are becoming the most prominent target in the firing-line. Nevertheless, the description O'Malley gives of the interactions between republicans, security services and loyalists is broadly accurate, even if his assertions about republi-can intentions are less well founded. Republicans certainly killed more RUC personnel in 1976 than in any year since the Troubles began, and twice as many as the previous year[298]; they also killed more UDR soldiers than any year since 1972.[299] The loyalists did also respond by killing more civilians: 107 compared to 99 in 1975. The republicans, however, killed more civilians in 1976 than in any other year. The Sutton Index records them only killing one more than in 1972, the bloodiest year of the Troubles, but given that in 1972 51% of the deaths were civilians compared to 67% in 1976, this was proportionally a higher level of civilian deaths.[300] So even if O'Malley is correct that the 'UDR man' was the ideal target for the Provisionals, the more striking trend of the year was republican murders of civilians.

Further, while O'Malley might be correct that part of the reason for this increase in violence was down to the PIRA needing to use Jujitsu Politics to provoke a loyalist backlash, the state's policy of Ulsterisation must also have been a huge causal factor by exacerbating CE. Peter Taylor claimed that 'the policy was, in the short-term, effective',[301] but it is hard to see how this is so. As the RUC and UDR increasingly became the main tool used by the state to deal with the paramilitaries, they naturally came into direct conflict with them more. Also, given that 90% of the RUC and 98% of the UDR were Protestants, it is hardly surprising that Catholics frequently complained about how their community was policed.[302] The British policy had 'effectively created an armed Protestant force of considerable magnitude.'[303] As already mentioned, by this time the British government knew that the UDR had been infiltrated by loyalists. Cadwallader has shown that many atrocities committed by loyalists were done so in collusion with RUC officers, and that the subsequent investigations were interfered with to protect people by elements within the British state. The Police Service of Northern Ireland's own Historical Enquiries Team stated that

> It is difficult to believe … when judged in concert with other cases emerging at the time that such widespread evidence of collusion in these areas was not a significant concern at the highest levels of the security forces and the government.[304]

It now seems clear that the RUC, including at least two chief constables,

> must have known that important investigations were contaminated, yet neither did anything. The RUC failed the nationalist community in Mid-Ulster during the 1970s… They knew who the killers were – yet they failed to put them behind bars, thus paving the way for more killings (including many of their own officers) and prolonging the conflict.[305]

Yet the decision was still made to allow these same forces to become the central policing agencies for a lethal sectarian conflict of which many of them were active participants.

The policies of criminalisation, Ulsterisation and normalisation were the three interlocking strands of the 'long-haul British blueprint for the North'.[306] Broadly speaking, the strategy aimed to undermine the PIRA's legitimacy as a republican force while simultaneously ensuring Ulster-born (rather than British) people took the brunt of the violence, a move which 'made broad political sense in that the drop in regular army casualties helped prevent any build-up of sentiment in Britain for a withdrawal from Northern Ireland.'[307] While this strategy may have helped Westminster to tackle the problems of Ulster over the long-term, it had a dramatic impact on the dynamic of CE.

Ulsterisation pitted the two communities against each other in a more direct way than they had experienced in years. The bigger role played by the overwhelmingly Protestant RUC and UDR exacerbated Catholic fears and led to more sectarian killings being committed by the PIRA. This in turn caused a backlash from the Protestant community, with similar results. Criminalisation had a similarly detrimental effect on the M/CM dynamic. Nationalists referred to the legal system as a 'conveyor belt', whereby 'unwanted members of the public' were arrested, convicted in a '[j]uryless court' (otherwise known as a Diplock court), interrogated (and allegedly tortured) 'in the purpose built interrogation centre at Castlereagh in Belfast' and then finally sent to the 'H-Blocks of Long Kesh' prison or 'the Women's Prison in Armagh'.[308] This, not unreasonable, view of the judicial system amongst the Catholic population of course further damaged what little credibility and legitimacy the system may have previously had, and further polarised the two communities. Ulsterisation and criminalisation may well have been a contributing factor in the drop in murders in Northern Ireland from 1977 onwards, but in the short term it facilitated processes of cumulative extremism; it led to more deaths in Northern Ireland in total, and specifically more deaths of civilians and Northern Irish security services.

As 1976 ended the M/CM contest seriously de-escalated. There were around 110 deaths in 1977, down from 297 in 1976, and the total deaths per year stayed between 50 and 110 until the mid-1990s.[309] Although the conflict would continue with a much lower intensity for more than two decades, the '"Troubles" in one sense were over'.[310]

Conclusion

This chapter began by looking at a period when a growing Catholic middle class began to press for change in an optimistic atmosphere with a Protestant Prime Minister seemingly attempting to help them improve their lot, and yet ended in one of the bloodiest feuds in Western Europe since the Second World War. The progression from non-violent civil rights activism to guerrilla war is, of course, a highly complex one. Yet here, more than with the previous chapters dealing with violent street movements in Britain, the concept of CE has a good deal of explanatory power to help us understand these events.

That the dynamic of CE began to emerge and radicalise the groups involved, and draw more people in to the conflict, boils down to five key factors. Firstly, as discussed in earlier chapters, the way in which an M/CM conflict unfolds is influenced by context and situations in which the opposing groups face each other. Groups engaging with each other primarily through courtrooms are less likely to have a radicalising influence on each other than those meeting in the streets during emotionally charged demonstrations. With NI's history of highly symbolic and provocative marches and commemorations, it was a perfect breeding ground for intergroup hostility. Further, as della Porta has stated, as these face-to-face encounters on the streets continue they become more likely to succumb to 'gradual reciprocal adaptation to increasingly dangerous weapons', which was demonstrated in Derry and Belfast in August 1969.[311]

Secondly, because of the structure and history of NI both the CRM and loyalist groups were widely perceived as representing 'the material and symbolic interests' of the Catholic and Protestant communities respectively,[312] while also being widely 'perceived to threaten the dominant values' and interests of the opposite community; far more so than the fascist and anti-fascist movements did to any broader social groups.[313] This dramatically increased the likelihood of people from those communities mobilising with the group that seemed to be championing their interests against the ones threatening them. As already mentioned, as the violence continued people in NI who were not yet part of a paramilitary group or SMO were motivated to become activists as people from their community were killed, hurt or attacked. This motivation through 'vicarious retribution' is demonstrated by Brendan Hughes, who would go on to be a heroic figure within the Provisional IRA, when he stated that

> … most of us at that time did not have a great deal of political ideology. It wasn't until later that we really began to learn what republicanism meant. We were motivated by the fact that Catholic homes and streets had been burned down, [that] Catholics had been forced out of their homes.[314]

This close proximity between the SMOs and their target constituencies also enabled the third factor: the use of Jujitsu Politics. Michael Farrell has admitted that the 'long march' to Burntollet was intended to provoke a reaction (although by no means to the extent that they actually did), and it is hard to imagine that the Derry Boys of Apprentice were not looking to do something similar in August 1969. This tactic is much more likely to lead to reciprocal radicalisation between groups when there is a large visible support base associated with the social movement for their opponents to attack. For instance, if the anti-fascists of AFA had succeeded in provoking the BNP in to attacking an event held by the labour movement this may have radicalised some people to join the anti-fascists, but the process would have likely halted at that point as there was no large community acting as a support base for the fascist movement. In Northern Ireland, where the M/CM contest was taking place in the context of a society divided into two communities, the use of Jujitsu politics was more likely to provoke revenge attacks on the wider communities (i.e. Protestants and Catholics) rather than just the SMOs, thereby leading to 'vicarious retribution' and spirals of violence.

The fourth factor was the intransigence of the NI state. While the CRM did radicalise to some extent through interactions with the loyalists, this would have been significantly less likely if the NI state had been seen as neutral or receptive to the Catholic communities' grievances. As stated, the CRM tried to achieve their goals through normal political channels. The Northern Ireland Labour Party attempted to achieve some of the CRM goals through Stormont. The CSJ had conducted research to try to bring to light the discrimination that the Catholic community experienced so as to convince the British to intervene on their behalf. And the NICRA and the PD attempted to hold peaceful marches and rallies to highlight their concerns and the demands of the CRM. Each of these efforts were either ultimately ignored, obstructed or attacked. As these attempts to achieve their goals using moderate means through the usual political channels failed, they became increasingly militant. The result of the inflexibility of the NI state was a channelling of the CRM towards a more radical protest strategy. This in turn alarmed the Protestant community more and provoked an increasingly violent reaction.

The fifth factor was the enormous influence the British state's interventions had on the M/CM relationship. The curfew imposed on the Lower Falls Road, the introduction of internment, and the tragedy on Bloody Sunday (amongst other incidents) all served to escalate M/CM interactions. Catholics (and republicans), feeling that they were being oppressed by a hostile state, reacted by taking to the streets and joining republican paramilitary groups. This in turn mobilised Protestants, who felt anxious over the radical reaction of the Catholic community.

However, the British state's interventions between 1973 and 1976 did also serve to curb the cycle of violence between the paramilitaries in Northern Ireland in the long term. Indeed, the longer a lethally violent M/CM contest continues, the more sophisticated the state's interventions are likely to become. Nevertheless, these interventions, even when they achieve the particular goal the state was aiming for, often do not actually mitigate the dynamic of cumulative extremism in the short term. Indeed, often they exacerbate it, and it was these interactions which mainly shaped the contest between the republicans and the loyalists after 1972.

This chapter has demonstrated that as processes of cumulative extremism drive an M/CM contest to lethal conflict, these same processes can then also serve to maintain that conflict at a relatively high level of intensity. Further, while these processes may also foster countervailing desires to bring the conflict to a close, the dominant trend is vicarious retribution which motivates actors to continue engaging in the conflict. Also, it seems clear that the state's interactions with the movement and countermovement can have an extremely strong effect on the M/CM dynamic. Rather than interrupting processes of cumulative extremism, the state's actions tended to exacerbate them (at least until the end of 1976). While the numbers of (non-Ulster) British soldiers killed went down across this period, numbers of civilian and Ulster security service personnel (UDR and RUC) deaths went up.

Notes

1 Material from this chapter has been published as: Carter, A. J. 'Cumulative Extremism: Escalation of Movement–Countermovement Dynamics in Northern Ireland between 1967 and 1972', *Behavioral Sciences of Terrorism and Political Aggression*, 9, no. 1 (2017), pp. 37–51.

2 This study, while referring to Catholics and Protestants, uses the terms to refer to ethnic groups, as is commonly accepted in the literature on Northern Ireland: see McGarry, John and Brendan O'Leary. *Explaining Northern Ireland* (Oxford: Blackwell Publishers, 1995), pp. 185–207; Ó Dochartaigh, Niall. *From Civil Rights to Armalites: Derry and the Birth of the Irish Troubles* (Cork: Palgrave Macmillan, 2005), p. 7.

3 Farrell, Michael. *Northern Ireland: The Orange State* (London: Pluto Press, 1976), p. 238.

4 Finn, Daniel. 'The Point of No Return? People's Democracy and the Burntollet March', *Field Day Review*, 9 (2013), pp. 4–21.

5 Throughout this book, the term CRM shall be used to refer to the movement as a whole. The CRM was a diverse and heterogeneous movement, though, which included many organisations with divergent views on how to accomplish their goals. It should not be confused with any one civil rights organisation.

6 Durkheim, Emile. *The Rules of Sociological Method* (New York: The Free Press, 1982), p. 52.

7 Bourke, Richard. *Peace in Ireland: The War of Ideas* (London: Pimlico, 2003), p. 11 & p. 47.

8 Ibid., p. 11 & p. 47.

9 Taylor, Peter. *Provos: The IRA and Sinn Fein* (London: Bloomsbury, 1998), p. 33.

10 Bourke, *Peace in Ireland*, p. 45.

11 Fraser, *Ireland in Conflict*, pp. 38–40.

12 The legitimate grievances of the Catholic population had in fact existed since the very establishment of the Northern Irish state in 1921. As Buckland argues, 'a tendency towards discrimination on matters of law and order developed almost accidentally out of the confused troubles of the years 1921–22, but … in respect of education and representation, discrimination became an integral part of government policy.' Buckland, Patrick. *The Factory of Grievances: Devolved Government in Northern Ireland 1921–39* (Dublin: Glenn and Macmillan, 1979), p. 6.

13 Farrell, *Northern Ireland*, p. 243.

14 *LondonDerry: One Man, No Vote*, Campaign for Justice in Northern Ireland, Castlefields, Dungannon, 19 February 1965, p. 1; Purdie, *Politics in the Street*, pp. 91–103.

15 Hancock, L. 'Northern Ireland: Troubles Brewing'. *CAIN Web Service – Conflict and Politics in Northern Ireland* [http://cain.ulst.ac.uk/othelem/landon.htm] (1998) Accessed on 1 February 2016.

16 Jackson, *Ireland 1798–1998*, pp. 358–359.

17 Bloomfield, *Tragedy of Errors*, p. 167.

18 Ibid., p. 15.

19 Buckland, Patrick. *The Factory of Grievances: Devolved Government in Northern Ireland 1921–39* (Dublin: Glenn and Macmillan, 1979), p. 2.

20 Ibid., p. 2.

21 Ibid., p. 68.

22 Ibid., p. 69.

23 Ibid., p. 69.

24 Ibid., p. 69.

25 Bew, Paul, Peter Gibbon and Henry Patterson. *Northern Ireland 1921/2001: Political Forces and Social Classes* (London: Serif, 2002), pp. 17–18.

26 Ibid., p. 18; Morgan, Austen. *Labour and Partition: The Belfast Working Class* (London: Pluto Press, 1991), pp. 265–269.

27 Bew, Paul, Peter Gibbon and Henry Patterson. *Northern Ireland 1921/2001: Political Forces and Social Classes* (London: Serif, 2002), pp. 17–18.
28 Farrell, Michael. *Northern Ireland: The Orange State* (London: Pluto Press, 1976), p. 17.
29 Buckland, Patrick. *The Factory of Grievances: Devolved Government in Northern Ireland 1921–39* (Dublin: Glenn and Macmillan, 1979), p. 71.
30 Bew, Paul, Peter Gibbon and Henry Patterson. *Northern Ireland 1921/2001: Political Forces and Social Classes* (London: Serif, 2002), p. 27.
31 Bourke, *Peace in Ireland*, p. 51.
32 Ibid., p. 51.
33 Taylor, Peter. *Loyalists* (London: Bloomsbury, 1999), p. 35.
34 Bruce, Steve. *The Red Hand: Protestant Paramilitaries in Northern Ireland* (Oxford: Oxford University Press, 1992), p. 22 & pp. 30–31; Taylor, *Loyalists*, p. 36.
35 Cusack, Jim and Henry McDonald. *UVF* (Dublin: Poolbeg Press, 1997), p. 38.
36 Boulton, David. *The UVF 1966–73: An Anatomy of Loyalist Rebellion* (Dublin: Torc Books, 1973), pp. 40–41; Cusack, Jim and Henry McDonald. *UVF* (Dublin: Poolbeg Press, 1997), p. 7.
37 Novosel, *Northern Ireland's Lost Opportunity*, p. 16.
38 Ibid., p. 17.
39 Purdie, *Politics in the Street*, p. 31.
40 Kenney, Mary Catherine. 'Ritualized Conflict and Ideological Polarization in Northern Ireland', *Michigan Discussions in Anthropology*, 7, no. 1 (1984), pp. 38–40.
41 NICRA, *'We Shall Overcome': The History of the Struggle for Civil Rights in Northern Ireland, 1968–1978* (Belfast: Northern Ireland Civil Right Association, 1978), p. 11.
42 Quoted in Taylor, Peter. *Provos: The IRA and Sinn Fein* (London: Bloomsbury, 1998), p. 34.
43 Cusack and McDonald, *UVF*, p. 21.
44 Purdie, *Politics in the Street*, p. 76.
45 Ibid., p. 73.
46 Ibid., p. 73.
47 Dixon, Paul. *Northern Ireland: The Politics of War and Peace* (Basingstoke: Palgrave Macmillan, 2008), pp. 78–79; Purdie, Bob. *Politics in the Street: The Origins of the Civil Rights Movement in Northern Ireland* (Belfast: The Blackstaff Press Limited, 1990), p. 133.
48 NICRA, *'We Shall Overcome': The History of the Struggle for Civil Rights in Northern Ireland, 1968–1978* (Belfast: Northern Ireland Civil Right Association, 1978), p. 11; Purdie, *Politics in the Street*, pp. 134–135.
49 *The United Irishman,* Vol. XXII, January 1967, p. 6.
50 De Fazio, 'The Radicalization of Contention', p. 483.
51 Zald, N. Mayer and Useem Bert. 'Movement and Countermovement Interaction: Mobilization, Tactics, and State Involvement', in *Social Movements in an Organizational Society: Collected Essays,* Edited by Mayer N. Zald and John D. McCarthy (Oxford: Transaction Publishers, 1984), pp. 247–248.
52 Meyer and Staggenborg, 'Movements, Countermovements', p. 1635.
53 Della Porta, Donatella. *Social Movements, Political Violence, and the State: A Comparative Analysis of Italy and Germany* (Cambridge: Cambridge University Press, 1995), pp. 152–155.
54 Bourke, *Peace in Ireland*, p. 43.
55 Ó Dochartaigh, *From Civil Rights to Armalites*, p. 18.
56 Farrell, *Northern Ireland*, p. 246.
57 Bew, *Ireland: The Politics of Enmity*, p. 489.
58 Ó Dochartaigh, *From Civil Rights to Armalites*, p. 18.
59 Purdie, *Politics in the Street*, pp. 155–156.
60 LHL: P933: *Explosion in Ulster: Religion and Class*, Gibbon / P D *Militants Discuss Strategy*, Baxter, Devlin, Farrell, McCann, Toman, p. 32.

61 Purdie, *Politics in the Street*, p. 147.
62 For example, see: Della Porta, Donatella. *Clandestine Political Violence* (Cambridge: Cambridge University Press, 2013), p. 32.
63 Buckland, Patrick. *The Factory of Grievances: Devolved Government in Northern Ireland 1921–39* (Dublin: Glenn and Macmillan, 1979), p. 20.
64 De Fazio, 'The Radicalization of Contention', p. 478.
65 Purdie, *Politics in the Street*, p. 206.
66 Farrell, *Northern Ireland*, p. 247.
67 Ibid., p. 247; Purdie, *Politics in the Street*, p. 207.
68 Farrell, *Northern Ireland*, p. 248.
69 Ó Dochartaigh, *From Civil Rights to Armalites*, p. 30.
70 Ibid., pp. 72–73.
71 Purdie, *Politics in the Street*, pp. 212–213.
72 Bloomfield, *Tragedy of Errors*, p. 172; Bourke, *Peace in Ireland*, p. 80; Purdie, *Politics in the Street*, pp. 212–213.
73 LHL: P1063A: December 1968; Towards a Programme of Campaign for 1969, p. 1.
74 Bourke, *Peace in Ireland*, p. 89.
75 Ibid., p. 89.
76 Bew, Paul. '"The Blind Leading The Blind"? London's Response to the 1969 Crisis', *History Ireland*, 17, no. 4 (2009), p. 47.
77 Della Porta, *Clandestine Political Violence*, pp. 167–168; Ó Dochartaigh, *From Civil Rights to Armalites*, p. 35.
78 Purdie, Bob. *Politics in the Street*, p. 215.
79 Ó Dochartaigh, *From Civil Rights to Armalites*, pp. 35–36.
80 Ibid., p. 37.
81 Farrell, *Northern Ireland*, p. 249.
82 Ó Dochartaigh, *From Civil Rights to Armalites*, p. 37 & pp. 31–32.
83 McCauley, Clark. 'JuJitsu Politics: Terrorism and Responses to Terrorism', in *Collateral Damage: The Psychological Consequences of America's War on Terrorism*, Edited by Paul R. Kimmel and Chris E. Stout (Westport: Praeger Publishers, 2006), p. 49.
84 Lickel, Brian, Norman Miller, Douglas M. Stenstrom and Thomas F. Denson. 'Vicarious Retribution: The Role of Collective Blame in Intergroup Aggression', *Personality and Social Psychology Review*, 10, no. 4 (2006), 372–373.
85 Farrell, *Northern Ireland*, pp. 250–251.
86 Arthur, Paul. *The People's Democracy 1968–73* (Belfast: Blackstaff Press Ltd, 1974), [http://cain.ulst.ac.uk/events/pdmarch/arthur74a.htm#chap1], Accessed on 30 March 2016.
87 P933: *Explosion in Ulster: Religion and Class*, Gibbon / P D Militants Discuss Strategy, Baxter, Devlin, Farrell, McCann, Toman.
88 Taylor, Peter. *Loyalists* (London: Bloomsbury, 1999), p. 50.
89 Swan, Sean. *Official Irish Republicanism, 1962 to 1972* (Self-published: Lulu, 2007), p. 251.
90 Reid, Colin. 'Protestant Challenges to the 'Protestant State': Ulster Unionism and Independent Unionism in Northern Ireland, 1921–1939', *Twentieth Century British History*, 19, no. 4 (2008), pp. 444–445.
91 Novosel, *Northern Ireland's Lost Opportunity*, pp. 55–56.
92 Hanley and Millar. *The Lost Revolution*, p. 125.
93 Boulton, *The UVF 1966–73*, p. 115.
94 Adams, Gerry. *Before the Dawn: An Autobiography* (New York: William Morrow and Company, Inc, 1996), p. 95.
95 Bourke, *Peace in Ireland*, p. 100.
96 Anderson, Brendan. *Joe Cahill: A Life in the IRA* (Dublin: The O'Brien Press Ltd, 2007), p. 172.
97 Adams, Gerry *Before the Dawn: An Autobiography* (New York: William Morrow and Company, Inc, 1996), p. 98.

98 Moloney, Ed. *A Secret History of the IRA* (London: Penguin Books, 2007). p. 67.

99 Moloney, *A Secret History of the IRA*, pp. 65–66.

100 Horowitz, Donald. L. *The Deadly Ethnic Riot* (Berkeley: University of California Press, 2002), p. 12.

101 Bourke, Richard. *Peace in Ireland: The War of Ideas* (London: Pimlico, 2003), p. 103.

102 Tarrow, Sidney. 'Charles Tilly and the Practice of Contentious Politics: From France to England and [Not quite] Back Again', Histoire@Politique. Politique, culture, société, 10 (2010): www.histoire-politique.fr.

103 Hanley and Millar. *The Lost Revolution*, p. 135.

104 Ibid., pp. 136–137.

105 Anderson, *Joe Cahill*, pp. 177–181.

106 Sutton, Malcolm. *An Index of Deaths from the Conflict in Ireland 1969–1993* (Dublin: Beyond the Pale Publications, 1994), p. 1; Sutton, Malcolm. *An Index of Deaths from the Conflict in Ireland 1969–1993* (Dublin: Beyond the Pale Publications, 1994), p. 76.

107 Ibid., p. 79.

108 *West Belfast Newsheet,* N.N., N.D., c.1970, p. 1.

109 Bourke, *Peace in Ireland*, p. 131.

110 Fraser, *Ireland in Conflict*, p. 49.

111 Sanders, Andrew. *Inside the IRA* (Edinburgh: Edinburgh University Press, 2011), p. 49.

112 Sanders, *Inside the IRA*, p. 49.

113 Hanley and Millar, *The Lost Revolution*, p. 156.

114 Wood, S. Ian. *Crimes of Loyalty: A History of the UDA* (Edinburgh: Edinburgh University Press, 2006), pp. 1–3.

115 Ibid., pp. 1–3.

116 Della Porta, *Social Movements*, p. 154.

117 Moloney, *Voices from the Grave*, pp. 55–56.

118 Moloney, *A Secret History of the IRA*, p. 91; Adams, *Before the Dawn*, p. 144.

119 Moloney, *A Secret History of the IRA*, p. 95.

120 *Resistance, Magazine of the University Republican Clubs,* No. 2, February 1971, pp. 11–13.

121 Bruce *The Red Hand*, p. 41.

122 Moloney, *A Secret History of the IRA*, p. 97.

123 HA/32/3/6: 'Note of a Meeting in London on 16 March', Meeting between British Home Secretary and the Prime Minister of Northern Ireland (16 March 1971).

124 Bew, *Ireland: The Politics of Enmity*, p. 502.

125 *People's Press: Newspaper of West Belfast People's Democracy*, 17 April 1971, p. 3.

126 De Fazio, Gianluca. 'The Radicalization of Contention in Northern Ireland, 1968–1972: A Relational Perspective', *Mobilization: An International Quarterly*, 18, no. 4 (2013), p. 477.

127 Wood, *Crimes of Loyalty*, p. 5.

128 Bishop and Mallie. *The Provisional IRA*, pp. 180–181.

129 English, *Armed Struggle*, p. 123.

130 *The United Irishman*, August 1971, Vol. XXV, p. 1.

131 *An Phoblacht*, Vol. 2, Issue 9, September 1971, p. 1.

132 Bourke, *Peace in Ireland*, pp. 114–115.

133 Farrell, *Northern Ireland*, pp. 283–287.

134 Hanley and Millar. *The Lost Revolution*, p. 166.

135 Kennedy-Pipe, Caroline. *The Origins of the Present Troubles in Northern Ireland* (Essex: Longman, 1997), p. 60.

136 Bourke, *Peace in Ireland*, pp. 114–115.

137 *The United Irishman,* September 1971, Vol. XXV, p. 5; Hanley, Brian and Scott Millar. *The Lost Revolution: The Story of the Official IRA and the Workers' Party* (London: Penguin, 2010), p. 166.

138 Boulton, David. *The UVF 1966–73: An Anatomy of Loyalist Rebellion* (Dublin: Torc Books, 1973), pp. 144–145.
139 Ibid., pp. 144–145.
140 Kennedy-Pipe, *The Origins of the Present Troubles*, p. 60; Wood, *Crimes of Loyalty*, p. 3.
141 Bishop and Mallie, *The Provisional IRA*, pp. 180–181.
142 Cusack and McDonald, *UVF*, pp. 92–93.
143 Sutton, Malcolm. 'An Index of Deaths from the Conflict in Ireland 1969–1993', *CAIN Web Service – Conflict and Politics in Northern Ireland* [http://cain.ulst.ac.uk/sutton/], Accessed on 27 February 2017.
144 Ibid.
145 Ibid.
146 Moloney, *Voices from the Grave*, p. 93.
147 Moloney, *A Secret History of the IRA*, p. 110.
148 Ibid., p. 110.
149 Fraser, *Ireland in Conflict*, p. 52.
150 Jackson, *Ireland 1798–1998*, p. 371.
151 *The United Irishman*, March 1972, Vol. XXVI, p. 3.
152 McCann, Eamonn. *War and an Irish Town* (London: Pluto Press, 1993), pp. 163–168.
153 Callaghan, 'Surveying Politics of Peace', pp. 33–49.
154 Hanley and Millar, *The Lost Revolution*, p. 180.
155 Ibid., p. 180.
156 *The United Irishman*, June 1972, Vol. XXVI, p. 1; Wood, S. Ian. *Crimes of Loyalty: A History of the UDA* (Edinburgh: Edinburgh University Press, 2006), pp. 102–103.
157 Moloney, *A Secret History of the IRA*, p. 112.
158 Cusack and McDonald, *UVF*, p. 98.
159 Ibid., p. 98.
160 Bruce, *The Red Hand*, p. 50.
161 Wood, *Crimes of Loyalty*, p. 104.
162 Cusack and McDonald, *UVF*, p. 98.
163 Bishop and Mallie, *The Provisional IRA*, pp. 235–237.
164 Ibid., pp. 235–237.
165 Moloney, *Voices from the Grave*, p. 103; Bourke, *Peace in Ireland*, p. 170.
166 *An Phoblacht*, Vol. 3, Issue 8, August 1972, p. 3.
167 Moloney, *Voices from the Grave*, p. 103; Bourke, *Peace in Ireland*, p. 107.
168 Ibid., p. 117.
169 Cusack and McDonald, *UVF*, pp. 111–114.
170 Ferguson, Neil, Mark Burgess and Ian Hollywood. 'Crossing the Rubicon: Deciding to Become a Paramilitary in Northern Ireland', *International Journal of Conflict and Violence*, 2, no. 1 (2008), p. 134.
171 *Loyalist News*, 29 July 1971, p. 1.
172 Moloney, *A Secret History of the IRA*, p. 117.
173 PRONI: CAB/9/G/27/6/3: 'Conclusions of Morning Meeting' (31 July 1972).
174 Moloney, *A Secret History of the IRA*, p. 117.
175 Wood, *Crimes of Loyalty*, p. 102.
176 Ibid., p. 102.
177 NAUK: DEFE 24/824.
178 *The United Irishman*, August 1972, Vol. XXVI, p. 3.
179 Cadwallader, Anne. *Lethal Allies: British Collusion in Ireland* (Cork: Mercier Press, 2013), p. 26.
180 Ibid., p. 26.
181 Ibid., pp. 6–29.
182 *An Phoblacht*, Vol. 3, Issue 8, August 1972, p. 2.
183 Wood, *Crimes of Loyalty: A History of the UDA* (Edinburgh: Edinburgh University Press, 2006), p. 6.

184 Sutton, *An Index of Deaths*, pp. 13–39; This does not include deaths of soldiers, republican or loyalist volunteers, or people killed in terrorist operations abroad such as the OIRA bomb blast in Aldershot.
185 Cusack and McDonald, *UVF*, pp. 120–123.
186 Ibid., pp. 120–123.
187 Ibid., pp. 120–123.
188 Sutton, Malcolm. *An Index of Deaths from the Conflict in Ireland 1969–1993* (Dublin: Beyond the Pale Publications, 1994).
189 Bruce, Steve. *The Red Hand: Protestant Paramilitaries in Northern Ireland* (Oxford: Oxford University Press, 1992), p. 87.
190 Cusack, Jim and Henry McDonald *UVF* (Dublin: Poolbeg Press, 1997), p. 124.
191 Bruce, *The Red Hand*, p. 87.
192 Sutton, *An Index of Deaths*.
193 Nelson, Sarah. *Ulster's Uncertain Defenders: Protestant Political, Paramilitary and Community Groups in the Northern Ireland Conflict* (Syracuse: Syracuse University Press, 1987).
194 McKittrick, David and David McVea. *Making Sense of the Troubles* (London: Penguin, 2001), p. 91.
195 Wood, S. Ian. *Crimes of Loyalty: A History of the UDA* (Edinburgh: Edinburgh University Press, 2006), pp. 28–30.
196 HM Government. *Northern Ireland Constitutional Proposals* (London: HMSO, March 1973), Paras. 30, 44.
197 Ibid., Paras. 67–70.
198 Ibid., Para. 110.
199 Ibid., Para. 112.
200 Coogan, Tim Pat. *The Troubles: Ireland's Ordeal and the Search for Peace* (London: Arrow Books, 1996), p. 192.
201 Wood, *Crimes of Loyalty*, pp. 28–30.
202 Cusack and McDonald, *UVF*, pp. 127–129.
203 Cadwallader, *Lethal Allies*, p. 35.
204 NA: DEFE 24/835: Ulster Defence Regiment (UDR): Recruitment and Medals; Subversion.
205 Dillon, Martin. *The Dirty War* (London: Arrow Books, 1991), p. xix.
206 White, Robert W. 'Comparing State Repression of Pro-State Vigilantes and Anti-State Insurgents: Northern Ireland, 1972–75', *Mobilization: An International Quarterly*, 4, no. 2 (1999), pp. 189–202.
207 Bruce, *The Red Hand*, p. 269.
208 Ibid., p. 271.
209 Campbell, B. 'Death Squads: Definition, Problems and Historical Context', in *Death Squads in Global Perspective: Murder with Deniability*, Edited by B. Campbell and A. Brenner (London: Macmillan, 2000), p. 3.
210 Cadwallader, *Lethal Allies*, pp. 264–278.
211 PREM 16/154: Defensive Brief D Meeting between the Prime Minister and the Taoiseach 5 April 1974 Army Plain Clothes Patrols in Northern Ireland.
212 Sluka, Jeffrey A. '"For God and Ulster": The Culture of Terror and Loyalist Death Squads in Northern Ireland', in *Death Squad: The Anthropology of State Terror* (Philadelphia: University of Pennsylvania Press, 2000), p. 134.
213 Rolston, Bill. '"An effective mask for terror": Democracy, Death Squads and Northern Ireland', *Crime, Law and Social Change*, 44, no. 2 (2005), p. 192.
214 Former MRF member, *BBC Panorama*, 'Britain's Secret Terror Force', Directed by John Ware (first aired BBC1, 21 November 2013).
215 Sanders, Andrew and Ian S. Wood. *Times of Troubles: Britain's War in Northern Ireland* (Edinburgh: Edinburgh University Press, 2012), p. 186.
216 *An Phoblacht*, 18 February 1973, p. 7.
217 *Resistance, Magazine of the New Lodge Resistance Council*, No. 37, 12 February 1973, p. 1.

218 Sluka, Jeffrey A. '"For God and Ulster": The Culture of Terror and Loyalist Death Squads in Northern Ireland', in *Death Squad: The Anthropology of State Terror* (Philadelphia: University of Pennsylvania Press, 2000), p. 134.
219 Kitson, Frank. *Gangs and Counter-gangs* (London: Barrie and Rockliff, 1960), pp. 121–122.
220 Hughes, James. 'Frank Kitson in Northern Ireland and the "British way" of counter-insurgency', *History Ireland*, 22, no. 1 (2014), p. 45.
221 Bloomfield, Kenneth. *Tragedy of Errors: The Government and Misgovernment of Northern Ireland* (Liverpool: Liverpool University Press, 2007), p. 43.
222 PRONI: OE/1/28: 'Communique on Tripartite Talks on Council of Ireland' (9 December 1973).
223 Ibid.
224 *Combat*, No. 1 Vol. 1, 18 March 1974, p. 1.
225 *The United Irishman*, January 1974, Vol. XXVIII.
226 *The Ulster Loyalist*, 3 January 1974, pp. 1–2.
227 Guelke, Adrian. 'Loyalist and Republican Perceptions of the Northern Ireland Conflict: The UDA and the Provisional IRA', in *Political Violence and Terror: Motifs and Motivations*, Edited by Peter H. Merkl (Berkeley: University of California Press, 1986), p. 106.
228 Novosel, Tony. *Northern Ireland's Lost Opportunity: The Frustrated Promise of Political Loyalism* (London: Pluto Press, 2013), p. 127.
229 *An Phoblacht*, 18 January 1974, p. 1.
230 Ibid., p. 7.
231 *An Phoblacht*, 25 January 1974, p. 3.
232 *Combat*, Vol. 1 No. 8, May 1974, p. 1.
233 *Combat*, Vol. 1 No. 5, April 1974, p. 1.
234 Novosel, Tony. *Northern Ireland's Lost Opportunity: The Frustrated Promise of Political Loyalism* (London: Pluto Press, 2013), p. 89.
235 Taylor, Peter. *Loyalists* (London: Bloomsbury, 1999), pp. 123–124; Hanley, Brian and Scott Millar. *The Lost Revolution: The Story of the Official IRA and the Workers' Party* (London: Penguin, 2010), p. 227.
236 Parsons, Michael. 'Auction of "Gusty" Spence archives casts new light on UVF's secret talks with IRA', *The Irish Times* [http://www.irishtimes.com/news/auction-of-gusty-spence-archives-casts-new-light-on-uvf-s-secret-talks-with-ira-1.478532] (10 March 2012), Accessed on 21 March 2017.
237 Ibid.
238 *An Phoblacht*, 8 March 1974, p. 1.
239 Cusack and McDonald, *UVF*, pp. 145–147.
240 Parsons, Michael. 'Auction of "Gusty" Spence archives casts new light on UVF's secret talks with IRA', *The Irish Times* [http://www.irishtimes.com/news/auction-of-gusty-spence-archives-casts-new-light-on-uvf-s-secret-talks-with-ira-1.478532] (10 March 2012), Accessed on 21 March 2017.
241 Stedman, S. J. 'Spoiler Problems in Peace Processes', *International Security*, 22 (1997), pp. 5–53.
242 Ibid., p. 8.
243 Wood, *Crimes of Loyalty*, pp. 32–33.
244 Holland, Jack. *Hope Against History: The Ulster Conflict* (London: Hodder & Stoughton, 1999), p. 104.
245 Nelson, *Ulster's Uncertain Defenders*, p. 155; Wood, *Crimes of Loyalty*, p. 34.
246 Anderson, Don. *Fourteen May Days: The Inside Story of the Loyalist Strike of 1974* (Dublin: Gill & Macmillan, 1994), p. 27.
247 Ulster Workers' Council, *Press Statement from the Ulster Workers Council*, 15 May 1974.
248 Anderson, *Fourteen May Days*, p. 27.

249 McKittrick and McVea, *Making Sense of the Troubles*, p. 103.
250 Ibid., p. 103.
251 Bruce, *The Red Hand*, pp. 98–99.
252 Moloney, Ed. *Voices From the Grave* (London: Faber and Faber, 2010), p. 167.
253 Bell, *The Irish Troubles*, pp. 405–406.
254 Holland, *Hope Against History*, pp. 109–110.
255 Bruce, *The Red Hand*, p. 296; Sutton, *An Index of Deaths*.
256 McKearney, Tommy. *Provisional IRA: From Insurrection to Parliament* (London: Pluto Press, 2011), p. 138.
257 Moloney, *Voices from the Grave*, p. 170.
258 PREM 16/515 IRELAND: Situation in Northern Ireland: Part 10; Bell, J. Bowyer. *The Irish Troubles: A Generation of Violence* (Dublin: Gill & Macmillan Ltd, 1993), p. 434.
259 Coogan, *The Troubles*, pp. 258–259.
260 Kelley, Kevin J. *The Longest War: Northern Ireland and the IRA* (London: Zed Books, 1988), p. 223.
261 *An Phoblacht*, 30 May 1975, p. 1.
262 Coogan, *The Troubles*, pp. 316–317; also see Adams, Gerry. *Before the Dawn: An Autobiography* (New York: William Morrow and Company Inc, 1996), pp. 249–250.
263 Moloney, *Voices from the Grave*, p. 169.
264 Ibid., p. 169.
265 Bishop and Mallie, *The Provisional IRA*, p. 273.
266 Holland, *Hope Against History*, p. 113.
267 Kevlihan, Rob. *Aid, Insurgencies and Conflict Transformation* (New York: Routledge, 2013), p. 49.
268 *The Ulster Loyalist*, 17 March 1975, p. 1.
269 *Combat*, Vol. 2 No. 31, N.D., c. February 1975, p. 5.
270 *The Ulster Loyalist*, 17 February 1975, p. 1.
271 Bell, *The Irish Troubles*, pp. 450–451.
272 Cusack and McDonald, *UVF*, pp. 166–167.
273 Cadwallader, *Lethal Allies*, p. 327.
274 Smith, *Fighting for Ireland?*, p. 120.
275 Cusack and McDonald, *UVF*, p. 161.
276 Dillon, *The Dirty War*, pp. 212–217.
277 *Combat*, August 1975, p. 22.
278 *An Phoblacht*, 15 August 1975, p. 3.
279 Cusack and McDonald, *UVF*, p. 163.
280 Irwin, Alistair and Mike Mahoney, 'The Military Response' in *Combating Terrorism in Northern Ireland*, Edited by James Dingley (London: Routledge, 2009), p. 203.
281 Sutton, Malcolm. *An Index of Deaths*.
282 Ibid.
283 Moloney, Ed. *A Secret History of the IRA* (London: Penguin Books, 2007), p. 147.
284 Ibid.
285 Taylor, *Provos*, p. 196.
286 Coogan, *The Troubles*, pp. 258–259.
287 Neumann, Peter R. *Britain's Long War: British Strategy in the Northern Ireland Conflict, 1969–98* (New York: Palgrave, 2003), p. 85.
288 Ibid., p. 85.
289 Moloney, *Voices from the Grave*, p. 172.
290 Kelley, *The Longest War*, p. 234.
291 Bell, *The Irish Troubles*, pp. 466–467.
292 Ibid., pp. 468–469.
293 Sutton, *An Index of Deaths*.
294 Taylor, *Provos*, p. 197.

295 Geraghty, Tony. *The Irish War: The Military History of a Domestic Conflict* (London: HarperCollins, 2000), p. 97.
296 Hillyard, Paddy. 'Political and Social Dimensions of Emergency Law in Northern Ireland', in *Justice Under Fire: The Abuse of Civil Liberties in Northern Ireland*, Edited by Anthony Jennings (London: Pluto Press, 1990), p. 192.
297 O'Malley, *The Uncivil Wars*, pp. 289 – 290.
298 Republicans killed 21 RUC personnel in 1976. The highest before that was in 1972 when they killed 14. Sutton, *An Index of Deaths.*
299 Republicans killed 15 UDR personnel in 1976, and 22 in 1972. Sutton, *An Index of Deaths.*
300 Sutton, *An Index of Deaths.*
301 Ibid., p. 202.
302 Moloney, Ed. and Andy Pollak. *Paisley* (Dublin: Poolbeg Press Ltd, 1986), p. 365.
303 Hillyard, Paddy. 'Political and Social Dimensions of Emergency Law in Northern Ireland', in *Justice Under Fire: The Abuse of Civil Liberties in Northern Ireland*, Edited by Anthony Jennings (London: Pluto Press, 1990), p. 194.
304 Cadwallader, *Lethal Allies*, p. 264.
305 *Index*, p. 278.
306 Kelley, Kevin J. *The Longest War: Northern Ireland and the IRA* (London: Zed Books, 1988), p. 259.
307 McKittrick, David and David McVea. *Making Sense of the Troubles* (London: Penguin, 2001), p. 123.
308 Adams, Gerry. *Free Ireland: Towards a Lasting Peace* (Niwot: Roberts Rinehart Publishers, 1994), p. 58.
309 Sutton, Malcolm. *An Index of Deaths.*
310 Holland, *Hope Against History*, p. 117.
311 Della Porta, Donatella. *Social Movements, Political Violence, and the State: A Comparative Analysis of Italy and Germany* (Cambridge: Cambridge University Press, 1995), p. 154.
312 De Fazio, Gianluca. 'The Radicalization of Contention in Northern Ireland, 1968–1972: A Relational Perspective', *Mobilization: An International Quarterly*, 18, no. 4 (2013), p. 477.
313 Fadaee, Simin. 'Social Movements, Counter-movements, and their Dynamic Interplay', in *Women's Movements and Countermovements: The Quest for Gender Equality in Southeast Asia and the Middle East*, Edited by Claudia Derichs and Dana Fennert (Newcastle: Cambridge Scholars Publishing, 2014), p. 19.
314 Moloney, *Voices From the Grave*, p. 47.

6

ISLAMISTS AND THE COUNTER-JIHAD IN BRITAIN, 2009–2018

Introduction

This chapter will now turn to the interactions between the counter-jihad movement (CJM) and the Islamist movement in Britain. This is an episode which has been at the centre of discussions of cumulative extremism since the formation of the English Defence League (EDL) in 2009. However, the degree to which the relationship between the two movements has actually involved interactive escalation, and produced tactical innovations of their respective protest repertoires, has not yet been investigated in a sustained and in-depth manner. Furthermore, at the outset it should be noted that the 'enduring cycle of violence or terrorist action' which some observers have warned of has not (yet) occurred. This begs the question: why not?[1] What are the necessary and sufficient conditions for the development of CE to escalate to the sustained use of extreme or lethal violence? What is the likelihood of this eventuality developing in the future? By closely analysing the evolution of the movements involved in this case study in the light of the analyses of the previous chapters, the present discussion will answer these questions.

2009–2011

The roots of this case study lay in the radical Islamist Omar Bakri Muhammad's attempt to establish a presence for the international pan-Islamic organisation Hizb ut-Tahrir (HT) in the United Kingdom. Throughout the 1990s HT was the most radical Islamist organisation in Britain. Despite this, they did not engage in violence but rather 'organized rallies, held public events and distributed ideological literature'.[2] However, this approach was judged to be too timid by Omar Bakri, whose militancy increasingly brought him into conflict with HT's international leadership. Bakri subsequently left HT and founded his own group, al-Muhajiroun (AM), with Anjem Choudary, a former lawyer from south London. In 2004 AM was proscribed under the Terrorism Act 'for inciting violence and racial hatred' and disbanded on 13 October 2004.[3] It seems very likely, though, that two groups formed shortly afterwards, al-Ghurabaa and The Saviour Sect, were little more than permutations of AM. Both of these organisations were also subsequently proscribed in 2006 following the 7 July 2005 bombings in London by Islamist terrorists. This pattern of proscription followed by re-branding and re-founding of Islamist extremist groups linked to Al-Muhajiroun – including the groups Islam4UK, Muslims Against Crusades and Need4Khilafah – continued until at least 2014.[4]

It was the actions of the front-groups for the AM-network that really galvanised organised anti-Muslim sentiment and ignited the counter-jihad movement in Britain. In the Bedfordshire town of Luton, a demonstration held on 10 March 2009 by members of the radical Islamist group Ahlus Sunnah wal Jamaah (itself another AM offshoot), in protest against British soldiers returning from service in Iraq, sparked off a series of counter-demonstrations by counter-jihad groups such as the United People of Luton (UPL) and March for England (MfE).[5] In the aftermath of these, often violent, demonstrations, members from UPL and various other counter-jihad groups, as well as members from a number of football hooligan 'firms', formed the English Defence League with the aim of forcing 'the Government to get Islamic extremists "off the streets"'.[6] From 2009 the organisation grew at a fairly impressive rate, and in 2010 alone they held at least seven demonstrations with between 1,000 and 2,000 members taking part, as well as a number of smaller events.[7]

During this period of growth, the leaders of the EDL attempted to capitalise on their good fortune by founding similar organisations throughout Europe in 2010. Working with the infamous American counter-jihad activists Pamela Geller and Robert Spencer, EDL leader Stephen Yaxley-Lennon (also known by his pseudonym Tommy Robinson) helped found the Norwegian, Swedish, Danish and Finnish defence leagues. Further, these 'alliances [were] officially consolidated online through a defence league umbrella group called the European Freedom Initiative (EFI), founded by Robinson and former EDL media head Steve Simmons.'[8] On the whole these efforts failed to produce long-lasting organisations with the scale of support that the English Defence League achieved; some have already ceased to exist, and the ones that continue to mobilise are 'smaller and much less important' than the EDL.[9] Indeed, the campaigning group Hope not Hate refers to them as 'the failed European Defence Leagues'.[10]

However, the efforts to develop an international network of 'Defence Leagues', as well as the EDL's and EFI's collaboration with the American 'Stop the Islamisation of Nations' (SION), should not be dismissed as entirely trivial. In the first place, through these networks of support (facilitated by the organisations' respective internet sites and shared internet forums), '[i]nformation, ideas, emotions and plans for the future have long been exchanged'.[11] As Hun and

Meleagrou-Hitchens argue, 'Defence leagues inspired by the EDL have emerged throughout Scandinavia and are organising joint rallies and conferences, helped on by so-called "ideas people", including Robert Spencer, who provides much of the ideological fuel, and Pamela Geller, whose organisational skills the [European Counter-Jihad Network] has employed to some effect.'[12] The EDL benefited, even if only marginally, from both the ideological resources and from extra activists (members of European Defence Leagues have attended EDL events in Britain and vice versa) that these networks have provided.[13]

This attempt to expand the movement throughout Europe on the part of the CJM was reflected by attempts to accomplish similar objectives on the part of the radical Islamists. At around the same time that Yaxley-Lennon was helping to develop other European 'Defence Leagues', at 'the end of the 2000s, Choudary began to export his group's strategy and methods to other parts of Europe.'[14] Soon groups such as Sharia4France, Sharia4Belgium and Sharia4Holland were founded in those respective countries. However, whereas the CJM's efforts in this area may have fuelled the M/CM contest in Britain, even if only in a small way, the radical Islamists' chief aim was to send jihadist fighters to places like Syria. This ultimately would have the effect of de-escalating the M/CM conflict by depriving Islamist groups of key activists in Europe. Indeed, this disparity in focus on the part of the two movements reflects a major aspect of this episode, which has gone some way in inhibiting sustained escalations: right from the outset the two movements have been asymmetrically coupled, with the CJM being far more tightly coupled to the Islamists than vice versa. While the EDL was formed in direct response to the provocative actions of radical Islamists, and the CJM movement in general frequently mobilises in response to the high-profile actions of Islamists, the Islamist movement is largely speaking unresponsive to their would-be antagonists.

There are some important exceptions to this: in June 2012 six Islamist extremists attempted to bomb an EDL rally but were arrested before they could carry out their attack.[15] Further, there have been a number of clashes between members of the counter-jihad and Islamist movements. Following the death of Al-Qaeda leader Osama Bin Laden in May 2011, Anjem Choudary and MAC organised a 'funeral service' for him outside the US Embassy in London. Unsurprisingly, this attracted the attention of a large group of EDL activists, and police struggled to keep the two groups apart from each other 'amid threats of violence from both sides.'[16] In September 2011 MAC attempted to protest a remembrance event for British victims of 9/11, again outside of the American Embassy in London. After the event, Islamist extremists and EDL members clashed in a series of fights around the Marble Arch and Edgware Road areas of London: 'Scotland Yard said four people, two from each side, were arrested around the Grosvenor Square site before police detained several more Islamists and about 20 EDL supporters as trouble spread to the West End.'[17]

Yet on the whole, the counter-jihad movement does not register as a major issue on the Islamists' list of priorities. Whereas virtually every communication coming from the EDL's website, Facebook page and Twitter account is related to the activities of Islamists or Muslims, or on atrocities carried out in Muslim countries, it is hard to find any mention of the EDL or any of their fellow-travellers on the archived websites for Islam4UK and MAC. In fact, one of the few posts on the Islam4UK website that mentions the EDL, titled 'An Invitation to the English Defence League by Islam4UK', strikes a strangely ameliorative tone towards them, while bizarrely criticising the anti-fascist organisation Unite Against Fascism (UAF) for their attacks on the EDL:

> As misinformed as they may be about Islam, recent events have also shown that [the EDL] are being poorly represented in the public arena by various media outlets; incorrect comparisons have been drawn between its members and those from among the British National Party, who are known for their particularly racist views…
>
> One such organisation, which has played a large role in distorting the reality of the English Defence League, is the Unite Against Fascism party. The UAF (Unite Against Fascism) party, who in an attempt to gain popular support among the British community, have taken it upon themselves to hijack protests led by members of the English Defence League to further their own socialist led policies, in a typical 'underdog' themed campaigns…[18]

Julia Ebner has recently warned of an escalating relationship between Islamists and the far right and introduces her book by describing events organised by both sides which she herself attended. Yet, tellingly, while the counter-jihad activists she met spoke unprompted about the problem of Islam (and spoke of little else), the Islamists did not mention the far right until Ebner herself asked them about the subject directly. While the far right serve to provide evidence for Islamists that the West is hostile to Islam, on the whole there is little evidence that Islamist animus springs from them.[19]

When movements are not tightly coupled, then it is less likely that they will meet each other in the 'arena' of street mobilisations, which are one of the sets of circumstances in which movements are more likely to develop strong ingroup loyalties and outgroup hatreds, in which people may become socialised to violence as they clash with members of an opposing movement, and in which people may engage in the 'gradual reciprocal adaptation to increasingly dangerous weapons'.[20]

However, because the Islamist movement has been unwilling to directly confront the EDL, the counter-jihad group has often engaged in violence with the perceived social base of the Islamist movement: the British Muslim community. Despite claims that they are motivated by a desire to tackle Islamist extremism, rather than Islam itself, members of the EDL have frequently clashed with young Muslim men, who are not extremists or part of any Islamist organisation, but merely locals from whatever area the EDL are protesting. In September 2009 a large EDL group clashed with a group of roughly 200 local young Muslims; the two groups fought and threw bricks at each other, leading to ninety arrests.[21] Similar scenes occurred days later on 11 September 2009, as an EDL demonstration on the anniversary of 9/11 near a Mosque in Harrow descended into a violent brawl between the counter-jihad activists and Asian youths. This resulted in riot police being called in, leading to ten arrests.[22] In Leicester, on 10 October 2010, EDL members broke through police lines and fought running battles with Asian youths in Muslim areas of the city.[23]

There is, of course, the possibility that these clashes might radicalise young British Muslims and push them into the arms of the Islamist movement. Indeed, Joel Busher has even stated that when the EDL holds a demonstration it makes it easier for Islamists to recruit in that area.[24] However, there is no evidence that this has occurred on a significant scale. Gauging precise levels of support enjoyed by the Islamist movement amongst British Muslims is difficult, partly because of the clandestine nature of the organisations involved, and partly because 'there are very few substantive studies and reports focusing' on them.[25] Pupcenoks and McCabe have stated that the now-exiled former leader of Al-Muhajiroun, Omar Bakri Muhammad, claimed that Islam4UK, one of the more recent iterations of AM proscribed on 14 January 2010, 'had 4500 supporters. However, it is more likely that the group never had more than 300 members from among more than two-million British Muslims.'[26]

The relatively tiny size of the AM network's membership base no doubt reflects the broader British Muslim community's feelings towards the Islamists; that is, relative hostility. Three factors may largely account for this: firstly, extremist Islamic doctrine is viewed as abhorrent by the vast majority of Muslims.[27] Secondly, their contentious actions are designed to sow discord between Muslim and non-Muslim communities, which no doubt contributes to increasingly negative feelings towards Muslims in general. Thirdly, there are extant, moderate community organisations who are much better placed to address the grievances of the Muslim community. The Muslim Council of Britain (MCB), for instance, is a well-known umbrella organisation which has developed a strong relationship with the British state. As Pedziwiatr points out, 'only six months after its launch, the MCB attended a meeting with Home Secretary Jack Straw, and by the end of its first year, had established regular contact with Straw and FCO ministers. This good relationship with the government continued to develop so that in its 2002 Annual Report the MCB claimed to conduct regular meetings with 'government ministers and other politicians and "movers and shakers" as well as senior civil servants.'[28]

The existence of efficacious institutional channels through which to address grievances provides a kind of pressure-valve, directing mobilisations away from taking radical paths and robbing extremist organisations of the chance to make political capital out of these issues. Fortunately, there seems to be evidence that the Muslim community in the United Kingdom is still sufficiently engaged with the extant political system. Maxwell found in 2010 that British Muslims were more likely to have trust in the government than Christians were. In addition,

Maxwell specifically highlighted 'the importance of general political satisfaction and political efficacy as opposed to the more specifically assimilation and segregation-related variables identified by the literature on minority attitudes.'[29] Very similar results were found by Goodhart *et al.* in 2016, when they found that 'Britain's Muslim population feels comparatively more able to exert influence upon the system. 51% felt they could influence decisions affecting their local area by engaging with local officials and 14% felt this "very strongly" – proportionally twice as many as the populace as a whole.'[30]

A further complicating factor to this episode of contention is the fact that, since 2009, it has become clear that the British far left are far more interested in opposing the CJM than Islamists are. The main far-left organisation that has strived to oppose the counter-jihad movement is the aforementioned Unite Against Fascism, a group formed through the merger of the Anti-Nazi League (ANL) and the National Assembly Against Racism (NAAR) in 2003.[31] The UAF's campaign against the CJM, and in particular the EDL, stemmed in large part from political developments elsewhere on the far right. The British National Party – long the UAF's primary concern – had had a number of electorally successful years, and by 2009 had managed to secure thirty-three local council seats and two European Parliamentary seats.[32] This obviously concerned the UAF, but more than just the BNP's successes, they were also driven by a belief that the

> BNP is a fascist organisation... As with fascist parties in the past, the BNP stands in elections to secure a veneer of respectability. This acts as a cover for its real agenda: promoting vicious race hatred and thuggery on our streets.[33]

Yet when, across 2009 and 2010, the BNP did not revert to their older aggressive form of 'street politics', the UAF's theoretical paradigm directed them to view the EDL as the BNP's foot soldiers. As Copsey argues, the UAF 'was inclined to conflate the BNP with the EDL', as they were sure that 'it was no coincidence that the EDL had formed at the high point of the BNP's electoral success... UAF now took on responsibility for organising the street-based opposition to the EDL.'[34] Indeed, in one of their first strategy papers written in regard to their anti-EDL campaign, they argued that '[t]he growth of the EDL street demonstrations, including outside Mosques, is a dangerous consequence of the election of the BNP to the European Parliament'.[35] Further, in an 'EDL factsheet' titled *The EDL: violent racists and fascists,* they argued:

> THE EDL IS RIDDLED WITH FASCISTS. EDL leader 'Tommy Robinson' – real name Stephen Yaxley Lennon – is a former member of the fascist British National Party. Founder EDL member Chris Renton was also in the BNP, as were other leading figures including North East organiser Alan Spence. Many more former members of the BNP, the Nazi National Front and other fascist organisations are also active in the EDL and its splinter groups...[36]

This opposition from the UAF had the effect of partially diverting the attention of the EDL away from Islamists towards left-wing targets. As Busher has noted, while 'most of the EDL leaders were keen to maintain their focus primarily on (militant) Islam, the fact that the main opposition to the EDL tended to come from overly left-wing groups such as UAF or Antifa meant that some EDL activists' focus shifted increasingly towards the left as clashes with these opponents gave rise to personal grievances and resentments.'[37] This new front of contention may well have actually aided EDL activists in their mobilisations, while simultaneously radicalising some of them. EDL leaders told Busher 'how disorganised and unprepared they had been and how ironically, they had at least initially learned quite a bit about how to conduct protests by observing their anti-fascist opponents.'[38]

Furthermore, the EDL physically clashed with anti-fascist opponents more frequently than with Islamists, leading to violent reprisals on left-wing targets – a tactic that does not seem to have been employed against Islamists. In June 2011 a group of nine EDL members violently attacked a pub that was holding a Rock Against Racism Event, throwing bricks and stones through windows and knocking one man's tooth out.[39] The same year members of the EDL and the EDL-offshoot group the Infidels attacked the protestors at the Occupy Newcastle camp, 'anti-racist and anti-cuts protesters, as well as attempting to target the Occupy movement which has camped outside St Paul's Cathedral'.[40] In December of that year the EDL attacked the Tyneside Irish Centre, mistakenly believing the Socialist Workers' Party were holding a meeting there.[41] In February 2015 a group of twenty EDL members disrupted an anti-fascist meeting which had been held to organise a counter-demo to a proposed counter-jihad march in Newcastle. The EDL members shouted abuse at the anti-fascists, stating that the women present should be sterilised.[42]

With their Islamist opponents often out of sight, the opportunity to clash with visible and active opponents may have helped to sustain the CJM. Hilary Pilkington found that the '"buzz" of demonstrations… cannot be detached from the thrill of the potential for, and actuality of, aggro with the opposition and even violence. The thrill of the eruption of violence between EDL and [Muslim Defence League] or UAF counter-demonstrators at a demo is described by [EDL activist] Tim as "just like Braveheart", while [EDL activist] Connor talks of the "adrenaline rush" of "having a good scrap"'.[43] Similarly, Busher found in his ethnographic research on the EDL that an important 'aspect of people's journeys into EDL activism concerns the emotions associated with entry into the group and its social scene… Every person I talked to about their journey into EDL activism spoke about the excitement or the "buzz" of the demonstrations… some described quite bluntly how they saw the EDL as an opportunity to "go and kick off" against "Muzzies" or "lefties"'.[44]

Between 2010 and 2011, the EDL's growth peaked: by October 2010 Nigel Copsey noted that they had ninety local divisions and 22,000 followers listed on Facebook and could mobilise several thousand activists for demonstrations.[45]

By November 2011 Bartlett and Littler estimated 'the total size of the [pool of supporters] to be at least 25,000–35,000 people', around half of whom 'have been involved in demonstrations and/or marches'.[46] Their first demonstration of 2011 was their biggest yet, with around 3,000 supporters joining in the march through Luton, the EDL's home town.[47] By May the group had held at least two more demonstrations with around 2,000 supporters, as well as many smaller ones.[48] However, 2011 was also the year that the EDL's luck began to change. On 22 July 2011, Anders Breivik carried out two terror attacks in Norway, killing 77 people including many children.[49] It subsequently came to light in the national media that 'Breivik wrote of having strong links with the EDL, saying he had met its leaders and had 600 EDL members as Facebook friends'.[50] Moreover, he claimed he 'was told he would be welcome at EDL demonstrations, and wrote about visiting Bradford and London. He is also reported to have attended an EDL rally in Newcastle.'[51] Furthermore, '[s]everal high profile EDL activists were recorded admitting their support for Breivik's actions'.[52]

2012–2013

In 2012 the EDL began to falter, with their pool of active supporters shrinking. In conjunction with the negative press the organisation had received in 2011, another reason contributing to their decline may well have been the efforts on the part of the leadership to moderate the image and behaviour of the rank and file members at demonstrations. After receiving consistently negative attention in the media for the violence which frequently occurred at their events, as well as for their connections to the far right and Anders Breivik, the leadership made a concerted effort to purge the grassroots of obviously far-right and violent individuals. However, in trying to prevent violence from occurring at their demonstrations, the leadership inadvertently robbed many members of their main motivation for attending them in the first place: that is, the visceral thrill of confrontation. As already stated, many of those who joined the EDL right from the outset were men involved with the football casuals scene: football 'hooligans', who enjoyed physical altercations. Pilkington has argued that the 'efforts of the leadership to rid the movement of the "thuggish" element and improve the public perception of it have been decisive in the decisions to leave of many of what Jack refers to as the "hard-core" that "look for the violent side of it"'.[53] Similarly, Busher has estimated 'that approximately 30%–40% of the core activist community in the area between March 2011 and May 2012 had entered EDL activism directly from the football-related public disorder scene, although their involvement waned more quickly than that of some other segments of the activist community when the group started to lose momentum in the course of 2011.'[54]

Developments in how the EDL were policed may have had a similar effect. When the EDL first appeared, their events were frequently volatile affairs, and often descended into violence. 'In that way it is understandable that a heavy handed and pro-actively aggressive approach to policing the EDL characterised the early style of policing them'.[55] This approach, however, was often counter-productive, and at times actually contributed to larger-scale conflicts between the EDL, counter-protesters and local communities, and the police. In October 2010 the strict control that the police attempted to hold over an EDL demo in Leicester – intentionally delaying some groups of protestors from arriving at the demo, banning them from marching in certain areas, and forcing them to be bussed from one place to another – provoked a concerted effort by many activists to break through police lines and attack the nearby Muslim community.[56]

However, since around February 2012 the police have employed a much softer approach, seeking 'dialogue and agreement with the EDL' in advance of an event.[57] This has seen a decrease in incidences of violence and large-scale public disorder at EDL events. Not only has this deprived some of the more aggressive and thrill-seeking members of the opportunity to engage in violence, it has also fairly successfully contained the M/CM contest. In Northern Ireland, the heavy-handed and one-sided behaviour of the RUC frequently antagonised members of the Catholic community and contributed to the dynamic of CE. While the members of the EDL do often feel they are treated unfairly by the police,[58] the general trends of de-escalation of the EDL's collective action repertoire and the decline in support for the movement suggests that, at the very least, the police are not feeding in to the dynamic of CE. Indeed, it seems likely that the police are interrupting the reciprocal radicalisation that can occur when antagonists frequently physically clash with each other, as happened between fascists and anti-fascists, and, to a much greater degree, to the Catholics and Protestants of Northern Ireland in 1968 and 1969. As Pilkington has observed '[o]rganised violence, however, is replaced by routinised scuffles which occur at easily identifiable trigger points. Corners along the route of a demonstration are one such point; as this is where the opposition often comes into view and the "banter" starts… observation at more than twenty demonstrations suggests the most peaceful marches are those where the opposition is kept consistently out of the line of vision.'[59]

On 22 May 2013, it appeared that the EDL's fortunes were reversing after the British soldier Lee Rigby was murdered by Islamist extremists Michael Adebolajo and Michael Adebowale in Greenwich, London. Three days later the EDL held one of their biggest rallies in months when around 2,000 activists marched through Newcastle. This led to fears over a resurgence and radicalisation of the EDL's behaviour, and specifically of the dynamic of CE developing. There was also a concern by observers at the time that processes of CE could end up radicalising more people, ultimately benefiting both the Islamist and counter-jihad movements. As Matthew Goodwin argued in *The Guardian* the day after Rigby's murder:

> The risk is that cumulative extremism leads to a spiral of mobilisation and then counter-mobilisation, which requires an altogether different set of policy and security tools than simply managing a renegade EDL

demonstration or a single terrorist attack. While at first this may produce hardened rhetoric or discourse on Facebook, it may have more serious long-term effects, by strengthening feelings of collective identity and loyalty among activists, sparking violent and sporadic reprisals and, at the absolute extreme, an enduring cycle of violent or terrorist action. We have seen this dynamic in cases such as Northern Ireland. Cumulative extremism arguably exposes the inadequacy of so-called 'counter-narratives' that focus simply on attempting to resolve particular grievances within particular extremist communities. We need to know far more about how and when this interplay occurs, how it escalates and how it can be stopped.[60]

Seemingly reinforcing Goodwin's warnings, Matthew Feldman and Mark Littler found that

[W]e [have] isolated one of the first concrete examples of [cumulative extremism], identifying an alarming rise in anti-Muslim attacks in the seven days that followed the murder of Drummer Lee Rigby. While the nature of the data prevents the identification of a directly causal relationship, and there remained a number of possible alternate explanations for the spike – for example, an increase in sensitivity to attacks amongst members of the Muslim community – our analysis nevertheless shows a clear pattern.[61]

Although the use of hate crimes committed by individuals as a measure of CE suggests a non-organisational understanding of CE by Feldman and Littler, which differs from the approach being taken in this book for reasons outlined in the introduction. More recently, Ebner similarly argued that 'Jihadist attacks tend to increase the support base of far-right movements. For example, in the days after Lee Rigby was murdered, the EDL's Facebook likes jumped by 100,000.'[62]

However, as reasonable as these concerns appeared in the context of a severely provocative radical Islamist attack and a spike in both EDL actions and anti-Muslim attacks, in reality the increased support and activities were short-lived. Macklin and Busher have argued that analysts of CE need to be sensitive to the ways in which 'shorter-wave arguments, confrontations, and emotional reflexes contribute to and fuel the longer-wave construction of oppositional identities and animosities'.[63] The murder of Lee Rigby certainly provoked a short-wave 'emotional reflex' as demonstrated by the increase in anti-Muslim crime and support for the EDL, but that this did not fuel 'the longer-wave construction of oppositional identities and animosities' demonstrates that the necessary conditions for CE to develop were not present at that time. In Northern Ireland there was a conflict fought across an extant and deep-seated communal cleavage, with community (or social movement) organisations that had long histories and/or strong ties to those communities. Thus when violence erupted across this cleavage, both the communal divisions and ties between communities and organisations were reinforced. In England in 2013 neither of these factors were present. Short-wave factors therefore have a lot more heavy lifting to do in order to translate into or fuel longer-wave identity formation (developing closer ties between social movement organisations such as AM or the EDL and the communities they claim to represent)[64] or fostering animosities (deepening the perceived cleavage between the Muslim and non-Muslim communities).

The EDL faced another blow to their campaign when their two most high-profile leaders, Stephen Yaxley-Lennon and Kevin Carroll, announced that they would be leaving the organisation following a series of meetings with the counter-radicalisation think tank Quilliam. In a press release sent out by Quilliam on 8 October 2013, Robinson stated that

> I have been considering this move for a long time because I recognise that, though street demonstrations have brought us to this point, they are no longer productive. I acknowledge the dangers of far-right extremism and the ongoing need to counter Islamist ideology not with violence but with better, democratic ideas.[65]

2014–2019

Hilary Pilkington, who was conducting ethnographic field research on the EDL at the time, noted that the 'humiliation of the resignation and realignment of Tommy Robinson and Kevin Carroll left the movement vulnerable. By January 2014, the initial spike in numbers following the murder of Lee Rigby had gone "flat".'[66] What is more, the new leader of the EDL, Steve Eddowes, felt sure that far-right parties now perceived the group as rudderless and thereby as a 'ready-made street army' to be recruited to their cause.[67] Of these far-right groups, the one most eager to 'court EDL activists' was the organisation Britain First (BF), which released a video in 2014 that criticised 'the EDL for lack of direct action, for cooperating with the police over planned demonstrations, not recognising that real change could only come about through being part of a political process and for wasting time idolising their old leader who had betrayed them.'[68]

In the fractured milieu of the CJM, the BNP splinter organisation Britain First stands out in terms of both the publicity it receives and the aggressive nature of their anti-Muslim protests. Formed in 2011, the party employed a clever social media strategy to successfully gain an impressive online presence which belies their modest size of active supporters. Indeed, in 2015 it was noted that Britain First became 'the first political party in the UK to receive more than 1 million supporters on its official Facebook profile',[69] although Hope not Hate have estimated their actual size to be between 800 and 1000 active members.[70] Surprisingly, unlike virtually the entire rest of the far right in Britain, the party initially paid no attention to Islam; until, that is, the murder of Lee Rigby. It was then decided that Anjem Choudary – who likely had been in contact with at least one of the killers – was responsible for the Islamists' radicalisation and so by extension for Rigby's murder. Subsequently, opposing the 'Islamification' of Britain was placed front and centre on BF's agenda.[71]

In 2014 the group gained notoriety in the UK when it began to use highly provocative anti-Muslim protest strategies; namely 'Christian patrols' and 'Mosque invasions'. The former was in response to the alleged introductions of 'Sharia controlled zones' by Anjem Choudary and his Muslims Against Crusades and Islam4UK organisations. The Islamist extremists put up fliers stating 'No Alcohol', 'No Gambling', 'No Music or Concerts', and other similar sentiments around areas of East London with large Muslim populations, as well as stating that '[w]e have hundreds, if not thousands, of people who are willing to go out and make sure our laws are obeyed… This is the best way of dealing with drunkenness, loutishness, prostitution and the sort of thug life you get in Britain.'[72] This was a specious statement, and was wholly intended to generate publicity – which it successfully did: the stunt garnered 'massive coverage' in the media.[73] BF's response to this was to drive three decommissioned army Jeeps through East London, and then film themselves 'emptying cans of beer outside a mosque during Friday prayers in what they described as an attempt to draw out the extremists.'[74] Just as had happened for Anjem Choudary's groups, Britain First successfully gained 'significant exposure in both the mainstream media and online'.[75]

The next tactical innovation of their protest repertoire was arguably even more aggressive. In May 2014 BF began what it referred to as 'Mosque invasions'. This entailed groups of activists entering mosques, 'refusing to remove their shoes and confronting worshippers and imams on a range of tenuously connected issues including Britain being a Christian country [and] the failure to stop members of Muslim communities from participating in grooming gangs.'[76] This tactic brought the group similar levels of attention in the press. However, as Hope not Hate have observed, despite the 'extraordinary… overexposure' they have consistently reaped 'few rewards.'[77] While there seems to be some evidence of the co-evolution of the collective action repertoires of BF and AM here, with some degree of reciprocal radicalisation taking place, this was entirely one-sided. The AM network never really responded to BF's actions with any tactical innovations of their own, and despite generating impressive levels of publicity, neither group managed to translate this into significant increases of active supporters. Indeed, it is possible that these publicity stunts actually hindered them. Both sides eventually fell afoul of the law, with BF leader Paul Golding being sentenced to prison in December 2016 for organising a Mosque invasion and Anjem Choudary being sentenced in September 2016 for supporting a terrorist organisation – a conviction which was likely arrived at in light of these activities.[78]

Indeed, 2014 was a damaging year for both the British Islamist and the counter-jihad movements, despite what should have been a very propitious year for the latter. Firstly, in early 2014 a new radical Islamist military force called

ISIS (Islamic State of Iraq and Syria; otherwise known as IS) operating in the Middle East came to international prominence as they took 'over Fallujah forty miles west of Baghdad as well as extensive territory in Anbar, the huge province encompassing much of western Iraq'.[79] Not only did the ISIS leadership, headed by radical Islamist Abu Bakr al-Baghdadi, proclaim their impressively sized territory to be a 'Caliphate' (an Islamic State),[80] but right from the beginning the group employed gruesome political violence to achieve its aims. Indeed, in a report published in September 2014, Amnesty International reported that

> [t]he group that calls itself the Islamic State (IS) has carried out ethnic cleansing on a historic scale in northern Iraq. Amnesty International has found that the IS has systematically targeted non-Arab and non-Sunni Muslim communities, killing or abducting hundreds, possibly thousands, and forcing more than 830,000 others to flee the areas it has captured since 10 June 2014.[81]

Secondly, in August 2014, an independent inquiry into child abuse in the town of Rotherham included a 'conservative estimate' that at least 1,400 children – some as young as eleven – were 'sexually exploited' between 1997 and 2013. Furthermore, and crucially as far as the counter-jihad movement was concerned, the report concluded that the vast majority of the victims were white and that most of the perpetrators were Muslims. As Hope not Hate observed at the time, these developments should have provided fertile ground for the counter-jihad to grow in, as '[m]any people – including people who would not normally vocalise such thoughts – start[ed] to make the connection and decide that there is something deeply troubling with Islam and its followers.'[82] Yet once again the CJM not only failed to capitalise on these developments, but actually continued its decline. Hope not Hate identified a number of factors to account for this failure: an inability for key leaders to distance themselves from more overtly racist ideologies and 'thuggish' behaviours, within-movement hostilities, and an 'increasingly active and aggressive anti-fascist movement' including 'street-militant groups' who have demoralised them.[83]

However, another factor could be that the counter-jihad movement's target, the Islamist movement, was itself declining, thereby starving them of the oxygen of conflict. One reason for this, ironically, was also the very same reason that the counter-jihad could have expected to find increased support amongst the British people; namely, the rise of ISIS. Hope not Hate described how '2014 was a year of tactical change for the' AM network as Choudary eschewed the 'regular large public demonstrations', and was instead to be found 'singing the praises and denying the crimes of the Islamic State' in television and online interviews.[84] This proselytising might well have decreased the AM network's capabilities by contributing to an 'exodus of AM activists to foreign war zones',[85] although in truth this may well have been Choudary (and the broader movement's) ultimate goal.[86]

Another reason was the intervention of British security services into the Islamist movement (no doubt partly motivated by intelligence that British radicals were attempting to head to fight for the IS). From the middle of 2014 onwards, there was the implementation of a concerted effort to disrupt AM activities by state forces: in June, the groups Need4Khilafah, the Shariah Project and the Islamic Dawah Association were all proscribed by the British Government under the Terrorism Act 2000. Then, in September Anjem Choudary and eight other high-profile AM leaders were arrested on suspicion of belonging to a proscribed organisation – 'just days before the UK government announced its intention to participate in air strikes against ISIS.'[87] Further, along with the arrests, the police seized all the groups' computer equipment, and thereby also gained valuable intelligence.[88]

This intervention by the state into the Islamist movement not only deprived the EDL and the other counter-jihad groups of the thrill of conflict which can sustain a social movement – especially one with its roots in angry confrontational protest – but, along with the foreign policy intervention into the IS, also probably eased anxieties amongst the broader population that the government was not taking the Islamist threat seriously; anxieties which could well have transformed into the motivation to become an active member of the counter-jihad movement had the government not acted.

Yet while this involvement of the state undoubtedly de-escalated this episode by assuaging the concerns of potential activists for the counter-jihad movement, there is still the possibility that in another way it may have quite the opposite result. Due, at least in part, to the clandestine nature of the Islamist movement's activities, the state has to a certain degree securitised the entire Muslim population of Britain. This has been done through the government's Prevent agenda, which is itself one of four strands of the broader CONTEST counter-terrorism strategy first developed in 2003.[89] The focus of Prevent was initially exclusively on Islamic extremism – leading to widespread feelings of victimisation amongst the British Muslim community. Later, in July 2015, the Government's Counter-Terrorism and Security Bill came into force, introducing new legislation which stated that a wide range of public bodies, including, but not limited to, schools, Doctors' Surgeries, hospitals and universities, were legally obliged to 'have due regard to the need to prevent people from being drawn into terrorism'.[90] While this is an ostensibly reasonable clause, in practice this has forced these bodies to comply with the much maligned Prevent strategy. The Muslim Council of Britain stated that the 'Government has rightly moved the emphasis of Prevent to the Home Office and has expanded the scope of Prevent to 'all forms of extremism'. Nevertheless, despite the British government's declared intentions, 'there still remains a strong perception that there is an unfair, unproductive and aggressive assumption of extremism when dealing with Muslim communities'.[91] The obvious lesson which can be taken from many of the policy blunders committed by the British government in Northern Ireland is that the careless use of counter-terrorism measures can easily backfire, potentially alienating and radicalising sections of the population.

The gradual decline of the CJM continued during 2015, and the attempt to hold a 'Muhammad Cartoon Competition' in September of that year sheds some light on another reason that the movement failed to maintain the progress it had achieved between 2009 and 2011. Organised by high-profile anti-Islam activist Anne Marie Waters, and modelled after similar events held in Denmark and Texas, the competition was cancelled in late August, allegedly over 'the very real possibility that people could be hurt or killed – before, during and after the event.'[92] In reality though, it seems that a significant contributing factor to the cancellation of the event was infighting between various members of the counter-jihad. While Anne Marie Waters, Stephen Yaxley-Lennon and Britain First financier Jim Dowson had an acrimonious argument over appropriate strategies, the far more telling divide was ideological.[93]

In the first instance, some members of the of the Lawyers Secular Society (LSS) were unpleasantly surprised to find out that their organisation had been sponsoring the CJM event, and that the group's secretary Charlie Klendjian had been scheduled to speak. After the angry LSS members called for, and lost, a vote to pull themselves from the event, Klendjian 'who works as an in-house lawyer for mobile network operator and internet service provider EE, was obviously feeling the heat [and in] the immediate aftermath of the exhibition's cancellation…resigned from the LSS'.[94] In the second instance, Waters had arranged for the leader of the far-right anti-Muslim political party Liberty GB, Paul Weston, to speak at the event. The presence of Weston caused much consternation amongst some of those planning to attend the event.[95] Speaking of Weston's involvement after the cancellation, and defending her decision to include him, Waters wrote on her blog:

> Some of the attacks aimed at us (from those who ought to support us) were allegedly made because of Paul Weston's planned presence at the event. Weston… has made some speeches about the future of white people, and according to those who set the rules, this is a step too far. The demographic-that-cannot-be-named was named, and this was more than enough to cancel Weston's speaking rights thenceforth[.][96]

What this episode illustrates is the heterogeneity and lack of cohesion inherent to the counter-jihad movement. Broadly speaking, it tries to present itself as a movement defending 'Western Civilization' against 'militant Islam'. However, this is a very coarse-grained description; in the fine-grain lay the issues which contribute to the movement's inability to maintain a sustained mobilisation. Not only do some organisations explicitly state that they are against Islam itself – rather than just the more extreme manifestations of it – but others still have different ideas about whom they are involving in their fight against (militant) Islam: for the EDL it is ostensibly any group (including moderate Muslims), for others it is Europeans, and for others still it is only white people.[97] For some groups the counter-jihad movement is just part of a broader project of racial supremacy, while others still make opposition to this sort of far-right ideology an important and prominent part of their group's identity. Some are vocally pacifist and eschew violence in favour of rhetoric, while others wilfully use political violence.

The example above of the 'Muhammad Cartoon Competition' represents the moderate, 'respectable' wing of the movement (as represented by Klendjian and the LSS) who clearly struggle to operate without suffering the stigma of being labelled as racist (a major problem for the counter-jihad movement). The more radical wing of the movement is represented here by Weston (although he pales in comparison to some of the more extreme elements of the movement), whose outspoken views are genuinely abhorrent to many in the movement and certainly seen as strategically counter-productive to others.

These confusing interactions between and within the different wings of the counter-jihad movement can partly be explained by the different motivations that members have for engaging with the movement. The more extreme groups see anti-Muslim activism as just one part of a broader ultra-nationalist project, and one which may prove more politically expedient than the more traditional extreme-right propaganda themes such as anti-Semitism. As Nick Griffin, then leader of the BNP, told his party in 2005

> … in real politics in the real world, one's proper choice of enemy is a group who you gain a worthwhile level of extra support by identifying, who you have a realistic chance of beating, and whose defeat will take you the furthest towards your goal. With millions of our people desperately and very reasonably worried by the spread of Islam and its adherents, and with the mass media… playing 'Islamophobic' messages like a scratched CD, the proper choice of enemy needn't be left to rocket scientists.[98]

The links between groups such as the BNP, the NF, the EDL and the EDL splinter-group the Infidels reflect the ideological overlap of specific members of those groups. While there has been concerted efforts by many EDL leaders to purge their organisation of extreme-right influence, there have also been similar efforts made by members of the extreme right to exert their influence, particularly during Yaxley-Lennon's time in prison and after his departure from the group.[99] At the same time, right from the EDL's formation, a significant number of founding members were men who had been active on the football hooligan scene, and for whom a major motivation for becoming an EDL activist was the opportunity for aggressive confrontation. The more successful that the moderate members of the EDL were in cultivating a non-violent protest repertoire, the less of an incentive many people had for active involvement with the group.

While the lowest common denominator for all these groups and people is hostility to Islamism, the genuinely held feelings of anti-racism and commitment to non-violent protest by some are anathema to the more extreme groups. Inversely, the overt racism and commitment to violence by people in the extreme wing are truly abhorrent to the more moderate members. The mutually exclusive ideological and strategic perspectives contained within the movement have been a serious impediment to mobilisation. Indeed, Busher's research has led him to estimate that, between February 2011 and May 2012, in London and the South East 'approximately 20%–30% of core EDL activists… had come to the EDL via their involvement in established far-right groups of one sort or another – in most cases political parties such as the BNP, English Democrats and the NF, and a handful had also been associated with more ideologically and tactically radical groupuscules such as Combat 18.'[100] As already stated, Busher had also found that '30%–40%' of EDL activists joined the organisation through their involvement with the football hooligan scene.[101]

Once the leadership seriously began attempting to present the EDL as a peaceful and non-racist organisation, and once the policing of their marches became more successful in maintaining order, it is hardly surprising that many of these people began to lose interest in the organisation and decide to join the more extreme outfits.[102] This contrasts strongly to the situation in, for example, Northern Ireland. While feuding within the republican and loyalist movements was far more violent than in any of the other case studies examined in this book, there was also much stronger agreement amongst all members of both movements over what their overarching goals were, as well as stronger agreement on the strategic approaches that should be taken (that is, lethal political violence).

This internal heterogeneity of the CJM could go some way in explaining why, since its formal launch in the UK, Pegida has failed to make any real headway in the UK. An abortive attempt to launch a UK branch in 2015, without the backing of the original organisation in Germany, failed to gain much momentum after the BNP, the NF, members of the EDL and other smaller far-right groups all struggled for control during a demo in Newcastle.[103] Subsequently, after Yaxley-Lennon gave a speech at an official Pegida event in October 2015 and had talks with the leadership there, the group was re-launched in Britain in February 2016 with the German Pegida's blessing.[104] Robinson stated that his vision for Pegida UK is for them to attract a 'middle-class' demographic and avoid 'loutish behaviour and alcohol-fuelled violence', stating that '[w]e are taking the whole football culture, which was embedded in the EDL, out of it and we are trying to create a safe environment'.[105]

The inaugural event was a 'silent march' in Birmingham with Yaxley-Lennon, Anne Marie Waters and Paul Weston at the head. It was hoped that by shedding the image of hooliganism, which was very much associated with the EDL in the public's mind's eye, that the group would gain wider support. However, in the event the march only managed to attract some 200 attendees, 'a large number of those being from the media.'[106] Their next event, a 'silent walk through Rotherham' in response to the child sex scandal that had occurred there, only managed to muster between 50 and 150 attendees.[107] Given that the demonstration held by the earlier incarnation of Pegida UK, which had involved the more extreme members of the counter-jihad movement such as the Infidels and the National Front, was not only larger than any of the events held by the later incarnation (it had around 300 people in attendance) but was also the biggest far-right event of 2015, it is clear that the lack of cohesion and divisions within the movement are a serious roadblock to mobilisation.

In attempting to remove violence and purge the overt expressions of racism, Pegida UK precluded much of their potential support base from engaging with them. As Jamie Bartlett, who was present on the Birmingham Pegida march, noted: 'Tommy had succeeded: the demonstration *was* respectable … But it was *too* respectable … Tommy's old group, the EDL, was popular not in spite of the drinking, the swearing, the chanting, and the ever present possibility of a fight with anti-fascists, but *because* of those things'.[108] At the same time, the high visibility of the far-right element in the movement has lent empirical credibility to the claims by groups like UAF that the movement is a fascist and/or racist one, which has created a serious barrier to the movement gaining broader popular appeal. As Gani argues, 'there is a need for a *common purpose* and a *collective identity* to drive the activists forward in a strategically astute way'.[109] These were two characteristics sorely lacking in the CJM.

By the summer of 2016, the leaders of Pegida UK were all devoting their efforts towards other projects, and so within 'six months of starting it was all over. Pegida-UK had failed.'[110] Yet just as the young organisation petered out, conditions seemed to become much more propitious for the counter-jihad movement. On 23 June the UK held its referendum on its membership in the European Union, with 52% of those voting opting to leave. In the wake of this decision, the incidence of hate crimes in the country rose sharply. Between July and September over 14,000 incidents were documented by police forces – the highest number in a comparable period since records began in 2012.[111] (Although, it should be noted that 'hate crimes have been on an upward trend since 2013, and always increase a lot in June and July – precisely when the referendum occurred.'[112]) However, on 16 June 2016 the Labour MP Jo Cox was tragically murdered outside of her constituency surgery by far-right activist Thomas Mair, who allegedly shouted 'Britain First' during the attack.[113]

Whereas the murder of Lee Rigby had animated the CJM, this had the effect of stalling it – particularly in the case of Britain First, who were seemingly implicated by Mair in the attack. This led to BF 'sitting out the subsequent by-election for fear of a local backlash',[114] as well as derailing the talks which had been ongoing between BF leader Paul Golding and Paul Weston of LibertyGB in the hopes of arranging a merger between the two parties.[115] The extreme right faced yet another hurdle in the form of the proscription of the neo-Nazi group National Action, who were banned on the grounds that they were 'concerned with terrorism.'[116] There was some concern that this would 'ban little more than its mere name', and just prompt an AM style re-branding with essentially the same actors still working together.[117] Indeed, subsequently two more groups – Scottish Dawn and NS131 – were also proscribed on the grounds that they were essentially synonymous with NA. As Macklin has observed, though, these concerns were 'unduly pessimistic; overestimating the capabilities and commitment of NA activists to weather the storm, whilst also underestimating the authorities' own commitment to dismantle the group'.[118] More importantly, in Spring 2017 the police arrested a leading member of NA, Alex Deakin, and subsequently gained access to his phone which contained incriminating messages between the former NA members detailing how they planned to subvert their ban. This led to a series of arrests, trials and convictions which effectively dismantled the group.[119]

However, Macklin has cautioned that these arrests, the appearance of former NA members in less extreme groups, and the formation of the group System Resistance Network (whose website uses very similar graphics to those used by NA) does indicate that there are former NA members still active and committed to the cause.[120] Further, the main threat in terms of extreme-right terrorism still comes more from solo actors, rather than directly from organisations such as National Action. Moreover, 'the bulk of contemporary lone actors' such as Thomas Mair, Jo Cox's murderer, 'appear "peripherally" involved in extreme-right groups while earlier cases had involved individuals who, despite acting alone, were, to some degree, "embedded" within the broader milieu. This currently constitutes a clear challenge for detection and interdiction.'[121]

The year 2017 seemed to signal that processes of CE were indeed spiralling towards a sustained shift towards deadly violence after three Islamist extremist and one anti-Muslim terrorist incidents occurred in the first half of the year. On 22 March 2017 Khalid Masood drove his car into pedestrians on Westminster Bridge, killing four, before fatally stabbing a police officer. Two months later, on 22 May, Salman Ramadan Abedi detonated an explosive device at a concert in the Manchester Arena, killing twenty-three people including himself (making this the deadliest terrorist attack in Britain since the 7/7 bombings). The following month three Islamist extremists crashed their van into pedestrians in London Bridge and then attacked pedestrians in the Borough Market area of London, killing eight people in total, before being killed themselves by armed police officers. Shortly afterwards, on 19 June, Darren Osborne drove a van into a crowd of Muslims near Finsbury Park Mosque, killing one of the group and injuring many others.[122]

Many have argued that these events are evidence of processes of CE developing, particularly Darren Osborne's terror attack.[123] Indeed, it does seem to be the case that Osborne's actions were to some degree motivated by the earlier Islamist attacks; what is more, he received messages from leading figures in the counter-jihad such as Jayda Fransen and Stephen Yaxley-Lennon regarding the perceived threat of Islam shortly before carrying out his attack.[124] Much like earlier Islamist terror attacks, the ones in early 2017 provoked a spike in anti-Muslim attacks – Osborne's was the most noteworthy of these. Julia Ebner has averred that the Islamist attacks can similarly be explained through vicarious retribution, arguing that the perpetrator of the Manchester Arena bombing – Salman Abedi – was radicalised after his friend was murdered in what he perceived to be a hate crime.

While it certainly seems to be the case that this event was a motivating factor in Abedi's pathway to radicalisation, some caution should be applied here in too quickly attributing the model of CE. In the first instance, Abedi had already made some progress in his journey towards radicalisation before his friend's murder. Not only is there evidence that he spent his school holidays fighting in Libya against the Gaddafi regime with his father when he was sixteen (both of whom had connections to radical cleric Abu Qatada),[125] but MI5 had a file on him from as early as January 2014.[126] Further, his sister has said that she thought his actions were motivated by US airstrikes in Syria, rather than events closer to home.[127]

Moreover, even if we did accept that Abedi's friend's murder was a prime motivational factor in his actions at Manchester Arena, it is important to be careful not to conflate racism and discrimination with the far right. While closely linked phenomena, they are nevertheless distinct. Being racist does not make one a member of the far right (though in likelihood racist attitudes generally mean one is much more likely to sympathise with the cause); and a racially motivated murder is by no means necessarily an action of the far right.

This is a point which warrants further attention. In analysing M/CM dynamics, it is necessary to be clear about who the individuals, groups and movements involved are. Ebner adroitly describes the radicalisation of Islamist and far-right extremists, but in describing the interaction between the two sometimes slips into conflating the far right with discrimination and racism. For example, as evidence of 'a symbiotic relationship between far-right and Islamist' exists,[128] Ebner quotes Al Muhajiroun's founder Omar Bakri Muhammad as saying 'People, when they suffer in the West, it makes them think. If there is no discrimination or racism, I think it would be very different for us'; elsewhere she explains that an Islamist terrorist's 'experiences of anti-Muslim hatred and racism played a crucial role in his radicalisation'; later Ebner describes how 'since the recent series of attacks on French territory, people are no longer ashamed of being openly racist. This new wave of outspoken hatred is likely to cause a backlash, because "the one thing that unites National Front and Al Qaeda is their hatred."'[129] Importantly, the National Front did not cause this hatred, as much as they may encourage it. Indeed, when one more carefully parses out the far right on the one hand and discrimination/racism on the other, there is much less clear evidence of reciprocal radicalisation existing between the far right and Islamist extremism; it is a much more asymmetrical dynamic.

The Islamist terror attacks breathed new life into the counter-jihad street movement. A new group, the Football Lads Alliance (FLA), emerged and succeeded in mobilising more activists on the streets of England than any far-right group since the BUF. On 24 June and 7 October the FLA held marches in London with around 5,000 and between 10,000 and 50,000 participants respectively.[130] The FLA is a 'self-proclaimed "anti-extremist"' group, but their events attract large numbers of far-right activists (and they often invite high-profile anti-Islam activists to speak at their rallies).[131] Indeed, the Premier League has warned football clubs that 'investigations have revealed that the group is using fans and stadiums to push an anti-Muslim agenda.'[132] These impressive mobilisations were given a further fillip in the form of mass outrage over the jailing of Stephen Yaxley-Lennon who was sentenced to prison for breaching reporting restrictions on an ongoing court case involving Muslims (although this sentence was later quashed on appeal and a new trial ordered). The FLA and other counter-jihad groups protested in London over Yaxley-Lennon's incarceration, with around 15,000 and 10,000 gathered together for 'Free Tommy Robinson' events on 9 June and 14 July respectively.

More troublingly, MI5 and counter-terrorism police successfully disrupted at least four extreme-right terrorist plots between 2017 and October 2018, indicating that there are indeed still anti-Muslim activists willing to use more extreme strategies to achieve their goals after the proscription of NA. These developments do seem to be driven by cumulative extremism.[133] As Max Hill Q.C. stated, in his role as Independent Reviewer of Terrorism Legislation, 'the threat we face from extreme right wing terrorism within the UK is considerable, and in my clear view it has grown in reaction to the terrorist atrocities on Westminster Bridge, London Bridge and at Manchester Arena last year.'[134] In the June 2018 iteration of the government's CONTEST counter-terrorism strategy, it was observed that before 2014 extreme-right activists *tended* to be older, espoused anti-immigration and white supremacist views, but crucially 'presented a very low risk to national security'.[135] However, NA's emergence seemed to have a lasting influence on the protest repertoire of the far right, which had the effect of increasing 'community tensions and the risk of disorder'; the document also added that other 'UK-based extreme right-wing groups also advocate the use of violence.'[136]

Nevertheless, it is also worth noting Hill's observation that despite 'the terrorist attacks and other events of 2017, the UK consistently avoids long-term elevation of the national threat level to the highest category, avoids recourse to Article 15 derogation and the declaration of a national state of emergency as seen in France, and benefits from policing and intelligence work which successfully disrupts terrorism-related activity almost every time.'[137] Crucially, this policing and intelligence work has been increasingly focussed on the threat from the extreme right (although still, understandably, is mainly concerned with that emanating from Islamist extremists). As Graham Macklin has argued, the 'authorities have moved toward an increasingly active, coordinated, and indeed multi-layered response to right-wing extremism', making it 'harder to substantiate the claim, in Britain at least, that the authorities still have a "blind spot" when it comes to extreme-right terrorism and political violence.'[138] Further, despite the seeming resurgence of the CJM in the form of the FLA, the infighting and lack of cohesion that has often characterised the far right has not abated. Indeed, the FLA experienced a schism and split into the FLA and the Democratic Football Lads Alliance (DFLA) by March 2018. It may be the case that the single-issue counter-jihad movement is not capable of sufficiently papering over the ideological differences possessed by the various individuals involved. As one member of a DFLA march said to

The Guardian: 'I detest some of the people I'm walking with. A lot of them hate people because of the colour of their skin. I'm a lefty, but I believe we should have a voice against the people who want to hurt everyone and cause harm.'[139] While the counter-jihad movement demonstrated that it could mobilise massive numbers of people on to the streets, it is by no means clear that this will translate into a cohesive long-lasting organisation or movement. Further, as Stocker and Feldman have noted, it has not 'proved capable of harnessing far-right activism into an even moderately successful political party.'[140] Indeed, Yaxley-Lennon's attempt to enter electoral politics, becoming a Special Political Advisor to the leader of UKIP, led to internal division and a spate of senior members resigning from the party in protest.[141] His subsequent attempt to run as an independent MEP candidate ended in 'humiliating defeat' as he snuck out of the vote count early, while a video was released seeming to show 'large sections of the audience' united in laughter as his vote count was later announced (receiving 2.2% of the vote, Yaxley-Lennon lost his deposit).[142] Further, UKIP, whose lurch to the far right from 2018 was typified by their association with Yaxley-Lennon and their invitation for notorious far-right internet figures Carl Benjamin and Mark Meechan to stand as candidates for them, precipitated an exodus of supporters and blanket electoral failure in the 2019 European elections in which they lost all twenty-four seats and gained none.[143]

Moreover, these events have once again largely speaking been ignored by Islamist extremists; the dominant M/CM dynamic has been that between the far right and anti-fascists. Indeed, the resurgence of the counter-jihad movement caused a flurry of activity amongst anti-fascist activists who developed new networks and worked hard to mobilise a significant number of activists to challenge their political adversaries.[144] In direct response to the formation of the Football Lads Alliance (and their erstwhile comrades in the DFLA) anti-fascists with experience organising campaigns at football grounds (such as the Celtic Fans Against Fascism) founded the Football Lads and Lasses Against Fascism (FLAF). These groups clashed violently at FLA and DFLA marches in 2018, with anti-fascists successfully disrupting a DFLA march in London on 13 October.[145]

Conclusion

The foregoing discussion has assessed the extent to which CE has developed between the CJM and the Islamist movement in Britain since 2009. This case study is notable since it has been the focus of much of the academic literature on CE. Academics including Eatwell & Goodwin, Feldman & Littler, and Nigel Copsey have all warned of the potential for processes of cumulative extremism to develop between these two movements. More recently, Andre has agreed with these assessments and argued that 'far-right extremism and Islamist extremism represent two sides of the same coin', adding that with each Islamist terror 'attack, populist far-right movements gain credibility and political support, and liberal democracies harden their illiberal policies, which in turn further alienates an already stigmatized and traumatized European Muslim community.'[146]

The emergence of the English Defence League and the subsequent growth of the broader counter-jihad movement certainly seemed to indicate that the potential for CE to develop exists. Despite this, on the whole this episode has not escalated to a sustained shift in tactics towards the consistent use of organised lethal violence, aside from several important incidents such as the four terrorist attacks committed by Islamist extremists and a far-right extremist across the first half of 2017. But given the presence of two militant and at times certainly adversarial movements in what has been, at times, a tinderbox situation, why has this episode not escalated further?

The first reason is that, more than any other set of opposing movements examined throughout this book, the counter-jihad and Islamist movements were extremely asymmetrically coupled. While the CJM was largely speaking ignited by the actions of Islamists, and its whole *raison d'être* has been to oppose Islamism, the reverse cannot be said to be true. With a few notable exceptions the existence and actions of the CJM have never been more than a passing concern to the Islamists. As has been described, the less closely that groups are coupled with each other, the less likely they are to frequently encounter each other in person or to experience 'rapid cycles of tactical innovation and adaptation.'[147] So, while the EDL's counter-demonstrations against Islamist events no doubt fuelled animosities and had some sort of radicalising effect on both sides, the fact that the Islamists never really responded to any of the CJM's numerous rowdy events meant that this effect was largely speaking less intense than it otherwise could have been.

The second reason lies with the quite wide distance that exists between the social movements' interests and aims and those of the communities which they claim to speak for, or from which they attempt to draw support. Certainly, the Islamist movement has never been more than a tiny, if disproportionately dangerous, fringe group within the relatively small Muslim community in Britain. As has already been explained, the group's extreme interpretation of Islam is considered odious by the vast majority of British Muslims. Furthermore, their intentionally incendiary actions and statements are seen to stoke anti-Muslim sentiments and thereby make life more difficult for the wider Muslim population. Similarly, the CJM has thus far been unsuccessful in framing their aims and objectives as significantly corresponding with the broader 'material and symbolic interests' or aims of their target audiences; be that the British public at large, or the white working class.[148] While the anti-immigration sentiment that is a broader interest of the CJM might well also be quite widely seen as being an interest of large parts of the British people, there are many channels and organisations which are perceived as being much more legitimate than the CJM through which to pursue that goal; for example, support for the Conservative party, or the right-wing populist Brexit Party. Expression of support for this issue through these channels comes at a much lower cost for people than does active involvement in the counter-jihad movement.

Indeed, this is directly related to the third reason that this episode did not escalate further: the internal heterogeneity, or 'identity crisis', of the CJM.

While the diverse array of groups and people that constitute the CJM could all agree on their opposition to militant Islam, there was little consensus on anything other than that one point. Everything else, from ideology and identity to strategy, was a source of strife. The more radical members' predilection for violence and overt racism was not only off-putting to more moderate members, but it also justified the cries of racism from their opponents on the left. By the same token, when the more moderate members attempted to exert control over the movement they denied many others of the thrill of conflict that had largely drawn them to the movement in the first place. These discrepancies in outlook and behaviour were not only a barrier to unity, thereby inhibiting mass mobilisations of the movement, but also prevented the movement from achieving more popular appeal.

The fourth reason that the contest did not escalate further than it did is the British Government's involvement in the episode which has, on the whole, been relatively balanced and effective. Many of the state interventions into the conflict in Northern Ireland, such as the one-sided introduction of internment that exclusively targeted Catholics or the ham-fisted imposition of a curfew so the British Army could search the Catholic area of the Falls Road, were astoundingly counterproductive and directly contributed to the radicalisation of parts of the Catholic community. By contrast, the British police forces and security services have managed to successfully contain the Islamist and CJM social movement organisations and interrupt processes of CE as well as acting in a manner likely to ease some of the concerns of the broader public which, if unchecked, could lead to increased support for one or the other movement.

A fifth factor which has thus far prevented the escalation of this episode is the constraints placed on the actors by the 'repertoires of contention' currently available to them. The EDL's genuine attempt to present itself as a moderate organisation is an impediment to the use of violence, an impediment which is shared by their leftist and community counter-protesters. Indeed, this commitment to nonviolence seems to have contributed to Pegida's failure to gain any traction. Even the Islamist groups associated with the AM network have tended to employ nonviolent forms of collective action in Britain. The few exceptions to this general rule have, of course, had dramatic impacts on the M/CM conflict: the terrorist attacks in 2017 breathed new life into the ailing CJM, and led to a spike in anti-Muslim violence.

However, while this analysis makes clear that CE has not significantly developed between the CJM and Islamist movement – and is unlikely to in the near future – it would still be somewhat myopic to conclude that it is certain never to. Indeed, it is important to be clear on just how it might yet develop. By comparing this case study to the previous ones examined in this thesis it is possible to identify which factors may be instrumental in the M/CM contest escalating towards CE. Unsurprisingly they are strongly related to the factors which have thus far inhibited an escalation in the episode.

There are three key variables in this episode which, if they developed in a certain way, could conceivably begin to generate processes of CE, with a resultant sustained shift in protest tactics and a growth of support for the social movement organisations:

1. If the conflict-cleavage solidified along ascriptive lines, with each movement drawing support from a separate and distinct community.
2. If the aims of the social movement organisations began to be perceived as aligning with the broader interests of these communities.
3. If the competing social movement organisations became more closely and symmetrically coupled.

While unlikely to occur, this confluence of factors developing is by no means beyond the bounds of the possible.

The conflict-cleavage between these two movements is a more complicated issue than it may at first appear. While the motivating issue for both movement and countermovement is, ostensibly, the proliferation of radical Islamism, in reality there are a set of broader factors such as class and ethnicity which also structure and drive the conflict. Pupcenoks and McCabe have argued that both the counter-jihad and the Islamist movements are the product of attempts to forge trans-national identities – a European identity in the case of the former, and the religious community of the Ummah in the case of the latter – which resemble competing nationalisms: 'Emerging Europeanized identities have been mirrored by trans-national identity-formation among Europe's Muslims… Thus, we can see the potential for a serious contentious episode between two antagonistic blocs, both of which are undergoing a process of identity construction along largely religious and ethno-nationalist lines, reflecting not an ethnic conflict per se, but an "ethnicized conflict".'[149] Akbarzadeh and Mansouri agree with this assessment, arguing that the 'perception of injustice and bridled aspirations' of many young Muslims who feel alienated and disenfranchised in Western society leads to them finding meaning, identity and a sense of purpose in Islamism: 'Here lies the attraction of neo-Islamism. Not being constrained by a national mind-frame and operating as a transnational force, it appeals to those who have lost their connection to their Muslim ancestral land but find it difficult to be accepted in their country of residence.'[150]

Thus, for some, it is their experience of exclusion from their national community which has fuelled their attachment to Islamism. Pantucci describes how the leaders of AM were quick to exploit the experiences of racism which coloured many Muslims' lives. As Anjem Choudary said to him: 'despite the fact that you have just as many qualifications as the next man and [have] gone to the same universities, there is still a feeling that you are disadvantaged or people are still discriminating against you'; AM founder Omar Bakri similarly stated that people 'are looking for an Islamic identity. You find someone called Muhammad, who grew up in Western society, he changes his name to Mike, he has a girlfriend, he drinks alcohol, he dances, he has sex, raves, rock and roll, then they say, "You are a Paki." After everything he gave up to be accepted, they tell him he is a bloody Arab, or a Paki.'[151] The problems faced by these people, then, in large part stem from their ascriptive identity and the perception (by both some Muslims and some white British) that Islam is not compatible with their country's shared identity.

As has been mentioned above, the counter-jihad movement is also hugely driven by anxieties felt by the white working class over issues such as immigration, multiculturalism and economic uncertainty. The description which one EDL member gave to Hilary Pilkington of her organisation consisting of members of 'the normal working class that are struggling to get by' suggests that the roots of their movement are broader than the single issue of anti-Muslim sentiment. Indeed, as Pilkington has argued, recognising 'the entwinement of class and race/ethnicity in patterns of contemporary inequality and marginalisation is central to understanding the context of activism in movements such as the EDL'. There is clearly the perception of a zero-sum game between the white working class and other disenfranchised communities developing in the minds of many, which fuels much of the support for the CJM. As another EDL member complained:

> Like a young English male like myself… we're not counted any more, we haven't got as much rights as say a young Islamic 28 year old, I think he's got more rights than me. You know, he can get more off the government than me. Say if I was not working… And I just think it's wrong.

Further, Treadwell and Garland argue that the efforts of the EDL to court more widespread support from the working class may not have been quite so fruitless as many observers have thought, and that in the future ongoing economic instability may help to channel public sentiment towards support for the EDL's goals: 'the EDL's presentation of itself as an organisation of 'moderation' that champions the issues and values that are important to ordinary people, may have more resonance than some would like to think… our fear is that the contemporary economic downturn will push working-class voters further in the direction that some have recently taken, from the ballot box and onto the streets.'[152]

So, while it may appear that the conflict-cleavage between the counter-jihad and Islamist movements is simply a single-issue, non-ascriptive one, it is apparent that these movements' continued existence is very much tied to the collective grievances of much larger groups. This demonstrates a stronger ascriptive element to this conflict than may appear at first glance. As argued before, this dynamic of an M/CM contest being fought across an ascriptive cleavage between two movements who do voice the genuinely felt grievances of larger populations is more conducive to CE developing than when not fought across ascriptive cleavages. The main concern here is that the radical CJM and Islamist extremist groups could grow in the eyes of their respective social bases as legitimate outlets for their grievances. Moreover, this process would also likely bring the counter-jihad and Islamist movements into closer competition, making them more tightly and symmetrically coupled. This could then lead to tactical escalations, vicarious retribution, and the use of Jujitsu Politics. Nevertheless, at the time of writing, Britain in 2019 bears very little resemblance in terms of CE to Northern Ireland in 1969.

Notes

1 Goodwin, Matthew. 'Woolwich Attack and the Far Right: Three Points to Consider When the Dust Settles', *Guardian Online* [https://www.theguardian.com/commentisfree/2013/may/23/woolwich-attack-far-right-three-points] (23 May 2013), Accessed on 5 February 2017.

2 Pupcenoks, Juris and Ryan McCabe. 'The Rise of the Fringe: Right Wing Populists, Islamists and Politics in the UK', *Journal of Muslim Minority Affairs*, 33, no. 2 (2013), p. 175.

3 Thomas, Dominique. 'Al-Muhajirun and Al-Ghuraba', in *Islamic Movements of Europe*, Edited by Frank Peter and Rafael Ortega (London: I.B. Taurus, 2014), p. 178.

4 Vidino, Lorenzo. 'Sharia4: From Confrontational Activism to Militancy', *Perspectives on Terrorism*, 9, no. 2 (2015), pp. 12–13.

5 Copsey, Nigel. *The English Defence League: Challenging Our Country and Our Values of Social Inclusion, Fairness and Equality* (London: Faith Matters, 2010).

6 Ibid., p. 11.

7 Jackson, Paul. *The EDL: Britain's 'New Far Right' Social Movement* (Northampton: RNM Publications, 2011), pp. 70–72.

8 Meleagrou-Hitchens, Alexander and Hans Bru. *A Neo-Nationalist Network: The English Defence League and Europe's Counter-Jihad Movement* (London: ICSR, 2013), p. 17.

9 Berntzen, Lars Erik and Sveinung Sandberg. 'The Collective Nature of Lone Wolf Terrorism: Anders Behring Breivik and the Anti-Islamic Social Movement', *Terrorism and Political Violence*, 26, no. 5 (2014), pp. 761–762.

10 *HOPE Not Hate*, Issue 23, January–February 2016, p. 13.

11 Godin, Emmanuel. 'The European Extreme Right: In Search of Respectability?', in *The Routledge International Handbook on Hate Crime*, Edited by Nathan Hall, Abbee Corb, Paul Giannasi and John Grieve (Oxon: Routledge, 2015), p. 148.

12 Meleagrou-Hitchens, Alexander and Hans Bru. *A Neo-Nationalist Network: The English Defence League and Europe's Counter-Jihad Movement* (London: ICSR, 2013), p. 24.

13 Lowles, Nick. 'Police Searches', *Hope Not Hate* [https://web.archive.org/web/20140707152934/http://www.hopenothate.org.uk/blog/nick/police-searches-1095] (5 February 2011), Accessed on 2 February 2017.

14 Neumann, Peter R. *Radicalized: New Jihadists and the Threat to the West* (London: I.B. Tauris, 2016), p. 116.

15 Pantucci, Raffaello. *We Love Death as You Love Life: Britain's Suburban Terrorists* (London: C. Hurst & Co. Ltd, 2015), pp. 276–277.

16 *Mail Online* [http://www.dailymail.co.uk/news/article-1384353/Osama-bin-Laden-mock-funeral-Fury-erupts-outside-US-Embassy-London.html] (7 May 2011) Accessed on 2 February 2017.

17 *Metro* [http://metro.co.uk/2011/09/11/muslims-against-crusades-and-english-defence-league-square-up-at-911-ceremony-145461/] (11 September 2011) Accessed on 2 February 2017.

18 Islam4UK, 'An Invitation to the English Defence League', *Islam4UK* [http://cryptome.org/islam4uk/341.html] Accessed on 12 December 2016.

19 Ebner, Julia. *The Rage: The Vicious Circle of Islamist and Far-Right Extremism* (London: I.B. Tauris, 2017), pp. 1–9.
20 Della Porta, Donatella. *Social Movements, Political Violence, and the State: A Comparative Analysis of Italy and Germany* (Cambridge: Cambridge University Press, 1995), p. 154.
21 *Mail Online* [http://www.dailymail.co.uk/news/article-1211414/Anti-fascists-clash-right-wing-protesters-Birmingham.html#ixzz4XdI7q7pE] (7 September 2009) Accessed on 3 February 2017.
22 *The Independent* [http://www.independent.co.uk/news/uk/home-news/riot-police-called-in-as-demonstrators-clash-at-anti-muslim-protest-1785797.html] (11 October 2009) Accessed on 3 February 2017.
23 Treadwell, James. 'Controlling the New Far Right on the Streets: Policing the English Defence League in Policy and Praxis', in Neil Chakraborti and Jon Garland (eds.), *Responding to Hate Crime: The Case for Connecting Policy and Research* (Bristol: Policy Press, 2015), p. 134.
24 Busher, Joel. *The Making of Anti-Muslim Protest: Grassroots Activism in the English Defence League* (Oxon: Routledge, 2016), p. 177.
25 Pupcenoks, Juris and Ryan McCabe. 'The Rise of the Fringe: Right Wing Populists, Islamists and Politics in the UK', *Journal of Muslim Minority Affairs*, 33, no. 2 (2013), p. 176.
26 Ibid., p. 176.
27 ICM Unlimited Survey 2015, *What Muslims Really Think* [https://www.icmunlimited.com/polls/icm-muslims-survey-for-channel-4/] Accessed on 12 December 2016.
28 Pędziwiatr, Konrad. 'Creating New Discursive Arenas and Influencing the Policies of the State: The Case of the Muslim Council of Britain', *Social Compass*, 54, no. 2 (2007), p. 273.
29 Maxwell, Rahsaan. 'Trust in Government Among British Muslims: The Importance of Migration Status', *Political Behavior*, 32, no. 1 (2010), pp. 89–109.
30 Goodhart, David, Martyn Frampton and Khalid Mahmood. *Unsettled Belonging: A Survey of Britain's Muslim Communities* (London: Policy Exchange, 2016), p. 28.
31 Copsey, Nigel. *Anti-Fascism in Britain* (London: Macmillan Press Ltd, 2000), p. 194.
32 Copsey, Nigel. *Anti-Fascism in Britain*, 2nd ed. (Oxon: Routledge, 2017), p. 202.
33 *The Times*, Saturday, 13 June 2009, p. 31.
34 Copsey, Nigel. *Anti-Fascism in Britain*, 2nd ed. (Oxon: Routledge, 2017), p. 216.
35 Unite Against Fascism, *Consequences of the Election of the BNP to the European Parliament* [http://uaf.org.uk/wp-content/uploads/2010/04/1002strategy1.pdf] (2010) Accessed on 3 February 2017.
36 Unite Against Fascism, *The EDL: Violent Racists and Fascists* [http://uaf.org.uk/wp-content/uploads/2015/04/EDLfactsheet2.pdf] (2015) Accessed on 3 February 2017.
37 Busher, Joel. *The Making of Anti-Muslim Protest: Grassroots Activism in the English Defence League* (Oxon: Routledge, 2016), p. 83.
38 Ibid., p. 14.
39 *Yorkshire Evening Post* [http://www.yorkshireeveningpost.co.uk/news/edl-gang-in-court-over-leeds-pub-attack-1-4893231] (4 September 2012) Accessed on 2 February 2017.
40 *The Guardian* [https://www.theguardian.com/uk/2011/nov/19/edl-splinter-group-target-unions] (19 November 2011) Accessed on 2 February 2017.
41 *Chronicle Live* [http://www.chroniclelive.co.uk/news/north-east-news/edl-gang-jailed-attack-newcastle-1407869#] (3 December 2011) Accessed on 2 February 2017.
42 *Chronicle Live* [http://www.chroniclelive.co.uk/news/north-east-news/pegida-newcastle-edl-tell-anti-fascists-8674533] (18 February 2015) Accessed on 2 February 2017.
43 Pilkington, Hilary. *Loud and Proud: Passion and Politics in the English Defence League* (Manchester: Manchester University Press, 2016), pp. 182–183.

44 Busher, Joel. *The Making of Anti-Muslim Protest: Grassroots Activism in the English Defence League* (Oxon: Routledge, 2016), p. 52.
45 Copsey, Nigel. *The English Defence League: Challenging Our Country and Our Values of Social Inclusion, Fairness and Equality* (London: Faith Matters, 2010), p. 20.
46 Bartlett, Jamie and Mark Littler. *Inside the EDL: Populist Politics in a Digital Age* (London: Demos, 2011), p. 4.
47 *The Guardian* [https://www.theguardian.com/politics/2011/feb/05/david-cameron-speech-criticised-edl] (5 February 2011) Accessed on 3 February 2017.
48 Jackson, Paul. *The EDL: Britain's 'New Far Right' Social Movement* (Northampton: RNM Publications, 2011), p. 72.
49 Berntzen, Lars Erik and Sveinung Sandberg. 'The Collective Nature of Lone Wolf Terrorism: Anders Behring Breivik and the Anti-Islamic Social Movement', *Terrorism and Political Violence*, 26, no. 5 (2014), p. 759.
50 *The Telegraph* [http://www.telegraph.co.uk/news/worldnews/europe/norway/8661139/Norway-killer-Anders-Behring-Breivik-had-extensive-links-to-English-Defence-League.html] (25 July 2011) Accessed on 3 February 2017.
51 *The Telegraph* [http://www.telegraph.co.uk/news/worldnews/europe/norway/8664159/Norway-killer-Anders-Behring-Breivik-emailed-manifesto-to-250-British-contacts.html] (26 July 2011) Accessed on 3 February 2017.
52 'The English Defence League', *Hope Not Hate* [http://www.hopenothate.org.uk/hate-groups/edl/] Accessed on 2 February 2017.
53 Pilkington, Hilary. *Loud and Proud: Passion and Politics in the English Defence League* (Manchester: Manchester University Press, 2016), pp. 183–185.
54 Busher, Joel. *The Making of Anti-Muslim Protest: Grassroots Activism in the English Defence League* (Oxon: Routledge, 2016), p. 38.
55 Treadwell, James. 'Controlling the New Far Right on the Streets: Policing the English Defence League in Policy and Praxis', in *Responding to Hate Crime: The Case for Connecting Policy and Research*, Edited by Neil Chakraborti and Jon Garland (Bristol: Policy Press, 2015), p. 134.
56 Ibid., p. 134.
57 Ibid., p. 135.
58 Pilkington, Hilary. *Loud and Proud: Passion and Politics in the English Defence League* (Manchester: Manchester University Press, 2016).
59 Ibid., pp. 183–185.
60 *The Guardian* [https://www.theguardian.com/commentisfree/2013/may/23/woolwich-attack-far-right-three-points] (23 May 2013) Accessed on 5 February 2017.
61 Feldman, Matthew and Mark Littler. *Tell MAMA Reporting 2014/2015: Annual Monitoring, Cumulative Extremism, and Policy Implications* (Middlesbrough: Centre for Fascist, Anti-Fascist and Post-Fascist Studies, 2015), p. 13.
62 Ebner, Julia. *The Rage: The Vicious Circle of Islamist and Far-Right Extremism* (London: I.B. Tauris, 2017), p. 144.
63 Busher, Joel and Macklin, Graham. 'Interpreting "Cumulative Extremism": Six Proposals for Enhancing Conceptual Clarity', *Terrorism and Political Violence*, 27, no. 5 (2014), p. 892.
64 Ibid., p. 892.
65 'Quilliam Facilitates Tommy Robinson Leaving the English Defence League', *Quilliam* [http://www.quilliaminternational.com/quilliam-facilitates-tommy-robinson-leaving-the-english-defence-league/] (8 October 2013) Accessed on 8 February 2017.
66 Pilkington, Hilary. *Loud and Proud: Passion and Politics in the English Defence League* (Manchester: Manchester University Press, 2016), p. 41.
67 Ibid., p. 41.
68 Ibid., p. 42.

69 *The Independent* [http://www.independent.co.uk/news/uk/politics/britain-first-far-right-group-claims-to-be-first-political-party-to-reach-1-million-likes-on-a6728991.html] (10 September 2015) Accessed on 3 February 2017.
70 *HOPE Not Hate*, Issue 23, January–February 2016.
71 Allen, Chris. 'Britain First: The "Frontline Resistance" to the Islamification of Britain', *The Political Quarterly*, 85, no. 3 (2014), p. 356.
72 Vidino, Lorenzo. 'Sharia4: From Confrontational Activism to Militancy', *Perspectives on Terrorism*, 9, no. 2 (2015), p. 7.
73 Ibid., p. 7.
74 Allen, Chris. 'Britain First: The "Frontline Resistance" to the Islamification of Britain', *The Political Quarterly*, 85, no. 3 (2014), p. 358.
75 Ibid., p. 358.
76 Ibid., p. 358.
77 *HOPE Not Hate*, Issue 23, January–February 2016, p. 16.
78 *HOPE Not Hate*, Issue 27, September–October 2016.
79 Cockburn, Patrick. *The Jihadis Return: ISIS and the New Sunni Uprising* (New York: OR Books, 2014), p. 32.
80 Neumann, Peter R. *Radicalized: New Jihadists and the Threat to the West* (London: I.B. Tauris, 2016), p. 71.
81 Amnesty International. *Ethnic Cleansing on a Historic Scale: Islamic State's Systematic Targeting of Minorities in Northern Iraq* (London: Amnesty International, 2014), p. 4.
82 *HOPE Not Hate*, Issue 17, January–February 2015, p. 22.
83 Ibid., pp. 22–23.
84 *HOPE Not Hate*, Issue 27, September–October 2016, p. 17.
85 Ibid., p. 17.
86 Neumann, Peter R. *Radicalized: New Jihadists and the Threat to the West* (London: I.B. Tauris, 2016), pp. 116–117.
87 *HOPE Not Hate*, Issue 27, September–October 2016, p. 17.
88 Ibid., p. 17.
89 HM Government. *Contest: The United Kingdom Government's Strategy for Countering Terrorism: Annual Report* (London: TSO, 2013).
90 HM Government, *Prevent Duty Guidance* (London: TSO, 2015), p. 3.
91 Muslim Council of Britain, http://www.mcb.org.uk/wp-content/uploads/2015/01/Response-to-the-Counter-Terrorism-and-Security-Bill.pdf, Accessed on 13 December 2016, p. 1.
92 *HOPE Not Hate*, Issue 21, September–October 2015, p. 12.
93 Ibid., p. 14.
94 Ibid., p. 14.
95 Ibid., p. 14.
96 Waters, Anne Marie, *Cancellation of Mohammed Cartoons* [http://www.annemariewaters.org/cancellation-of-mohammed-cartoons/] (18 August 2015) Accessed on 3 February 2017.
97 EDL, *About Us* [http://www.englishdefenceleague.org.uk/mission-statement/] Accessed on 14 March 2017.
98 Feldman, Matthew. *From Radical-Right Islamophobia to Cumulative Extremism* (London: Faith Matters, 2012), p. 1.
99 *HOPE Not Hate*, Issue 22, November–December 2015, p. 24.
100 Busher, Joel. *The Making of Anti-Muslim Protest: Grassroots Activism in the English Defence League* (Oxon: Routledge, 2016), pp. 38–39.
101 Ibid., p. 38.
102 Ibid., pp. 38–39.
103 *HOPE Not Hate*, Issue 23, January–February 2016, p. 32.
104 *HOPE Not Hate*, Issue 27, September–October 2016, pp. 35–36.
105 *BBC News* [http://www.bbc.co.uk/news/magazine-35432074] (29 January 2016) Accessed on 1 March 2017.

106 *HOPE Not Hate*, Issue 27, September–October 2016, p. 36.
107 *The Yorkshire Post* [http://www.yorkshirepost.co.uk/news/far-right-group-stages-silent-anti-muslim-protest-in-rotherham-1-7948087] (5 June 2016) Accessed on 21 February 2017.
108 Bartlett, Jamie. *Radicals: Outsiders Changing the World* (London: Windmill, 2017), p. 92.
109 Gani, Jasmine. 'Contentious Politics and the Syrian Crisis: Internationalization and Militarization of the Conflict', in *Contentious Politics in the Middle East: Popular Resistance and Marginalized Activism beyond the Arab Uprisings*, Edited by Fawaz A. Gerges (New York: Palgrave Macmillan, 2015), p. 148.
110 Bartlett, Jamie. *Radicals: Outsiders Changing the World* (London: Windmill, 2017), p. 93.
111 *The Independent* [https://www.independent.co.uk/voices/hate-crime-figures-racism-brexit-trump-isnt-going-to-solve-the-problem-a7583201.html] (17 February 2017) Accessed on 1 November 2018.
112 Devine, Daniel. 'Hate Crime Did Spike after the Referendum – Even Allowing for Other Factors', *LSE Brexit Blog* [http://blogs.lse.ac.uk/brexit/2018/03/19/hate-crime-did-spike-after-the-referendum-even-allowing-for-other-factors/] (19 March 2018) Accessed on 1 November 2018.
113 *HOPE Not Hate*, Issue 30, January–February 2017, p. 7.
114 Ibid., p. 20.
115 Ibid., p. 7.
116 Macklin, Graham. '"Only Bullets will Stop Us!" – The Banning of National Action in Britain', *Perspectives on Terrorism*, 12, no. 6 (2018), p. 109.
117 Allen, Chris. 'Proscribing National Action: Considering the Impact of Banning the British Far-Right Group,' *The Political Quarterly*, 88, no. 4 (2017), pp. 652–659.
118 Macklin, p. 109.
119 Ibid., p. 109.
120 Ibid., p. 116.
121 Macklin, Graham. 'The Evolution of Extreme-Right Terrorism and Efforts to Counter It in the United Kingdom', *CTC Sentinel*, 12, no. 1 (2019), p. 18.
122 Walker, Clive. *Counterterrorism Yearbook 2018: United Kingdom* (Canberra: Australian Strategic Policy Institute, 2018), p. 142.
123 *The Guardian* [https://www.theguardian.com/commentisfree/2017/jun/21/us-and-them-extremism-terror-attacks] (21 June 2017) Accessed on 30 June 2017.
124 *The Independent* [https://www.independent.co.uk/news/uk/crime/finsbury-park-attack-trial-live-darren-osborne-court-muslims-mosque-van-latest-news-updates-a8173496.html] (23 January 2018) Accessed on 1 November 2018.
125 *BBC News* [https://www.bbc.co.uk/news/uk-40019135] (12 June 2017) Accessed on 1 November 2018.
126 Anderson, David. *Attacks in London and Manchester March–June 2017 Independent Assessment of MI5 and Police Internal Reviews* (London: David Anderson, 2017), p. 8.
127 *BBC News* [https://www.bbc.co.uk/news/uk-40019135] (12 June 2017) Accessed on 1 November 2018.
128 Ebner, Julia. *The Rage: The Vicious Circle of Islamist and Far-Right Extremism* (London: I.B. Tauris, 2017), p. 155.
129 Ibid., pp. 144–146.
130 *Searchlight* [http://www.searchlightmagazine.com/2017/10/football-lads-alliance-the-far-right-march-plus-six-things-you-need-to-know/] (11 October 2018) Accessed on 1 November 2018.
131 *The Times* [https://www.thetimes.co.uk/article/premier-league-clubs-warned-over-far-right-football-lads-alliance-0mgq2lppv] (30 March 2018) Accessed on 1 November 2018.
132 Ibid.

133 Hill, Max. *The Terrorism Acts in 2017: Report of the Independent Reviewer of Terrorism Legislation on the Operation of the Terrorism Acts 2000 and 2006, The Terrorism Prevention and Investigation Measures Act 2011, and the Terrorist Asset Freezing Etc. Act 2010* (London: Her Majesty's Stationery Office 2018), pp. 20–21.

134 Ibid., p. 13.

135 HM Government. *Contest: The United Kingdom Government's Strategy for Countering Terrorism: Annual Report* (London: TSO, 2018), p. 21.

136 Ibid., p. 21.

137 Hill, Max. *The Terrorism Acts in 2017: Report of the Independent Reviewer of Terrorism Legislation on the Operation of the Terrorism Acts 2000 and 2006, The Terrorism Prevention and Investigation Measures Act 2011, and the Terrorist Asset Freezing Etc. Act 2010* (London: Her Majesty's Stationery Office, 2018), p. 33.

138 Macklin, Graham. 'The Evolution of Extreme-Right Terrorism and Efforts to Counter It in the United Kingdom', *CTC Sentinel*, 12, no. 1 (2019), p. 19.

139 *The Guardian* [https://www.theguardian.com/world/2018/oct/13/anti-fascists-block-route-of-democratic-football-lads-alliance-london-march] (13 October 2018) Accessed on 1 November 2018.

140 Feldman, Matthew and Paul Stocker. 'The Post-Brext Far-Right in Britain', in *Violent Radicalisation and Far-Right Extremism in Europe*, Edited by Aristotle Kallis, Sara Zeiger and Bilgehan Öztürk (Istanbul: SETA Publications, 2018).

141 *The Guardian*, [https://www.theguardian.com/politics/2018/nov/27/patrick-oflynn-ukip-mep-quits-tommy-robinson-gerard-batten] (27 November 2018) Accessed on 1 December 2018.

142 *The Mirror* [https://www.mirror.co.uk/news/politics/tommy-robinsons-european-election-result-16207595] (27 May 2019) Accessed on 3 June 2019.

143 *The Guardian* [https://www.theguardian.com/politics/2019/may/27/ukip-defeat-in-eu-elections-cast-doubts-on-party-future] (27 May 2019) Accessed on 3 June 2019.

144 Anon. 'Building coalitions outside SUTR/SWP (9th Dec write up)', *London Anarchist Federation* [https://aflondon.wordpress.com/2018/12/18/building-coalitions-outside-sutr-swp-9th-dec-write-up/] (18 December 2018) Accessed on 20 December 2018.

145 *The Guardian* [https://www.theguardian.com/world/2018/oct/13/anti-fascists-block-route-of-democratic-football-lads-alliance-london-march] (13 October 2018) Accessed on 1 November 2018.

146 Andre, Virginie. 'Merah and Breivik: A Reflection of the European Identity Crisis', *Islam and Christian–Muslim Relations*, 26, no. 2 (2015): 183–204.

147 Busher, Joel and Graham Macklin. 'Interpreting "Cumulative Extremism": Six Proposals for Enhancing Conceptual Clarity', *Terrorism and Political Violence*, 27, no. 5 (2014), p. 898.

148 De Fazio, Gianluca. 'The Radicalization of Contention in Northern Ireland, 1968–1972: A Relational Perspective', *Mobilization: An International Quarterly*, 18, no. 4 (2013), p. 477.

149 Pupcenoks, Juris and Ryan McCabe. 'The Rise of the Fringe: Right Wing Populists, Islamists and Politics in the UK', *Journal of Muslim Minority Affairs*, 33, no. 2 (2013), p. 174.

150 Akbarzadeh, Shahram and Fethi Mansouri. *Islam and Political Violence: Muslim Diaspora and Radicalism in the West* (London: I.B. Tauris, 2010), p. 11.

151 Pantucci, Raffaello. *We Love Death as You Love Life: Britain's Suburban Terrorists* (London: C. Hurst & Co. Ltd, 2015), p. 53.

152 Garland, Jon and James Treadwell. 'The New Politics of Hate? An Assessment of the Appeal of the English Defence League Amongst Disadvantaged White Working-Class Communities in England', *Journal of Hate Studies*, 10, no. 1 (2012), p. 138.

7

CONCLUSION

Since Roger Eatwell introduced the concept of cumulative extremism in 2006 it has gained traction among academics and policy makers, and is often discussed in academic reports,[1] newspapers[2] and government strategy documents.[3] Yet for the most part the concept is taken at face value, with relatively little work being undertaken to rigorously interrogate it; in short, the breadth of acceptance has not yet provoked a corresponding effort to gain a deeper understanding of this developing concept.[4] To redress this issue, this book has provided the first sustained, in-depth analysis of the concept of cumulative extremism (CE).

By conducting a comparative examination of different movement-countermovement contests – namely British fascism and anti-fascism in the interwar period and in the second half of the twentieth century, the escalation of the Troubles in Northern Ireland up unto their violent peak between 1972 and 1976, and the Islamist and counter-jihad movements since 2009 – it has been possible to answer the central research questions which have driven this study: when is the dynamic of cumulative extremism likely to develop, and when is it not likely to? What are the key factors that are likely to escalate an M/CM conflict towards the use of increasingly violent and radical means, or de-escalate towards more moderate tactics? Under what conditions are opposing movements likely to draw in larger numbers of supporters, rather than just repeatedly mobilising the same pool of activists, and so further expand the conflict?

Cumulative extremism: A general framework

With the analyses of the previous chapters' case studies now complete, it is time to induce a general framework for understanding when and where processes of CE can develop. In constructing this framework, it is useful to group the key variables into three separate areas. Firstly, the social movement organisations themselves, their relationship with the social base with which they claim to represent, and the nature of the cleavage between the opposing movements. Secondly, the nature of the relationship between the opposing social movements and the ways in which they interact with each other. Thirdly and finally, the environmental factors; that is, the broader political and social context in which the M/CM contest occurs. This includes the structure of political opportunities, government policy interventions and styles of policing the conflict, and the broader domestic and international social and political settings.

Social bases, social movement organisations and conflict-cleavages

The first major observations to be highlighted from the previous chapters are the way in which the onset of CE is affected by the nature of the M/CM cleavage. Movements and countermovements may be divided along ascriptive (e.g. ethnicity, race, nationality) or non-ascriptive (e.g. ideology, class) lines.[5] This distinction is important for if the cleavage is non-ascriptive, then the movement and countermovement may be competing for support from the same social base. Contests fought under these circumstances are less likely to develop processes of cumulative extremism. As has been demonstrated, sometimes lethal categorical violence is employed by SMOs, either to dissuade their opposing movement's social base from supporting their opposing SMOs or to generate goodwill and support amongst their own social base for taking retribution against their perceived enemies. Both aims have been suggested by observers and activists of the paramilitaries in Northern Ireland as motivations for their use of lethal violence.[6]

However, when the opposing movements are both competing for support of the same constituency they are obviously much less likely to engage in these types of violence. For instance, it would have been astoundingly stupid for the British National Party or Red Action to have bombed a white working class area (from which both sides were mainly drawing their support), for obvious reasons. Rather, when the cleavage of an M/CM conflict is non-ascriptive, and both movements are competing for the support of the same constituency, the case studies here suggest that both sides are likely to adopt a 'hearts and minds' approach to achieve hegemonic dominance in a given constituency. This was really the dominant aspect of the work of fascist and anti-fascist activists between the 1970s and 1990s, who worked and organised in areas of working class culture, such as the music and football scenes, so as to eventually be a dominant ideological force within that demographic. However, it is likely, judging from similar but larger conflicts in places like Spain in the 1930s and in post-war Italy, that if either side was successful in gaining a foothold in their target constituency, and actually became a formidable political force, then CE could have developed much further.[7]

Further, whereas engagement with elections may de-escalate some M/CM contests – as happened in the 1990s when the BNP sought electoral success – a conflict which is fought along ascriptive lines, and maps on to extant divisions within the broader society, may actually be exacerbated by an election. In his analysis of how ethnic party systems tend to foster competition rather than co-operation, Donald Horowitz has broached this subject. Horowitz argues that when elections are organised along ethnic divisions, party competition between ethnic groups creates a strong incentive for parties to outbid each other in their assertions for exclusively ethnic demands. In his view, 'because ethnicity is a largely ascriptive affiliation, the boundaries of party support stop at the boundaries of ethnic groups. There are many working-class Tories, but there are very few Hindu Akalis – to take an example from among the least rigidly ascriptive ethnic groups and parties. In an ascriptive system, it is far more important to take effective steps to reassure ethnic supporters than to pursue will-o'-the-wisps by courting imaginary voters across ethnic lines. The near-impossibility of party competition for clientele across ethnic lines means an absence of countervailing electoral incentives encouraging party moderation on ethnic issues.'[8] This goes some way towards explaining why the British National Party's attempt to make a big impact electorally led to their gradual de-escalation away from violence from 1993, as they tried to moderate and become more appealing to the centre ground, whereas elections in Northern Ireland failed to bridge the conflict in any way between 1969 and 1976.

The second point to be made is that the greater the extent to which the SMOs' aims are genuinely perceived as representing those of their social base, and the greater the extent to which they 'are perceived as threatening the material and symbolic interests of other groups', the more likely processes of CE are to develop.[9] For instance, no matter how successful the anti-nuclear movement becomes, it is unlikely that it will ever generate a large, communal counter-mobilisation like the loyalist reaction to the Civil Rights Movement (CRM). The goals of the CRM (reformation of the state) and of the loyalists (maintaining the status quo) were not only mutually exclusive but were, to a greater or lesser extent, the same 'material and symbolic interests' of the two wider communities who formed the social bases for the two movements. As Fadaee has observed, if a 'given movement is perceived to threaten the dominant values of a group or of a society in general, then the formation of an influential countermovement gains high probability.'[10] This observation goes some way towards explaining the behaviour of the National Front in the 1970s: they hoped that by provoking a race war they would then come to be seen as the organisation best placed to protect the interests of the white British 'race'.[11]

The third variable that affects the development of CE between opposing movements is the degree of internal heterogeneity of values and agreement on strategy. Whereas complete ideological and tactical unanimity is of course largely unheard of outside of the realms of cults, nevertheless most groups and movements studied throughout this book were broadly in agreement over what their overarching goal was, be it to stop the spread of fascism or to form a United Ireland. Yet, in the case of the counter-jihad movement the wildly divergent views on what was an appropriate form of protest as well as differences in ideological outlook has been a real obstacle to cooperation. The overt white supremacism of the far-right groups such as the Infidels and the National Front has tarnished the image of the movement and made it difficult for more moderate people to join or remain within the movement without being considered racists themselves.

Moreover, many genuinely find their extreme ideology abhorrent and refuse to associate with them on principle. When the more moderate members of the EDL tried to exert their influence and prevent violence from occurring at their events this deprived ex-football hooligans, who had comprised a sizeable portion of the original organisation, of one of their main reasons for attending – the emotional rush of conflict. These disagreements over aims, ideology and strategy have inhibited the counter-jihad movement. Similarly, while the NF did not have quite the same degree of conflicting opinions and attitudes, it did nevertheless lack cohesion. Consequently infighting led to the National Party splitting from the NF and taking a significant amount of the party's membership and resources with it.

The final issue to consider here is how the opposing movements' 'strategies and their broader aims' differ, and how these differences affect the evolution of the M/CM contest.[12] As Macklin and Busher have argued, most groups and activists involved in an M/CM contest are also 'engaged in multiple contests with multiple opponents and their actions [are] shaped by efforts to influence political decision makers and to engage, or at least not alienate, broader constituencies (real or imagined) of support.'[13] Thus, the BNP's desire to become a serious electoral force in the 1990s precluded them from engaging in continued street-based violence with their anti-fascist antagonists. The IRA, however, following the riots of 1969, had a growing incentive to stockpile weapons and use political violence. These strategies, informed by the aim of garnering support from 'broader constituencies', had an impact on the M/CM contest as their respective countermovements reacted by either escalating or de-escalating with them.

Movement-countermovement interactions

This brings us on to the nature of the interactions between the social movements and social movement organisations themselves. Firstly, whether or not processes of CE will develop between a movement and a countermovement depend in large part on how closely or symmetrically 'coupled' the two movements are. As an example, the loyalists and republicans of Northern Ireland were much more tightly and symmetrically coupled than any of the fascist and anti-fascist groups examined here, whereas the counter-jihad movement was almost entirely asymmetrically coupled to the Islamist movement. This disparity in degrees of symmetry and 'tightness' of coupling across the case goes some way in explaining why each of those experienced more or less intense processes of CE. Where movements are less symmetrically and tightly coupled 'their campaigns would be less likely to be organised in direct opposition to one another', therefore, presenting less opportunities for direct confrontations, violence and increased feelings of animosity.[14]

Another factor which influences whether M/CM relations will escalate is the type of 'arena' in which they mobilise. There are many 'arenas', or 'battlefields', that the movement and countermovement can operate in – from pursuing legal action in courts to addressing different audiences at rallies. This study reinforces Zald's and Useem's argument that radicalisation is more likely to occur when the two movements encounter each other face-to-face 'on the streets' at demonstrations and counter-demonstrations.[15] For example, during the violent confrontation between fascists and anti-fascists in Lewisham on 13 August 1977, different activists involved in the fighting described how much they enjoyed the intense emotions they experienced through the physical conflict with their enemies.[16]

Rallies, marches and demonstrations were major forms of claim-making by most of the movements considered here. However, the aforementioned relationship between social movement organisations and their social bases strongly influences the degree to which radicalisation may occur in these arenas: one of the main differences between the case studies presented here is that in Northern Ireland there was a strong tradition of marches and parades by the social movement *bases*, and not just the SMOs themselves. Because these interactions frequently involved people who were often not actually already activists – in stark contrast to the episodes involving fascists and anti-fascists or Islamists and the CJM – when these encounters turned violent they had the effect of radicalising a wider pool of people. Once Protestants or Catholics had been socialised to violence in this way, it was much easier for them to then address their grievances through a paramilitary organisation such as the IRA or UVF. When fascists and anti-fascists in Britain had violent encounters with each other, this was often between roughly the same groups of activists each time, and so rarely drew in and radicalised new people.

When movements are fairly closely coupled and regularly meet on the streets, della Porta has argued that the activists involved become more likely to succumb to the 'gradual reciprocal adaptation to increasingly dangerous weapons'.[17] As has been demonstrated, in Northern Ireland from 1968 onwards this process was not so gradual, whereas in Britain lethal weapons have been very rarely used. But close examination of the case studies can offer some explanation as to why activists will start using weapons in some conflicts, but not in others. A useful conceptual tool to aid in this endeavour is Charles Tilly's 'repertoires of contention', which he defines as 'inherited forms of collective action… arrays of performances that are currently known and available within some set of political actors.'[18] Importantly, 'on the whole, when people make collective claims, they innovate within limits set by the repertoire already established for their place, time, and pair.'[19] As Tilly suggests, forms of collective action are often constrained by the historical and cultural traditions and mores of the time and place in which they occur. In Britain, there has long been fairly deeply entrenched norms against the use of political violence: the progress of both the British Union of Fascists and the National Front was severely hindered by their association with violence in the public eye.[20] When the British National Party wanted to be taken seriously as an electoral force they attempted to distance themselves from political violence, and even accounts 'of [fascist/anti-fascist] street violence are peppered with recollections of more experienced activists stepping in when someone had "had enough"'.[21]

In contrast, republicans and loyalists in Northern Ireland in the 1960s were the inheritors of a relatively long tradition of lethal political violence. From the very act of partition with the Government of Ireland Act of 1920 – itself a product of bloody civil war – armed militias such as the Irish Republican Army, the original Ulster Volunteer Force and the Ulster Imperial Guards employed lethal violence in the pursuit of their political goals. With the events of the Irish Northern and Border campaigns (1942–44 and 1956–62 respectively) and the formation of the second UVF in 1966, lethal violence by armed groups was a fairly regular feature of life in Northern Ireland. Given this observation, it is hardly surprising that when faced with a growing social movement which was perceived as threatening their groups' interests, activists in Northern Ireland were much more quick to use weapons and lethal violence than activists in Britain.[22]

However, the nature of the M/CM coupling can, under the right circumstances, also lead to a de-escalation of the contest. When a movement is tightly coupled to another movement, it is more or less compelled to follow its rival when it alters the 'arena' in which it operates. This means that when a movement de-escalates and shifts its focus from operating in 'the streets' to electioneering, the countermovement faces strong pressure to de-escalate also. This explains the demise of AFA and the creation of the Independent Working Class Association (IWCA) after the BNP 'modernised'.[23] Of course, this gives an advantage to a movement which is less closely coupled to its countermovement than vice versa, as it creates opportunities to outmanoeuvre them.

There are two dynamics of interaction which can contribute towards the onset of CE which are much more likely to occur when the M/CM contest if fought along ascriptive lines. These are the mechanisms of 'vicarious retribution' and 'Jujitsu Politics'. Both of these mechanisms are more likely to lead to reciprocal radicalisation when there is a large visible support base for people to attack. A loyalist would have much more luck in radicalising Protestants by attacking Catholics (thereby provoking counterattacks) than AFA would have had in attacking members of the white working class. In terms of 'vicarious retribution', in contests between fascists and anti-fascists, it is likely that known activists were attacked by their enemies for actions that other members of their groups undertook. However, given the small size of the groups involved, this would have necessarily been on a fairly small scale. There was no wider pool of people, or potential supporters, with ascriptive identities, which would mark them out as such, to attack. In Northern Ireland, by contrast, where the contest was fought along ascriptive lines and mapped on to extant social groups, 'vicarious retribution' occurred frequently as Protestants and Catholics looking to take revenge for violent acts visited upon them or their kin searched out for any member of the opposing group – creating a cycle of violence and revenge.

Environmental factors: Public policy, policing and the structure of political opportunities

A strong factor influencing how M/CM interactions will develop is the structure of political opportunities.[24] This study has found that one of the elements of the political opportunity structure which most influences a social movement's tactical decision to engage in direct action, including the use of political violence, is the efficacy of institutional means of campaigning to achieve political goals. On the whole, if institutional channels of redress (such as lobbying politicians, publishing research, campaigning during elections and so on) are closed to movements, they will likely start to employ tactics of direct action and civil disobedience.[25] This observation goes some way in explaining why Catholics in Northern Ireland escalated their collective action strategies in the mid-1960s. The Civil Rights Movement (CRM) had attempted to achieve its goals through a variety of methods before taking to the streets. The Campaign for Social Justice had carried out research and written propaganda to attempt to convince the British to intervene. The Northern Ireland Labour Party had attempted to achieve some of the CRM's goals through Stormont, but had failed.[26] Thereafter, civil rights groups had attempted to hold a number of peaceful marches through NI which were faced with state and loyalist violence. The failure of each of these peaceful attempts to achieve their goals through the usual political channels resulted in the adoption of an increasingly more militant and confrontational strategy, which then brought the CRM in direct confrontation with both the loyalists and the RUC.

In Britain, the perceived efficacy of electoral politics to attain organisational goals had differing effects on the M/CM contest. In May 1978, after the National Front fared poorly in local Council elections, they redoubled their more aggressive, extra-parliamentary forms of collective action.[27] However, their failure at the 1979 election, while leading to an increase in violence by smaller splinter groups, more-or-less hobbled the fascist movement for a few years. In Northern Ireland there was a feeling that Catholics simply could not achieve their goals through normal political channels because the system was designed to maintain the Protestant ascendancy. In Britain, by contrast, although the National Front were no doubt unhappy with their electoral defeat in 1979, it is unlikely that many of them seriously thought that the election had been rigged and that to achieve their goals they would have to employ more radical means.

Fadaee argues that, 'one must bear in mind that the political opportunities are not only dependent on political structures, but also on the social setting and the cultural environment of a society.'[28] This point has been further demonstrated by the case studies presented here: between 1968 and 1972 the National Front gained significant attention and support after skilfully cashing in on growing anti-immigration sentiment amongst the wider British population. In particular, following Enoch Powell's 'Rivers of Blood' speech on 20 April 1968, and the influx of Ugandan Asians in August 1968, the National Front organised high-profile anti-immigration campaigns which generated a good deal of new supporters. What is more, and importantly for the current study, when political developments such as these benefit one movement, they can also then stimulate a concomitant growth in activity in the countermovement.

However, this study suggests that it is not just the social setting and cultural environment of the national society which affects the structure of political opportunities, but also global currents and the intersection of domestic and international political developments. For example, MI5 linked the BUF's growth between its founding in October 1932 and the spring of 1933 to the successes of continental fascism.[29] Similarly, the American civil rights movement of the 1960s 'proved an important guide for the Northern Ireland activists… Civil rights leaders in Ireland had been receiving literature from the civil rights movement in the US from the early 1960s, and by the early 1970s several visits had been exchanged across the Atlantic.'[30]

A further aspect of the political opportunity structure crucial to the development of M/CM conflicts is the ability of SMOs to disseminate their specific 'frames' of the central issues of the contest to the wider public. A key way of doing this is by having access to the mainstream media, or by at least being able to attract positive or sympathetic media coverage of the movement's activities and aims. The BUF's impressive growth from January 1934 and their subsequent decline following the events at Olympia on 7 June 1934 were strongly linked to the support which Lord Rothermere and his media empire gave to their movement, and which was subsequently retracted. Similarly, in Northern Ireland, the footage of police violence towards the Civil Rights Marchers on 5 October 1968 provided a massive boon to the movement. Of course, this cuts both ways, and if a movement's enemies succeed in generating negative media attention about them then this can seriously hamper their efforts. For example, the National Front's failures were in part caused by a hostile media, who they considered to be their 'number one enemy'.[31]

Another major element of the political opportunity structure which influences if and how CE may grow and evolve is the way the state acts towards one or all of the movements concerned. Indeed, by far the most influential actor in any episode of contentious politics – let alone any M/CM conflict – is the state. That is not to say that the state's actions always have the desired effect; the often careless way in which public policy was applied in Northern Ireland frequently had the effect of encouraging the development of CE. For example, on 3 October 1968, the Home Affairs Minister issued a banning order against the proposed civil rights march through Derry under the Public Order Act.[32] This action backfired, inflaming Catholic opinion and bringing more marchers onto the streets and into direct confrontation with the RUC. Yet the following year, the highly provocative loyalist procession on 12 August was permitted to go ahead; this led to the August riots and attacks against Catholics. Neither of these decisions were the right ones in terms of maintaining public order.

When policies designed to mitigate the escalation of an M/CM conflict are applied unevenly, focusing on one side at the expense of the other, the likely result is the opposite of what was intended. This is further demonstrated when the state interventions in Northern Ireland are compared to similar efforts by the government to quell political violence in Britain. When the state introduced the 1936 Public Order Act, they introduced the 'prohibition of political uniforms, the outlawing of paramilitary organisations and the regulation and control of public processions and assemblies' across the board – rather than just focusing on one side of the M/CM conflict.[33] Even though there have been mixed assessments of the efficacy of the Public Order Act by historians, in the long term and on the whole it probably did lead to a de-escalation in the M/CM conflict.

A different but related point is the specific way in which both movements in the M/CM conflict are policed. Donatella della Porta has argued that inconsistent repression of social movements can contribute towards the likelihood of terrorist atrocities taking place in M/CM conflicts, as the actors who are receiving preferential treatment become emboldened by the apparent indifference, or even collusion, of the state.[34] This certainly seems to have been the case in Northern Ireland, where there was not only inconsistent repression, but actual also some degree of collusion between state forces and loyalist paramilitaries.

All of this served to legitimise the Provisionals as the guardians of the Catholic community, increasing the support received by the organisation, while simultaneously emboldening the loyalists who felt they were being tacitly legitimised by the state's covert support. In stark contrast, the police's fairly even-handed and increasingly sophisticated attempts to prevent political violence and extremism in Britain seem to have been a large factor in why radical groups de-escalated their campaigns against their enemies. Indeed, both Red Action[35] and Combat 18[36] stated that advancements in police strategies and capabilities in the mid-1990s made it increasingly difficult for them to organise themselves. Similarly, the changes in style of policing of the counter-jihad movement since 2012 have generally led to more calm and sedate demonstrations (with some noteworthy exceptions) and so have helped to de-escalate the episode.[37]

This research has not only demonstrated the heuristic value of the concept of cumulative extremism in understanding M/CM interactions, but has also begun to set out a framework for better understanding when CE is likely to develop between competing groups. Viewing the historical case studies in this book through the lens of this framework has shed new light on them, allowing for a deeper understanding of why the various group actors have acted, and reacted, in the ways that they have. Nevertheless, while this study has presented the first extensive historical study of cumulative extremism, more work is needed to be done to further understand the concept.

In the first instance, comparative studies with much more widely differing cases are needed. Those examined here have differed sufficiently in terms of the strategies, aims, behaviour and identities of the actors involved – as well as in terms of the context within which the contests have developed – to draw some important conclusions about how and why movement-countermovement contests may develop processes of cumulative extremism. But nevertheless, they were all within the United Kingdom during the twentieth and early twenty-first centuries. A 'most different systems' comparative methodology, between cases from other continents in differing political circumstances, could yield more information pertaining to conditions which are conducive to the escalation or de-escalation of M/CM contests. Furthermore, conducting interviews with activists may shed light on the role emotions play in radicalisation, attachment to a movement or cause, and the development of in-group loyalties/out-group hostilities. Overt or covert ethnography within SMOs – observing meetings as well as protest actions – would shed light on the back-stage attitudes, strategic-planning, and emotional responses of an SMO with regard to their opposing movement(s).

Notes

1 See: Feldman, Matthew. *From Radical-Right Islamophobia to Cumulative Extremism* (London: Faith Matters, 2012), p. 4; Goodwin Matthew. *The Roots of Extremism: The English Defence League and the Counter-Jihad Challenge* (London: Chatham House, 2013), p. 5;

2 See: *The Guardian* [https://www.theguardian.com/commentisfree/2013/may/23/woolwich-attack-far-right-three-points], (23 May 2013) Accessed on 5 February 2017; and *The Independent* [http://www.independent.co.uk/voices/berlin-christmas-market-attack-terrorism-terrorist-refugees-far-right-neo-nazi-extremes-reciprocal-a7489946.html], (22 December 2016) Accessed on 14 February 2017.

3 See: HM Government. *Contest: The United Kingdom Government's Strategy for Countering Terrorism: Annual Report* (London: TSO, 2013), p. 22; and Home Affairs Select Committee. *The Roots of Violent Radicalisation* (London: TSO, 2012), pp. 20–21.

4 Several excellent articles have been written probing deeper into the subject, notably: Busher, Joel and Graham Macklin. 'The Missing Spirals of Violence: Four Waves of Movement–Countermovement Contest in Post-War Britain', *Behavioral Sciences of Terrorism and Political Aggression*, 7, no. 1 (2015), pp. 65–66; Busher, Joel and Graham Macklin. 'Interpreting "Cumulative Extremism": Six Proposals for Enhancing Conceptual Clarity', *Terrorism and Political Violence*, 27, no. 5 (2014), pp. 884–905. Yet all of these articles argue the need for further work to better understand the concept.

5 Alimi, Y. Eitan, Charles Demetriou and Lorenzo Bosi. *The Dynamics of Radicalization: A Relational and Comparative Perspective* (Oxford: Oxford University Press, 2015), p. 48.

6 For example, see: Sanders, Andrew. *Inside the IRA: Dissident Republicans and the War for Legitimacy* (Edinburgh: Edinburgh University Press, 2011), p. 49; Wood, S. Ian. *Crimes of Loyalty: A History of the UDA* (Edinburgh: Edinburgh University Press, 2006), p. 104.

7 For Spain, see: Preston, Paul. *The Spanish Holocaust: Inquisition and Extermination in Twentieth-Century Spain* (London: Harper Press, 2012); for Italy see Della Porta, Donatella. *Social Movements, Political Violence, and the State: A Comparative Analysis of Italy and Germany* (Cambridge: Cambridge University Press, 1995).

8 Horowitz, Donald. L. *Ethnic Groups in Conflict* (Berkeley: University of California Press, 1985), pp. 345–346.

9 De Fazio, Gianluca. 2013 'The Radicalization of Contention in Northern Ireland, 1968–1972: A Relational Perspective', *Mobilization: An International Quarterly*, 18, no. 4 (2013), p. 477.

10 Fadaee, Simin. 'Social Movements, Counter-Movements, and Their Dynamic Interplay', in *Women's Movements and Countermovements: The Quest for Gender Equality in Southeast Asia and the Middle East*, Edited by Claudia Derichs and Dana Fennert (Newcastle: Cambridge Scholars Publishing, 2014), p. 19.

11 Pearce, Joseph. *Race with the Devil: My Journey from Racial Hatred to Rational Love* (Charlotte: Saint Benedict Press, 2013), p. 62.

12 Busher, Joel and Graham Macklin. 'The Missing Spirals of Violence: Four Waves of Movement–Countermovement Contest in Post-war Britain', *Behavioral Sciences of Terrorism and Political Aggression*, 7, no. 1 (2015), p. 10.

13 Ibid., p. 10.

14 Busher, Joel and Graham Macklin. 'Interpreting "Cumulative Extremism": Six Proposals for Enhancing Conceptual Clarity', *Terrorism and Political Violence*, 27, no. 5 (2014), p. 898.

15 Zald, Mayer N. and Bert Useem. 'Movement and Countermovement Interaction: Mobilization, Tactics, and State Involvement', in *Social Movements in an Organizational Society*, Edited by Mayer N. Zald and John D. McCarthy (Oxford: Transaction Books, 1987), p. 259.

16 Hann, Dave. *Physical Resistance: A Hundred Years of Anti-Fascism* (Alresford: Zero Books, 2013), p. 268.

17 Della Porta, Donatella. *Social Movements, Political Violence, and the State: A Comparative Analysis of Italy and Germany* (Cambridge: Cambridge University Press, 1995), p. 154.

18 Tilly, Charles and Sidney Tarrow. *Contentious Politics*, 2nd ed. (Colorado: Paradigm Publishers, 2007), pp. 7–14.

19 Ibid., p. 16.

20 Lawrence, Jon. 'Fascist Violence and the Politics of Public Order in Inter-War Britain: The Olympia Debate Revisited', *Historical Research*, 76, no. 192 (2003), pp. 238–267.

21 Busher, Joel and Graham Macklin. 'The Missing Spirals of Violence: Four Waves of Movement–Countermovement Contest in Post-war Britain', *Behavioral Sciences of Terrorism and Political Aggression* (Published online: 10 November 2014), p. 13.

22 Della Porta, Donatella. *Clandestine Political Violence* (Cambridge: Cambridge University Press, 2013), p. 72.

23 Copsey, Nigel. 'From Direct Action to Community Action: The Changing Dynamics of Anti-fascist Opposition', in *British National Party: Contemporary Perspectives*, Edited by Nigel Copsey and Graham Macklin (Oxon: Routledge, 2011).

24 Meyer, D. S. and S. Staggenborg. 'Movements, Countermovements, and the Structure of Political Opportunity', *American Journal of Sociology*, 101, no. 6 (1996), p. 1634.

25 Della Porta, Donatella. *Clandestine Political Violence* (Cambridge: Cambridge University Press, 2013), p. 34.

26 Purdie, Bob. *Politics in the Street: The Origins of the Civil Rights Movement in Northern Ireland* (Belfast: The Blackstaff Press Limited, 1990), pp. 73–76.

27 Bethnal Green and Stepney Trades Council. *Blood on the Streets: A Report* (London: Bethnal Green and Stepney Trades Council, 1978), p. 32.

28 Fadaee, Simin. 'Social Movements, Counter-Movements, and Their Dynamic Interplay', in *Women's Movements and Countermovements: The Quest for Gender Equality in Southeast Asia and the Middle East*, Edited by Claudia Derichs and Dana Fennert (Newcastle: Cambridge Scholars Publishing, 2014), p. 14.

29 See the National Archives (NA) NA: HO 45/25384 Home Office: Registered Papers. Registered Papers, 1920 onwards. DISTURBANCES: British Union of Fascists: Reports on meetings and activities.

30 Dooley, Brian. *Black and Green: The Fight for Civil Rights in Northern Ireland & Black America* (London: Pluto Press, 1998), p. 4.

31 Copsey, Nigel. *Anti-Fascism in Britain* (London: Macmillan Press Ltd, 2000), p. 115.

32 Farrell, Michael. *Northern Ireland: The Orange State* (London: Pluto Press, 1976), p. 246.

33 Thurlow, Richard. *The Secret State: British Internal Security in the Twentieth Century* (Oxford: Blackwell, 1994), p. 201.

34 Della Porta, Donatella. *Clandestine Political Violence* (Cambridge: Cambridge University Press, 2013), pp. 67–68.

35 *Red Action Bulletin*, Issue 74, Spring 1997, p. 14.

36 *The Order*, Issue 12, 1995.

37 Treadwell, James. 'Controlling the New Far Right on the Streets: Policing the English Defence League in Policy and Praxis', in *Responding to Hate Crime: The Case for Connecting Policy and Research* (Bristol: Policy Press, 2015), p. 135.

INDEX

Note: Page numbers in italic refer to figures.
Page numbers followed by n refers to notes.

Printed in Great Britain
by Amazon